Microsoft® Office 2010

Transition from Office 2003 (First Look)

Microsoft® Office 2010: Transition from Office 2003 (First Look)

Part Number: 084574
Course Edition: 1.0

NOTICES

DISCLAIMER: While Element K Corporation takes care to ensure the accuracy and quality of these materials, we cannot guarantee their accuracy, and all materials are provided without any warranty whatsoever, including, but not limited to, the implied warranties of merchantability or fitness for a particular purpose. The name used in the data files for this course is that of a fictitious company. Any resemblance to current or future companies is purely coincidental. We do not believe we have used anyone's name in creating this course, but if we have, please notify us and we will change the name in the next revision of the course. Element K is an independent provider of integrated training solutions for individuals, businesses, educational institutions, and government agencies. Use of screenshots, photographs of another entity's products, or another entity's product name or service in this book is for editorial purposes only. No such use should be construed to imply sponsorship or endorsement of the book by, nor any affiliation of such entity with Element K. This courseware may contain links to sites on the Internet that are owned and operated by third parties (the "External Sites"). Element K is not responsible for the availability of, or the content located on or through, any External Site. Please contact Element K if you have any concerns regarding such links or External Sites.

TRADEMARK NOTICES Element K and the Element K logo are trademarks of Element K Corporation and its affiliates.

Microsoft® Office 2010 is a registered trademark of Microsoft Corporation in the U.S. and other countries; the Microsoft products and services discussed or described may be trademarks of Microsoft Corporation. All other product names and services used throughout this course may be common law or registered trademarks of their respective proprietors.

Copyright © 2010 Element K Corporation. All rights reserved. Screenshots used for illustrative purposes are the property of the software proprietor. This publication, or any part thereof, may not be reproduced or transmitted in any form or by any means, electronic or mechanical, including photocopying, recording, storage in an information retrieval system, or otherwise, without express written permission of Element K, 500 Canal View Boulevard, Rochester, NY 14623, (585) 240-7500, (800) 478-7788. Element K Courseware's World Wide Web site is located at www.elementkcourseware.com.

This book conveys no rights in the software or other products about which it was written; all use or licensing of such software or other products is the responsibility of the user according to terms and conditions of the owner. Do not make illegal copies of books or software. If you believe that this book, related materials, or any other Element K materials are being reproduced or transmitted without permission, please call (800) 478-7788.

HELP US IMPROVE OUR COURSEWARE

Your comments are important to us. Please contact us at Element K Press LLC, 1-800-478-7788, 500 Canal View Boulevard, Rochester, NY 14623, Attention: Product Planning, or through our Web site at **http://support.elementkcourseware.com**.

Microsoft® Office 2010: Transition from Office 2003 (First Look)

Lesson 1: Getting Started with Microsoft Office 2010

    A. Customize the User Interface 2

    B. Work with Contextual Tabs 11

    C. Save Files 20

    D. Print Files 26

Lesson 2: Modifying Documents Using Microsoft Office Word 2010

    A. Use the Navigation Pane 32

    B. Apply Text Styles 36

    C. Work with SmartArt Graphics 43

    D. Insert Screenshots in a Document 49

    E. Compare Reviewed Documents 53

Lesson 3: Working with Spreadsheets Using Microsoft Office Excel 2010

    A. Work with Tables in Excel 2010 60

    B. Apply Conditional Formatting 65

    C. Apply a Formula 69

    D. Work with Charts 77

    E. Create Sparklines 85

    F. Work with PivotTables and PivotCharts 89

Lesson 4: Creating Dynamic Presentations Using Microsoft PowerPoint 2010

- A. Apply Themes 98
- B. Apply Picture Effects to Presentations 103
- C. Applying Animation Effects 107
- D. Add Videos to a Presentation 110
- E. Divide a Presentation into Sections 114

Lesson 5: Working with Databases Using Microsoft Office Access 2010

- A. Work with Tables 120
- B. Work with Forms 130
- C. Work with Macros 138
- D. Work with Reports 145
- E. Work with External Data 155
- F. Design a Database for the Web 161

Lesson 6: Managing Tasks with Microsoft Office Outlook 2010

- A. Manage Mail Messages 172
- B. Locate Information Quickly 179
- C. Share Calendar Information 184
- D. Share Information by Using an Electronic Business Card 195
- E. Add RSS Feeds Through Outlook 2010 204

Lesson 7: Sharing Microsoft Office 2010 Files

- A. Protect Files 210
- B. Share Files Using Office Web Apps 215

Lesson Labs 223

Solutions 231

Glossary 233

Index 237

About This Course

Having worked with the applications in *Microsoft® Office 2003*, you must also get to know the features present in the latest release of the application. *Microsoft® Office 2010: New Features Transition from Office 2003* focuses on the enhanced features for improving the management, organization, presentation, and distribution of data. In this course, you will work with the new features in Office 2010.

When projects and deadlines are piling up, it is necessary to streamline your tasks and maximize productivity. *Microsoft® Office 2010* helps you achieve this with its new user-friendly interface, along with a host of new and enhanced results-oriented features. Even if you will be using the Office 2010 application only to create and format documents, it is important to have a working knowledge of the interface changes and the enhanced capabilities. This will help when you want to create better documents by using features that are not only enhanced, but are also simple and non-time consuming.

Course Description

Target Student

Users with prior experience of previous versions of the Microsoft Office suite, who are looking to transition to 2010 and want to know what the new features of Office 2010 are.

Course Prerequisites

To be successful in this course, you should be familiar with prior versions of the Microsoft Office suite of products (Excel, PPT, Word, Access, Outlook).To ensure your success, we recommend you first take one of Element K's Level 1 courses, such as either of the following, or have equivalent skills and knowledge:

- *Microsoft® Office Excel® 2003 Level 1*
- *Microsoft® Office Word® 2003: Level 1*
- *Microsoft® Office Access® 2003 Level 1*
- *Microsoft® Office PowerPoint® 2003 Level 1*
- *Microsoft® Office Outlook® 2003 Level 1*

Course Objectives

In this course, you will work with the new and updated features of Microsoft Office 2010.

You will:

- Identify the features that are common to all applications in the Microsoft Office suite.
- Modify documents using Microsoft Office Word 2010.
- Present spreadsheet data using Microsoft Office Excel 2010.
- Create Microsoft Office PowerPoint 2010 presentations.
- Work with databases using Microsoft Office Access 2010.
- Manage tasks using the new features in Microsoft Office Outlook 2010.
- Share files in Microsoft Office 2010.

How to Use This Book

As a Learning Guide

This book is divided into lessons and topics, covering a subject or a set of related subjects. In most cases, lessons are arranged in order of increasing proficiency.

The results-oriented topics include relevant and supporting information you need to master the content. Each topic has various types of activities designed to enable you to practice the guidelines and procedures as well as to solidify your understanding of the informational material presented in the course.

At the back of the book, you will find a glossary of the definitions of the terms and concepts used throughout the course. You will also find an index to assist in locating information within the instructional components of the book.

In the Classroom

This book is intended to enhance and support the in-class experience. Procedures and guidelines are presented in a concise fashion along with activities and discussions. Information is provided for reference and reflection in such a way as to facilitate understanding and practice.

Each lesson may also include a Lesson Lab or various types of simulated activities. You will find the files for the simulated activities along with the other course files on the enclosed CD-ROM. If your course manual did not come with a CD-ROM, please go to **http:// elementkcourseware.com** to download the files. If included, these interactive activities enable you to practice your skills in an immersive business environment, or to use hardware and software resources not available in the classroom. The course files that are available on the CD-ROM or by download may also contain sample files, support files, and additional reference materials for use both during and after the course.

As a Teaching Guide

Effective presentation of the information and skills contained in this book requires adequate preparation. As such, as an instructor, you should familiarize yourself with the content of the entire course, including its organization and approaches. You should review each of the student activities and exercises so you can facilitate them in the classroom.

Throughout the book, you may see Instructor Notes that provide suggestions, answers to problems, and supplemental information for you, the instructor. You may also see references to "Additional Instructor Notes" that contain expanded instructional information; these notes appear in a separate section at the back of the book. PowerPoint slides may be provided on the included course files, which are available on the enclosed CD-ROM or by download from http://elementkcourseware.com. The slides are also referred to in the text. If you plan to use the slides, it is recommended to display them during the corresponding content as indicated in the instructor notes in the margin.

The course files may also include assessments for the course, which can be administered diagnostically before the class, or as a review after the course is completed. These exam-type questions can be used to gauge the students' understanding and assimilation of course content.

As a Review Tool

Any method of instruction is only as effective as the time and effort you, the student, are willing to invest in it. In addition, some of the information that you learn in class may not be important to you immediately, but it may become important later. For this reason, we encourage you to spend some time reviewing the content of the course after your time in the classroom.

As a Reference

The organization and layout of this book make it an easy-to-use resource for future reference. Taking advantage of the glossary, index, and table of contents, you can use this book as a first source of definitions, background information, and summaries.

Course Icons

Icon	Description
	A **Caution Note** makes students aware of potential negative consequences of an action, setting, or decision that are not easily known.
	Display Slide provides a prompt to the instructor to display a specific slide. Display Slides are included in the Instructor Guide only.
	An **Instructor Note** is a comment to the instructor regarding delivery, classroom strategy, classroom tools, exceptions, and other special considerations. Instructor Notes are included in the Instructor Guide only.
	Notes Page indicates a page that has been left intentionally blank for students to write on.
	A **Student Note** provides additional information, guidance, or hints about a topic or task.
	A **Version Note** indicates information necessary for a specific version of software.

Course Requirements and Setup

You can find a list of hardware and software requirements to run this class as well as detailed classroom setup procedures in the course files that are available on the CD-ROM that shipped with this book. If your course manual did not come with a CD-ROM, please go to **http://www.elementk.com/courseware-file-downloads** to download the files.

1 Getting Started with Microsoft Office 2010

Lesson Time: 1 hour(s), 15 minutes

Lesson Objectives:

In this lesson, you will identify the features that are common to all applications in the Microsoft Office suite.

You will:

- Customize the Microsoft Office 2010 user interface.
- Work with Microsoft Office contextual tabs.
- Save files in different formats.
- Print files.

Introduction

You worked with earlier versions of Microsoft Office to create documents, spreadsheets, reports, and presentations, and exchange mail messages. The user-friendly interface and enhanced features of Microsoft Office 2010 are designed to streamline your work and maximize productivity. In this lesson, you will identify the redesigned user interface components and changes to file formats in Microsoft Office 2010.

Suppose your office workstations are upgraded to the latest release of the Microsoft suite of Office applications—Office 2010. The purpose of any upgrades would be to increase efficiency and make it easier for the user to work with the applications. You would, therefore, need to familiarize yourself with the features of Office applications to take full advantage of the suite.

TOPIC A
Customize the User Interface

In this topic, you will identify the features that are common to the applications of the Microsoft Office suite. The most obvious common feature is the user interface. In this topic, you will customize the components of the Microsoft Office 2010 user interface.

While working with the application user interface, you could potentially waste a significant amount of time accessing certain commands which you use frequently in the work environment. A working knowledge of the user interface and the ability to customize the application element prevents time from being wasted and helps you achieve the output that you are seeking.

The Microsoft Office [Application] User Interface

There are various interface elements that are common to all Office applications. The major elements include the Ribbon, Quick Access toolbar, Microsoft Office Status Bar, and Dialog Box Launchers.

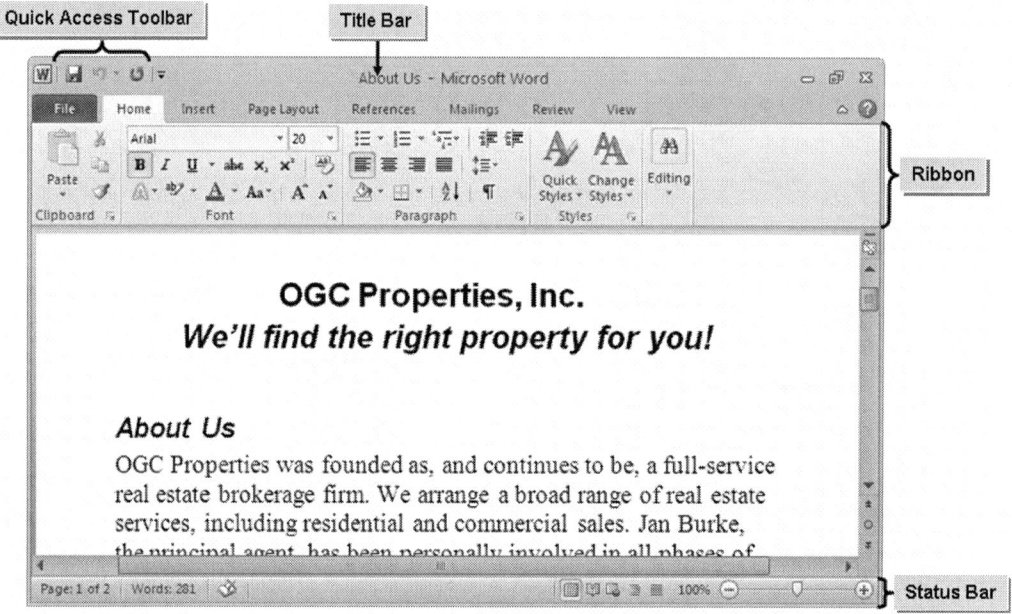

Figure 1-1: Common interface elements in Word 2010.

Interface Element	Description
The Ribbon	A panel that is present at the top of the interface. It has several *tabs* that are organized in the order in which they will be used during file creation. The tabs carry a group of commands that you may need to work in a file, and are organized in an easy-to-browse manner. You can hide the Ribbon by double-clicking any active tabs.

Interface Element	Description
The Quick Access toolbar	By default, it is displayed at the top of the window, above the Ribbon. It provides easy access to commonly used commands such as **Save, Undo,** and **Repeat.** It can also be customized to include other commands.
	You can also move the Quick Access toolbar below the Ribbon. The commands on the Quick Access toolbar are available irrespective of the primary tab that is displayed.
The Microsoft Office Status Bar	Located at the bottom of the application window, it displays a number of tasks relating to an open file's functionality, in a well-organized manner. The Microsoft Office Status Bar can also be customized to add or remove displayed tasks.
Dialog Box Launchers	Located at the bottom-right corner of certain command groups, they appear as small downward-pointing arrow buttons on a tab. They are used to launch the relevant dialog box with advanced setting options, reducing the time users spend locating the required set of commands.

Benefits of the Ribbon

Most of the commands and controls are accessible from the Ribbon, rather than through menus and dialog boxes. It helps users identify the desired functions and perform both simple and advanced operations, without having to extensively navigate through the application.

Ribbon Tabs

The Ribbon organizes commands on different tabs. Each tab is divided into logical *groups* that contain sets of commands. These groups represent a collection of features designed to perform a specific set of tasks, based on their priority and sequence. The commands in the different groups are divided and represented as large and small buttons. The large buttons represent the features that are commonly used and the smaller buttons represent the minor features that are designed to work together to achieve a common result.

The **Home** tab is the default tab that is displayed in the Microsoft Office interface. It generally contains clipboard commands, commands to format the font, alignment, and various other frequently used commands. The Microsoft Office 2010 interface also hosts numerous other tabs to help complete a task. Each tab contains commands that are related to a specific activity and grouped together. For example, the **Page Layout** tab in Word and Excel contains commands that help format the layout of the page by setting the margins, orientation, and other layout-specific features.

Screen Resolution and Ribbon Size

The new user interface is optimized for multiple screen resolutions. As screen resolution decreases, the groups appear smaller, and as the resolution increases, the groups appear larger. On large screens, the Ribbon shows large versions of groups. This means that users with large monitors will be able to view and access more options.

Customizable Ribbon Tabs

Office 2010 allows users to create custom tabs to arrange commands to suit a personal workflow, and to provide better access to frequently used commands. It not only allows users to create custom groups but also to hide default and custom tabs on the Ribbon. While custom tabs can be removed, the default tabs cannot.

Status Bar Display Differences

The status bar in various Office applications is displayed differently.

1. **Word:** The status bar displays the page number of the document, the number of sections, the line and column numbers, a live word count, and a contextual spell checker. The Microsoft Office Status Bar also displays whether the Track Changes mode is turned on or off. You can use the Microsoft Office Status Bar to switch between different views or to instantaneously zoom the document in or out to any desired size by using the **Zoom** slider. Additionally, it displays the number of authors editing the particular document, and its current upload status. It also provides options for recording macros.
2. **Excel:** The status bar displays the current cell, selection modes, page number, average, and sum. It also provides access to the **Macro Record** dialog box. You can also use the Microsoft Office Status Bar to navigate to the different view modes or zoom the spreadsheet in or out.
3. **PowerPoint:** The status bar displays the slide number and theme used. You can also use the Microsoft Office Status Bar to navigate to the different view modes or zoom the presentation in or out. In addition, you can zoom out to fit slide content into one page. Additionally, it displays the number of authors editing the presentation, and its current upload status.
4. **Access:** The status bar displays the current view of the table, report, query, or form. You can also switch between different views by using the Microsoft Office Status Bar.
5. **Outlook:** The status bar displays information about the active folder, quota, filter, reminders, shortcuts, and zoom options.

The Backstage View

The *backstage view* in Office 2010 applications is an interface that has simplified access to various features. Displayed when you select the **File** tab, the backstage view replaces both the Microsoft Office Button in Office 2007 applications and the traditional **File** menu in applications in Office 2003 and earlier versions. It contains not only a series of tabs that help group similar commands, but also displays the compatibility, permission, and version information for a specific file. It lets you save, share, print, and publish files with just a few clicks of the mouse.

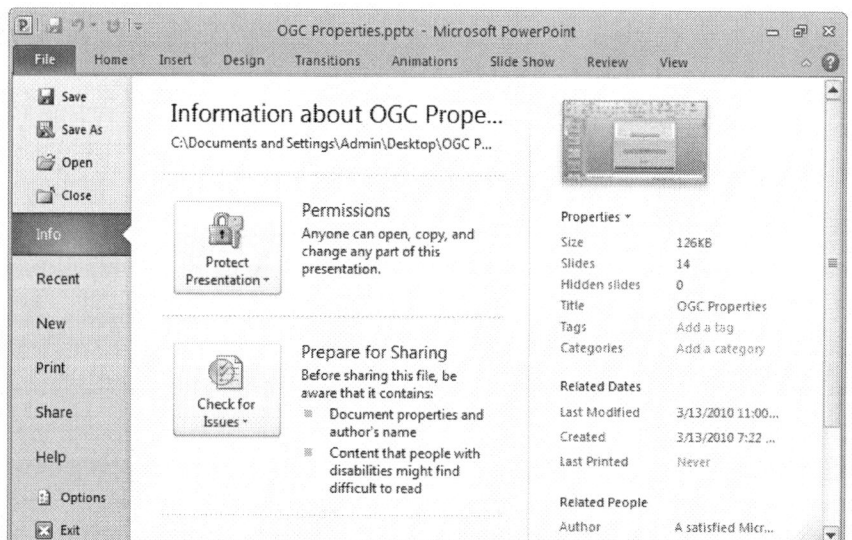

Figure 1-2: The backstage view as displayed in the PowerPoint application.

The backstage view can be customized to a user's personal workflow and procedures.

The Print Tab
With the **Print** tab in the backstage view of Office 2010, the print preview and print options are now easier to access. The integrated print preview option makes it convenient to preview the printed output.

Protected View
Protected view is a view that opens a file in read-only mode and is a safe mode that allows the user to check whether or not the file is from a trusted source. The file is blocked until then and is opened in a protected area called a "sandbox" so that it cannot affect other files or system data. Clicking the **Enable Editing** option allows the file to open in normal mode. The **Trust Center** contains options for opening files in protected view.

The [Application] Options Dialog Box
The **[Application] Options** dialog box contains a series of tabs, each with commands required to customize the environment.

Tab	Allows You To
General	Personalize your work environment by setting options such as the color scheme, user name, and ScreenTip style. It has an option to enable the Live Preview feature. In Excel, it allows you to specify options for new workbooks. In Outlook, the **Start up options** section allows you to specify whether Outlook should be the default program for mailing, contacts, and the calendar. In Access, it allows you to specify options for new databases. This tab is present in Access, Word, Excel, Outlook, and PowerPoint.
Display	Modify how text content is displayed on screen and in print. You can opt to show or hide certain page elements such as highlights, formatting marks, and tooltips. This tab is unique to Word.
Proofing	Customize various options to set the auto-correct, spelling, and formatting settings. It enables you to specify how textual content should be corrected and formatted. It also allows you to choose the settings to ignore certain words or spelling errors in certain files. Contextual spelling checks and evaluates words contextually to catch more spelling errors. It also allows you to include words from other languages such as French and Spanish. This tab is present in Word, Excel, and PowerPoint.
Save	Customize saving options. You can choose the frequency with which you want Microsoft Office to save a backup of files, and also specify the location and format in which they will be saved. It also provides you with the option to choose the location in which server drafts will be saved. This tab is present in Word, Excel, and PowerPoint.
Language	Modify Office language preferences. This tab is present in Word, Excel, Outlook, and PowerPoint.
Advanced	Specify advanced options for editing, formatting, displaying, calculating, presenting, printing, saving, and accessing options for files. This tab is present in Word, Excel, Outlook, and PowerPoint.

Tab	Allows You To
Customize Ribbon	Customize the Ribbon and shortcut options. Using this tab, you can select tabs that you want added to the Ribbon, and hide the ones that you do not need. This tab is present in Access, Word, Excel, Outlook, and PowerPoint.
Quick Access Toolbar	Customize the Quick Access toolbar. Using this tab, you can select those commands that you want added to the Quick Access toolbar. You can also opt to position the Quick Access toolbar below the Ribbon. This tab is present in Word, Excel, Outlook, and PowerPoint.
Add-Ins	Manage Office add-ins, if you are using extensions to enhance Office applications. Add-ins extend the capabilities of a function. Many of these add-ins ship with Office 2010. This tab is present in Word, Excel, Outlook, and PowerPoint.
Trust Center	Secure the system and documents. Using the **Advanced Trust Center Settings** button on this tab, you can set security measures needed to keep a document secure. This tab is present in Word, Excel, Outlook, and PowerPoint.

Other Tabs in the [Application] Options Dialog Box

In addition to the tabs mentioned, a few more tabs are present in the **[Application] Options** dialog box that is specific to that application. In Access, in the **Access Options** dialog box, three other tabs named **Current Database, Object Designers,** and **Datasheet** are available. These tabs help customize the options in the current database and how database objects and data sheets look like in Access, respectively. Access also has a **Client Settings** tab to specify the client behavior.

In Excel, the **Excel Options** dialog box contains the **Formulas** tab with options to calculate formulae and manage performance and errors. Outlook's **Outlook Options** dialog box contains additional tabs such as **Mail, Calendar, Contacts, Tasks, Notes and Journal, Search,** and **Mobile.**

ScreenTips

A *ScreenTip* is a label that appears when the mouse pointer is placed over a tool. It contains a description of the task performed by the tool. It helps users identify the functionality of the features and commands that they are not familiar with. You can customize a ScreenTip on the **General** tab of the **[Application] Options** dialog box by selecting any of the three available options: **Show Feature Descriptions in ScreenTips, Don't Show Feature Descriptions in ScreenTips,** and **Don't Show ScreenTips.**

How to Identify the User Interface

Procedure Reference: Open a File

To open a file:

1. Launch the desired application.
2. Open a file.
   - Open an existing file.
     a. Select the **File** tab and choose **Open.**
     b. If necessary, in the **Open** dialog box, navigate to the desired location.
     c. Select the file and click **Open.**
   - Open a new file.
     a. Select the **File** tab and then select the **New** tab.
       - In Word, in the **Available Templates** section, select **Blank document.**
       - In Excel, in the **Available Templates** section, select **Blank workbook.**
       - In PowerPoint, in the **Available Templates and Themes** section, select **Blank presentation.**

> The **Getting Started With Microsoft Office Access** window is displayed as soon as you launch the Access application. This window has options to open a new blank database.

     b. Click **Create.**

Procedure Reference: Customize the Microsoft Office 2010 User Interface

To customize the Microsoft Office 2010 user interface:

1. Select the **File** tab and choose **Options** to display the **[Application] Options** dialog box.
2. In the left pane of the **[Application] Options** dialog box, select the desired tab.
3. In the right pane, modify the desired options.
4. Click **OK** to customize the interface, based on the changes made.

Procedure Reference: Customize the Quick Access Toolbar

To customize the Quick Access toolbar:

1. Display the **[Application] Options** dialog box.
   - Use the **File** tab to display the **[Application] Options** dialog box.
   - Or, from the **Customize Quick Access Toolbar** drop-down list, select **More Commands.**
2. If necessary, in the **[Application] Options** dialog box, select the **Quick Access Toolbar** tab.
3. In the right pane of the **[Application] Options** dialog box, below the **Choose Commands From** section, select the desired command.
4. Click **Add** to add the selected command to the Quick Access toolbar.
5. If necessary, below the **Customize Quick Access Toolbar** section, select the desired command and click **Remove.**

6. If necessary, organize the commands in the **Customize Quick Access Toolbar** section by using the **Move Up, Move Down**, or **Reset** button to set the appearance of commands on the Quick Access toolbar.
7. If necessary, below the **Choose Commands From** section, click **<Separator>**, and then click **Add** to add a separator between the commands on the Quick Access toolbar.
8. If necessary, use the **Move Up** or **Move Down** button to reposition the separator.
9. If necessary, check the **Show Quick Access Toolbar below the Ribbon** check box to position the Quick Access toolbar below the Ribbon.
10. Click **OK** to apply the settings.

Procedure Reference: Add a Group to the Quick Access Toolbar

To add a group to the Quick Access toolbar:

1. On the Ribbon, select the tab that has the desired group.
2. Within the desired group, right-click the text region that is available below the buttons and choose **Add To Quick Access Toolbar.**

You can add any number of groups to the Quick Access toolbar. However, the Ribbon cannot be added to the Quick Access toolbar.

3. On the Quick Access toolbar, click the group to verify that all the commands have been added.

If you need to add only one command button from a tab on the Ribbon to the Quick Access toolbar, right-click the command and choose **Add to Quick Access Toolbar.**

Procedure Reference: Customize the Microsoft Office Status Bar

To customize the Microsoft Office Status Bar:

1. On the Microsoft Office Status Bar, right-click, and from the **Customize Status Bar** menu, choose the option to add to, or remove the option from, the Microsoft Office Status Bar.
2. Click away from the menu to close it.

ACTIVITY 1-1
Customizing the Microsoft Office Word 2010 Interface

Data Files:

Management.docx

Scenario:

Your company has just purchased and installed the Microsoft Office 2010 package. Because you will frequently be working with Word, you decide to spend some time exploring the new user interface elements of the Word environment. As you work with Word, you realize that it will be helpful if you have the commands that you intend to use most often, such as **New, Open,** and **Close** available on the interface itself, for increased efficiency. In addition to the default information available, such as the page number and word count of the document, you also want information pertaining to the section, column, and line number that you are currently working on, to be displayed on the Microsoft Office Status Bar.

1. Explore the user interface.

    a. Click **Start→All Programs→Microsoft Office→Microsoft Word 2010 (Beta)** to launch the Microsoft Office Word 2010 application.

    b. If necessary, in the **User Name** dialog box, click **OK.**

    c. If necessary, in the **Welcome to Microsoft Office 2010** dialog box, select the **Don't make changes** option and click **OK.**

    d. Select the **File** tab, observe the options on the tab, and choose **Open.**

    e. Navigate to the C:\084574Data\Getting Started with Microsoft Office 2010 folder and open the **Management.docx** file.

    f. On the Quick Access toolbar, place the mouse pointer over each button to view its ScreenTip.

    g. On the Ribbon, select the different tabs to view their related commands.

    h. On the Microsoft Office Status Bar, hover the mouse pointer over each button to view the screentip of each view button.

    i. Observe that the view is changed.

2. Add the necessary commands to the Quick Access toolbar.

    a. Click the **Customize Quick Access Toolbar** drop-down arrow, and select **New.**

    b. Observe that the **New** button has been added to the Quick Access toolbar.

    c. From the drop-down list, select **Open.**

d. From the drop-down list, select **More Commands** to display the **Quick Access Toolbar** tab in the **Word Options** dialog box.

e. In the right pane of the **Word Options** dialog box, from the **Choose commands from** drop-down list, select **File Tab**.

f. In the list box below the **Choose commands from** drop-down list, select **Close** and click **Add**.

g. Click **OK** to apply the settings.

h. Observe that the **New**, **Open**, and **Close** buttons have been added to the Quick Access toolbar.

3. Add options to the Microsoft Office Status Bar.

   a. Right-click the blank space on the Microsoft Office Status Bar to display the **Customize Status Bar** menu.

   b. Observe that a check mark is displayed next to the **Page Number** option, indicating that the option has been added to the Microsoft Office Status Bar.

   c. From the **Customize Status Bar** menu, choose **Section** to add the option to the Microsoft Office Status Bar.

   d. Similarly, add the **Line Number** and **Column** to the Microsoft Office Status Bar.

   e. Click elsewhere to close the **Customize Status Bar** menu.

   f. Observe that the **Section**, **Line Number**, and **Column** have been added to the Microsoft Office Status Bar.

   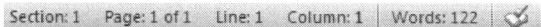

   g. Click the **Close** button in the Quick Access toolbar to close the document.

   h. If necessary, click **Don't Save** in the **Microsoft Word** dialog box.

TOPIC B
Work with Contextual Tabs

You identified various components of the Microsoft Office user interface. Unlike the regular options available on the Ribbon tabs, certain commands and options are available contextually when selecting specific object types such as tables, charts, and graphics. In this topic, you will work with contextual tabs.

Imagine a workspace where you have all the tools, tabs, and options occupying the interface. Searching for a specific option is like searching for that one piece of paper in an overstuffed file cabinet. Microsoft Office provides a set of contextual command tabs that appear only when relevant object types are selected. This provides you with an uncluttered workspace and ensures quick access to relevant commands for editing and formatting specific objects.

Contextual Tabs
Definition:
Contextual tabs are specialized commands that are displayed when the object they operate on, such as a table, picture, or drawing, is selected. These tabs are displayed next to the existing command tabs. They are context-based, so the scope of their commands and tools is restricted to only the objects they are specialized for. You can switch between contextual and core tabs as needed. However, when you deselect the object, contextual tabs disappear.

Example:

Figure 1-3: Contextual tabs displayed when an object is selected in the PowerPoint application.

Objects Displaying Contextual Tabs
There are various types of contextual tabs that are activated based on the application and the actions you perform.

Application	Objects Displaying Contextual Tabs
Word	Displayed when you select or insert a table, a picture, a text box, a shape, a chart, WordArt, equations, SmartArt, headers/footers, or clip art.
Excel	Displayed when you select or insert a table, a drawing, a text box, WordArt, or a chart.
PowerPoint	Displayed when you select or insert a table, picture, drawing, shapes, chart, SmartArt, audio files, or a movie file.

Application	Objects Displaying Contextual Tabs
Access	Displayed when you select or insert a table, form, or report, or when you query the database.
Outlook	Displayed when you select or insert a table, a picture, chart, SmartArt, WordArt, a text box, or an equation.

Types of Contextual Tabs

Office 2010 provides several types of contextual tabs to enable you to access commands relevant to an object. The groups and commands in each of the contextual tabs vary based on the object type.

Contextual Tab	Description
Format	This tab is displayed when you insert or select pictures, shapes, charts, SmartArt graphics, ClipArt, reports, forms, or sound and movie clips. The commands on this tab can be used to format the selected object. You can change the object's style, modify its color or size, or change its position.
	You can also remove the background in a picture, make corrections, add effects, and crop the picture. This tab also allows you to preview a movie clip, make corrections, change styles, and add video effects. It also contains commands to format a form or report.
Design	This tab is displayed when you insert or select tables, charts, reports, forms, or SmartArt graphics. The commands on this tab can be used to make layout and design changes, such as the style in which the object is presented.
Layout	This tab is displayed when you insert or select tables and charts. The commands on this tab can be used to change the layout of the existing chart or table by merging, splitting, or inserting rows, in addition to changing the layout of charts.
Playback	This tab is displayed when you insert media clips such as sound and movie. The commands on this tab can be used to adjust the volume, edit and preview a sound or movie clip, add bookmarks, and specify playback options.
Arrange	This tab is displayed when you insert or open a form or report in Microsoft Access. It contains commands to set the layout of a form or report. It contains options to merge, split, move, and position table rows and columns.
Page Setup	This tab is displayed when you open a report in Microsoft Access. It contains commands to set the page size and layout of a report.

 The Playback tab replaces the Options tab that no longer appears when a sound or movie clip is inserted.

Contextual Tab Groups

Contextual tab groups in Office 2010 vary with the objects inserted or selected in a file.

Contextual Tab Group	Description
Table Tools	This group is used to insert or draw a table. It consists of the **Design** and **Layout** tabs. • The **Design** tab provides options to draw a table, set various styles to the rows and columns, apply shading effects, and erase the borders of a table. • The **Layout** tab provides options to insert rows and columns, align cells and text, and set the cell size of a table.
Picture Tools	This group is used to insert a picture from a file. It consists of the **Format** tab that provides options to compress a picture, apply brightness and contrast, and recolor or resize a picture. You can change the picture style by making a selection from a gallery, or by giving it different effects. You can give images an outline and arrange them in coordination with other images. You can also position the object as desired by ensuring that text wraps around it. Unwanted portions of the image can also be cropped.
Drawing Tools	This group is used to insert shapes like rectangles, circles, lines, arrows, callouts, and flow chart symbols. It consists of the **Format** tab which provides options to insert various shapes, apply styles, shadow effects and 3D effects, and alter the shape and size of shapes and arrange them. It is also used to insert preformatted text boxes in a document. You can edit existing WordArt text, increase or decrease word spacing, pick alternate styles, and add effects.
Chart Tools	This group is used to insert a chart and compare its data. It consists of the **Design**, **Layout**, and **Format** tabs. • The **Design** tab provides options to change the chart type, save a newly created template, apply layout styles, and edit source data. • The **Layout** tab can be used to include pictures and shapes, if needed. Using this tab, you can also add chart elements such as titles, labels, gridlines, and axes, among others. • The **Format** tab provides options to apply outlines, a fill color, an outline color, shape effects, and various styles to the chart.
SmartArt Tools	This group is used to insert a SmartArt graphic to visually communicate information. It consists of the **Design** and **Format** tabs. • The **Design** tab provides options to create the SmartArt graphic, change the layouts of the graphic, apply various styles to the graphic, and reset the graphic to its original format. • The **Format** tab provides options to apply styles, effects, outlines, and colors to each shape of the graphic, arrange the shapes of the graphic, and set the size for each shape. It also provides options to apply formatting styles to only the text in the graphic.
Equation Tools	This group is used to insert common mathematical equations or to build your own equations by using the library. It consists of the **Design** tab which provides options to insert common mathematical equations and symbols, and to add some additional features such as fractions, radices , integrals , and matrices to the equation.

Contextual Tab Group	Description
Header & Footer Tools	This group is used to insert and customize the header and footer sections. It consists of the **Design** tab. Using this contextual tab, you can customize the header and footer sections by selecting the header and footer styles from their respective galleries. You can also add details such as date, time, page numbers, and images, among others. You can align and position them in select pages, as desired. Within this tab, you can also switch between headers and footers to make modifications to the elements within them.
Audio Tools	This group is used to insert and edit audio clips in a file. It consists of the **Format** and **Playback** tabs. • The **Format** tab provides various editing options. • The **Playback** tab is used to adjust the volume, and edit and preview a sound clip.
Video Tools	This group is used to insert and edit video clips in a file. It consists of the **Format** and **Playback** tabs. • The **Format** tab provides various options for a video including editing options, video styles, and effects. • The **Playback** tab is used to play, edit, and preview a movie clip.

Table Tools in Excel

When you select a table on a worksheet, the **Table Tools** tab category is displayed on the title bar next to the title of the spreadsheet. The tab category consists of the **Design** tab, which is a contextual tab that holds commands specific to formatting tables. Groups on this tab include **Properties, Tools, External Table Data, Table Style Options,** and **Table Styles.** Each group contains related options that apply similar types of formatting. You can use the options on the **Design** tab to enhance the appearance and layout of a selected table.

The Mini Toolbar

The *Mini toolbar* is a floating toolbar that is displayed when you select text. It consists of commonly used font and paragraph tools. It includes options for the font name, size, color, format painter, bold, italics, and text alignment. You can use one or more of these available commands, without having to navigate to the main toolbar. The Mini toolbar disappears when you move the mouse pointer away from the selected text.

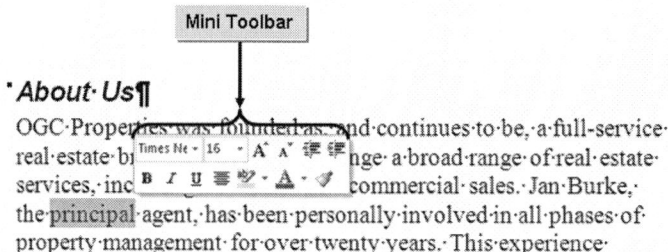

Figure 1-4: *The Mini toolbar for a selected piece of text in a Word document.*

The Mini toolbar is also accessible when you select and right-click text.

Galleries

Galleries are a set of libraries that lists outcomes depending on what command is used from the Ribbon. In Office 2010, most of the functional groups on the Ribbon contain galleries, each of which provides you with a set of predefined styles. These styles become active as you work with text.

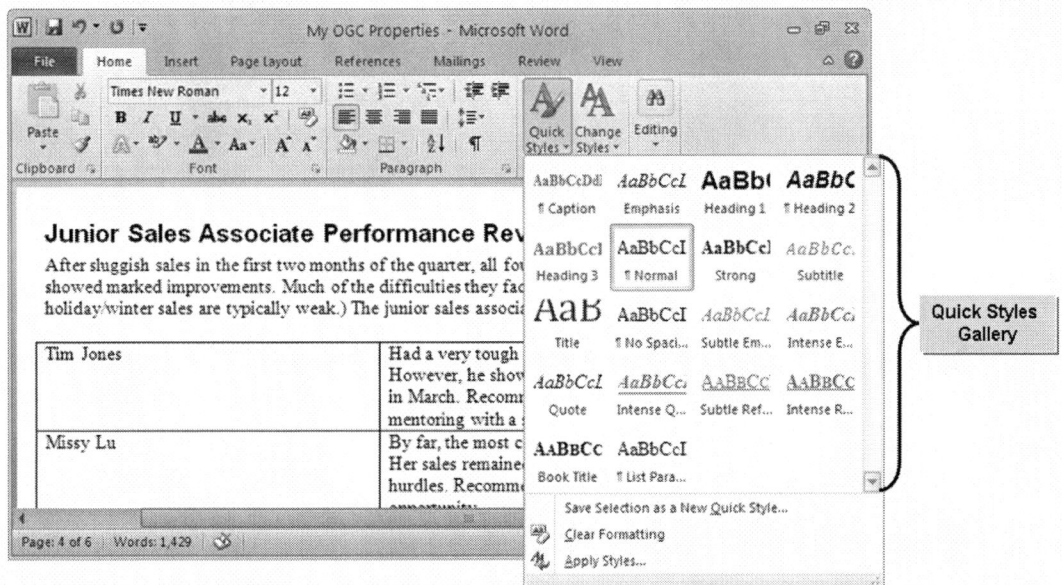

Figure 1-5: The QuickStyles gallery displaying various selections.

 Some gallery options are also available on shortcut menus that can be accessed by a simple right-click. These options allow the user to quickly access the relevant galleries.

The Live Preview Feature

The *Live Preview* feature enables you to view the result of a command when certain editing and formatting changes are made. Hovering the mouse pointer over an option displays an associated change for you to then apply the change to the active Office application.

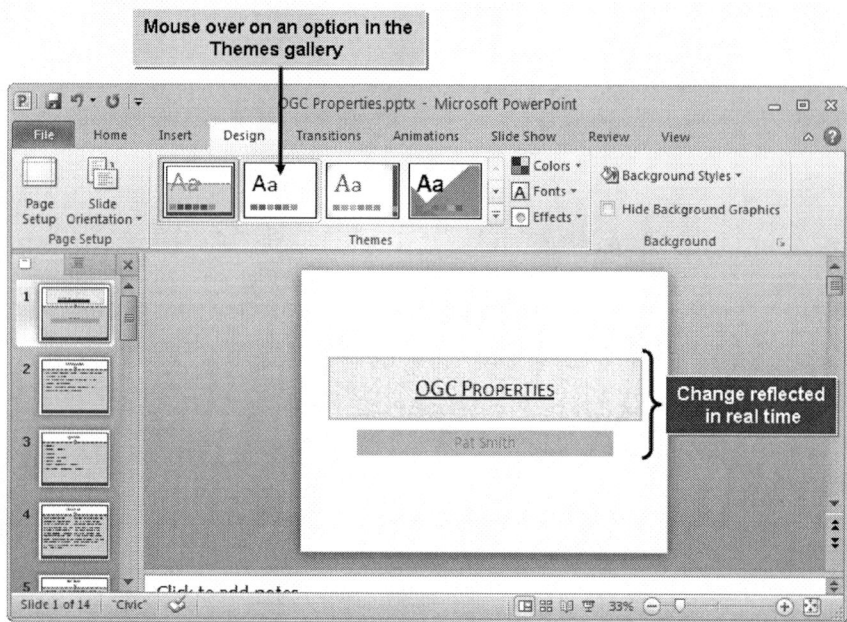

Figure 1-6: The Live Preview feature displaying real-time changes.

Paste Preview Options

Office 2010 provides paste options that are displayed once you copy content and hover the mouse over the **Paste Options** menu. Also accessed either by right-clicking the selected content or using the **Paste** drop-down list on the **Home** tab of the Ribbon, these options use the Live Preview functionality to preview effects.

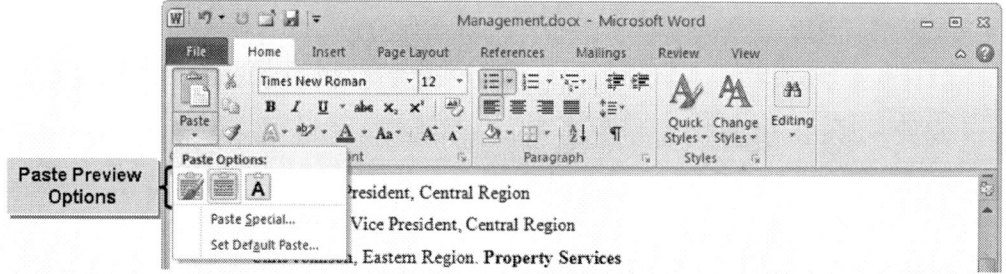

Figure 1-7: The three Paste Preview options in Microsoft Word.

How to Work with Contextual Tabs

Procedure Reference: Format Objects by Using Contextual Tabs

To format an object by using contextual tabs:

1. Open a file.
2. Select the object to be formatted.
3. From the displayed contextual tab, select the desired format command.
4. If necessary, select a Ribbon tab and click a command to perform any additional tasks.
5. Deselect the object to close the contextual tab.

Procedure Reference: Format Text by Using the Mini Toolbar

To format text by using the Mini toolbar:

1. Select the text to be formatted, to display the Mini toolbar.
2. Move the mouse pointer over the transparent Mini toolbar to make it visible.
3. On the Mini toolbar, click a command button to format the selected text.
4. Move the mouse pointer away from the Mini toolbar or deselect the text, to hide the Mini toolbar.

ACTIVITY 1-2
Inserting a Header Using Contextual Tabs

Data Files:

Tabs.docx

Before You Begin:

Navigate to the C:\084574Data\Getting Started with Microsoft Office 2010 folder and open the Tabs.docx file.

Scenario:

With the page border and consistent line spacing applied, the Tabs.docx document looks quite formal. You are now ready to hand off the document to your manager for approval. Upon a final check, you realize that you have not added a header to the document.

---

1. Insert a header.

    a. Select the **Insert** tab.

    b. In the **Header & Footer** group, click **Header** to view the **Header** gallery.

    c. In the gallery, in the **Built-In** section, scroll down and select **Mod (Odd Page)**.

    d. Observe that a header is inserted in the document and the **Design** contextual tab is displayed in the **Header & Footer Tools** tool tab on the Ribbon.

    e. In the header section, triple-click the text **About Us** to select it.

    f. Observe that the Mini toolbar is displayed beside the text "About Us."

    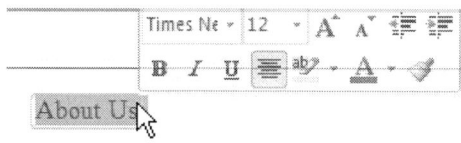

    g. Move the mouse pointer over the transparent Mini toolbar to make it visible.

    h. On the Mini toolbar, click the **Bold** button.

    i. From the **Font Size** drop-down list, select **18**.

    j. Click outside the selected text to view the changes.

    k. In the header section, select the "About Us" text again.

    l. Type **WELCOME TO OGC PROPERTIES**

---

2. Format the header using the contextual tabs.

a. At the top-right corner of the header, select the image.

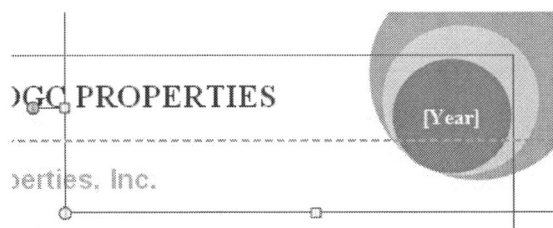

b. Observe that the **Format** contextual tab is displayed in the **Drawing Tools** tool tab on the Ribbon.

c. Select the **Format** contextual tab.

d. In the **Shape Styles** group, click the **More** button to view the gallery.

e. In the gallery, in the fourth row, sixth column, click the **Subtle Effect — Aqua, Accent 5** option.

f. Click the word "[Year]" in the image at the top-right corner of the header, to display the drop-down arrow and click the drop down arrow to display the calender.

g. In the displayed calendar, click **Today.**

h. Select the **Design** contextual tab, and in the **Close** group, click **Close Header and Footer** to close the contextual tabs.

3. Save and close the document.

   a. Select the **File** tab and choose **Save As.**

   b. In the **Save As** dialog box, in the **File name** text box, type *My Tabs* and click **Save.**

   c. Select the **File** tab and choose **Close.**

   d. Close the Word application.

TOPIC C
Save Files

You worked with contextual tabs to add effects to files by using tools provided in Microsoft Office 2010. Apart from knowing how to work in the interface, it is essential to be able to retrieve and share information. In this topic, you will save files in different formats to help share content with different users.

Sharing information with your colleagues, senior officials, and clients is an integral part of working in a corporate world. When dealing with different clients, you need to ensure that your documents are compatible with their applications. However, creating compatible documents can be a daunting and time-consuming task. Office 2010 allows you to save a file in different formats for easy integration of Office 2010 files into other applications and platforms.

The XML File Format

Office 2010 uses XML as the default file format. The XML format is a compact and robust file format that enables easy integration of Office 2010 files with other applications and platforms. The following table lists the file formats used with different applications.

Application	*Description*
Excel	Excel 2010 provides a varied list of file formats: ● Excel workbook (.xlsx) is the default Excel 2010 XML file format. ● Excel macro-enabled workbook (.xlsm) is the XML-based file format that is used to save workbooks with VBA macro code or Excel 4.0 macro sheets (.xlm). ● Excel template (.xltx) is the default Excel template file format. ● Excel macro-enabled template (.xltm) is the Excel macro-enabled template format that can contain VBA macro code or Excel 4.0 macro sheets. ● Excel binary workbook (.xlsb) is the Excel binary file format (BIFF12) that allows the use of VBA projects, Excel 4.0 macro sheets, and Office Excel 2010 new features. ● Excel add-in (.xlam) is an XML-based macro-enabled supplemental program that runs additional code and allows the use of VBA projects and Excel 4.0 macro sheets.

Application	Description
Word	Word 2010 provides a varied list of file formats: • Word document (.docx) is the default Office Word 2010 file format. • Word macro-enabled document (.docm) is the default Word 2010 file format for macro-enabled documents. It uses the same basic XML format as the Word 2010 XML Document format, but can store VBA macro code. • Word Template (.dotx) is the default format for a Word template. It is created while saving document styles and formatting. • Word macro-enabled template (.dotm) is the default format for a Word macro-enabled template. Word 2010 stores macro code for use with other Word documents. By default, documents are saved as .docx files even when created from a Word 2010 XML macro-enabled template.
Access	Access 2010 provides a varied list of file formats: • Access database (.accdb) is the default Access database format. It supports features such as multivalue fields and attachments. • Access executable (.accde) is an executable file format and replaces the .mde file format that was available in the previous versions of Access. • Access template (.accdt) is the file format for database templates. • Access runtime (.accdr) is the file format for runtime files.
PowerPoint	PowerPoint 2010 provides a varied list of file formats: • PowerPoint presentation (.pptx) is the default PowerPoint XML format. • PowerPoint macro-enabled presentation (.pptm) is also a basic XML format like the .pptx format, but can store VBA macro code. • PowerPoint template (.potx) is an XML-based PowerPoint template. • PowerPoint macro-enabled template (.potm) is an XML-based PowerPoint template that can store VBA macro code. • PowerPoint show (.ppsx) is an XML-based PowerPoint slide show that runs automatically when opened. • PowerPoint macro-enabled show (.ppsm) is an XML-based slide show that runs automatically when opened and contains VBA macro code. • PowerPoint add-in (.ppam) is an XML-based macro-enabled presentation that is run as a supplemental program.

 The "x" in Office 2010 file extensions stands for XML.

Advantages of XML File Formats

The new formats provide several benefits to end users.

Advantage	Description
Smaller file size	The new format uses zip compression to reduce file size by as much as 75 percent. These new file formats reduce the disk space required to store files and the bandwidth used to share documents across networks.
Improved information recovery	The files saved in these new formats are modularly structured. Different data components in the file are stored separately. Therefore, the file can be opened even if a component within the file has been damaged or corrupted.
Easier detection of documents with macros	The new file formats with their distinct file name extensions make it easy to distinguish files that contain macros, from those that do not. File extensions ending with 'x' cannot contain VBA macros or ActiveX controls, whereas file extensions ending with 'm' can.
Easy integration and interoperability of information	Information created within Office applications can be easily used by other business applications.

Interconversion of Access Databases in Different Formats

When working with databases in the previous versions of Access, you can use the **Convert** option available on the Microsoft Office button to upgrade the databases to the Access 2010 file format. However, to save the latest *.accdb file format to the *.mdb file format, the database must not include any of the enhanced features that are available in Access 2010.

The Compatibility Checker

The *Compatibility Checker* feature enables you to determine the compatibility of objects used in an Office 2010 document when you save the document in an earlier version. When you save an Office 2010 file in an earlier version, some of the contents, such as new text, shape effects, and SmartArt graphics, are converted to pictures for consistent presentation. These converted objects, however, cannot be modified using earlier versions of the application.

The Tabbed Document Viewing Feature

When a database created in the previous versions of Access is opened in Access 2010, the elements may be displayed as overlapping windows. To switch to tabbed document viewing, in the **Access Options** dialog box, in the **Current Database** category, in the **Application Options** section, under **Document Window Options,** select the **Tabbed Documents** option.

The PDF and XPS File Formats

Using Microsoft Office 2010, you can export or save any Microsoft Office system program files that are embedded in documents. Program files are embedded either in the Portable Document Format (PDF) or in the XML Paper Specification (XPS) file format. The PDF or XPS file format is a fixed-layout electronic format that preserves the file format exactly as intended, both in the print and online views. It also ensures that the file cannot be easily edited.

How to Save Files

Procedure Reference: Upgrade a File to the XML File Format

To upgrade a file to the XML file format:

1. In Office 2010, open a file saved in an earlier version.
2. Select the **File** tab and choose **Save As.**
3. If necessary, in the **Save As** dialog box, navigate to the desired location to save the file.
4. From the **Save as type** drop-down list, select the XML file format in which to save the file.
5. Click **Save**.

Procedure Reference: Save a File in the File Format of an Earlier Version

To save a file in the file format of an earlier version:

1. In Office 2010, open a file with the new XML file extension.
2. Select the **File** tab and choose **Save As.**
3. If necessary, in the **Save As** dialog box, navigate to the desired location to save the file.
4. From the **Save as type** drop-down list, select **[Application] 97–2003 [File Type] [Extension]**.
5. Click **Save** to save the file in the file format of the earlier version.
6. In the **Microsoft [Application] Compatibility Checker** dialog box, click **Continue** to modify as an uneditable object the features that are not supported in the earlier version.

ACTIVITY 1-3
Saving a Presentation

Data Files:

Company Introduction.pptx

Scenario:

You intend to work from home the following week and therefore want to save the presentation to your laptop. You need to save the presentation in the PowerPoint 2003 format because you have not installed PowerPoint 2010 on your laptop. You need to check whether you will be able to display all the objects properly in the PPT format when you work on the presentation at home.

1. Check for compatibility.

    a. Click **Start→All Programs→Microsoft Office→Microsoft PowerPoint 2010 (Beta)** to launch the Microsoft PowerPoint 2010 application.

    b. Navigate to the C:\084574Data\Getting Started with Microsoft Office 2010 folder and open the Company Introduction.pptx file.

    c. Select the **File** tab and, in the Information pane, from the **Check for Issues** drop-down list, select **Check Compatibility**.

    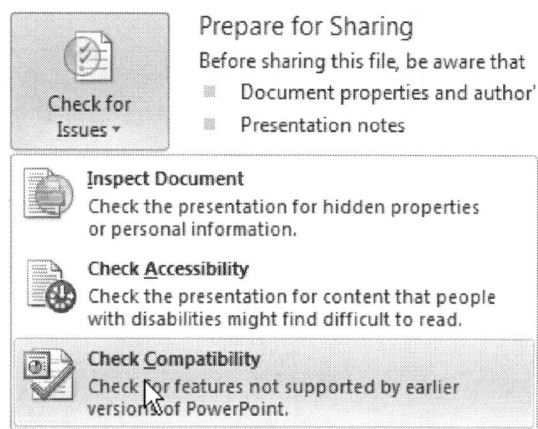

    d. In the **Microsoft PowerPoint Compatibility Checker** dialog box, observe that the features not supported in the PowerPoint 97–2003 format are displayed and click **OK**.

2. Save a presentation in the PPT format.

    a. Click **File→Save As** to open the **Save As** dialog box, and in the **Save As** dialog box, in the **File name** text box, type *My Company Introduction 2003*

    b. Observe that, in the **Save as Type** text box, the default file extension is (*.pptx).

c. From the **Save as type** drop-down list, select **PowerPoint 97–2003 Presentation (*.ppt)** and click **Save**.

d. In the **Microsoft PowerPoint Compatibility Checker** dialog box, observe that the objects that are incompatible with the PPT file format have been summarized.

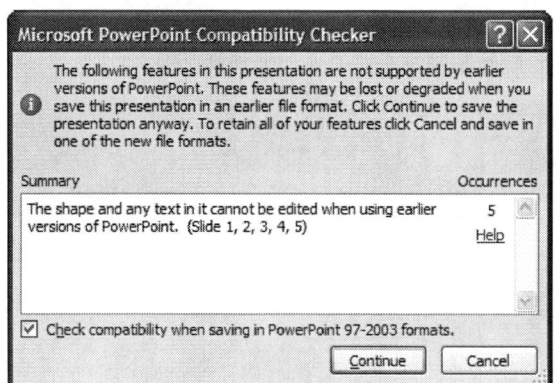

e. Click **Continue** to save the file.

f. Observe that the title bar displays the file name and close the presentation.

TOPIC D
Print Files

You saved a file. However, if you intend to share the information of your files as hard copies, you need to print the files. In this topic, you will print files.

At times it is necessary to have a hardcopy of a file. For example, when you are making a presentation in PowerPoint, providing hard copies of the presentation to the audience allows them to follow and refer to the content that you are presenting. It also provides them with a place to jot down any notes to use as reference material after the presentation.

Print Options in the Backstage View

In Office 2010, the **Print** option on the **File** tab in Backstage view enables you to either get a **Print Preview** of a document or **Print** it. **Print Preview** is an integrated option that allows you to view how a document will look when printed. In the PowerPoint application, the **Print** option in Backstage view displays two panes that let you preview and print a slide. The left pane is divided into three sections. The first section, **Print,** displays options to select the number of copies that need to be printed, as well as options to print them. The second section, **Printer,** allows you to select a printer and set printer properties. The third section, **Settings,** allows you to select the range of slides that need to be printed, set the orientation of slides, and choose the color option to print slides in a color, grayscale, or black and white printer. The right pane is where you preview slides before they are printed. You can also navigate through slides and set zoom options available at the bottom of the right pane, to magnify slides.

Figure 1-8: Print options as displayed in PowerPoint's Backstage view.

How to Print a Presentation

Procedure Reference: Preview a Presentation

To preview a presentation before printing it:

1. Select the **File** tab and choose **Print.**
2. In the right pane, view a print preview of the selected slide.
3. In the preview section, click the left and right arrow buttons to preview all the slides.

Procedure Reference: Print Slides by Using the Options in Backstage View

To print slides by using the options in Backstage view:

1. On the **File** tab, choose **Print.**
2. Apply the desired print settings.
   - In the **Settings** section, click the first drop-down arrow, and in the displayed gallery, select the slides that you want to print.
   - In the **Slides** text box, enter the slide numbers separated by commas or specify the range of slides to be printed, separated by a hyphen.
   - Click the third drop-down arrow, and from the displayed gallery, select a print layout option.
   - Click the fourth drop-down arrow, and from the displayed gallery, select the **Collated** option to print a copy of all slides, before printing the next copy, or select the **Uncollated** option to print the required number of copies of each slide, before moving on to the next slide.
   - Click the fifth drop-down arrow, and from the displayed gallery, select an option to print using the color, grayscale, or black and white option.
3. In the **Printer** section, from the drop-down list, select a printer and, if necessary, click the Printer Properties link to set printer properties such as Layout and Paper Quality.
4. In the **Print** section, in the **Copies** text box, enter the number of copies you want to print.
5. Click **Print** to print the copies.

ACTIVITY 1-4
Printing a Presentation

Data Files:

OGC Properties Overview Presentation.pptx

Before You Begin:

Navigate to the C:\084574Data\Getting Started with Microsoft Office 2010 folder and open the OGC Properties Overview Presentation.pptx file.

Scenario:

Your presentation is ready for delivery. Before you begin the presentation, you want to print the titles and main text of each slide for reference. However, you need to verify whether paper size and slide orientation have been set to ensure that the print output is perfect. You also want to print the notes associated with the slides, to use them as reference. Your manager has informed you that the presentation is going to be included as an appendix in the company's annual report. Therefore, you decide to print the presentation to append it to the report.

1. Set the slide orientation and paper size for printing.

    a. Select the **Design** tab and, in the **Page Setup** group, click **Page Setup**.

    b. In the **Page Setup** dialog box, in the **Slides** section, verify that the **Landscape** option is selected.

    c. In the **Notes, handouts & outline** section, verify that the **Landscape** option is selected.

    d. From the **Slides sized for** drop-down list, select **A4 Paper (210x297 mm)**.

    e. Click **OK** to apply the page settings to the presentation.

2. Print an outline of the presentation.

    a. Select the **File** tab and choose **Print**.

    b. In the **Settings** section, from the **Full Page Slides** drop-down list, in the **Print Layout** section, select **Outline**.

    c. Observe that the outline of the slide content is displayed in the preview pane.

    d. Click **Print** to print the presentation.

3. Print the speaker notes.

    a. Select the **File** tab and choose **Print**.

    b. In the **Settings** section, below the **Slides** text box, click **Outline** and, in the displayed gallery, in the **Print Layout** section, select **Notes Pages**.

    c. At the bottom-left corner of the preview pane, in the text box, click **1**, type *14* and press **Enter** to view the notes on the Revenue Highlights slide.

d. Click **Print** to print the notes.

4. Print the handouts.

    a. Select the **File** tab and choose **Print.**

    b. In the **Settings** section, in the first drop-down list, verify that **Print All Slides** is selected.

    c. Click **Notes Pages** and, in the displayed gallery, in the **Handouts** section, select **4 Slides Horizontal.**

    d. In the preview pane, observe that the four slides are horizontally displayed.

    e. Click **Print** to print the selected slides.

    f. Save and close the application.

Lesson 1 Follow-up

In this lesson, you identified the new components of the Microsoft Office user interface and the new file formats for saving files. You also customized the Microsoft Office environment to suit your requirements. This will enable you to customize the workspace, streamline your tasks, and work more efficiently with the new versions of the Office applications.

1. **What do you think are the advantages of the new user interface?**

2. **Of the new formatting options provided, which ones will you use in your everyday work?**

2 Modifying Documents Using Microsoft Office Word 2010

Lesson Time: 1 hour(s)

Lesson Objectives:

In this lesson, you will modify documents using Microsoft Office Word 2010.

You will:

- Move within a document using the navigation pane.
- Apply text Quick styles to documents.
- Work with SmartArt graphics to enhance a document with a visual effect.
- Screencapture images.
- Compare reviewed documents.

Introduction

You identified features in the new user interface in which commands have been organized into different groups in the Ribbon and contextual tabs. Word 2010 has additional options for the appropriate use of font styles and graphics, and the reusability of frequently appearing chunks of information. In this lesson, you will modify documents using Microsoft Word 2010.

Whether you are preparing a report for your boss or a proposal for a client, creating a multi-page document is invariably a tedious task. Therefore, while working on official documents, it is important to include a cover page and, at times, create visual elements that enhance the look and message of the document. You may also have to maintain standard formatting across different documents. Word 2010, with its simple commands and galleries, helps you create documents that reach the target audience in the intended manner.

TOPIC A
Use the Navigation Pane

You identified features in the new user interface in which commands are organized into different groups in the Ribbon and contextual tabs. You are now ready to access various types of information in a document and restructure the content. In this topic, you will navigate within a document to access and restructure information using the navigation pane.

Search engines make it easy and convenient to locate information on the web. Similarly, the navigation pane in Word 2010 makes it easy to access the document's content, and navigate between the sections, regardless of the length or number of pages. You also do not need to move through numerous pages in the document to go to a particular section. The navigation pane allows easy navigation between different sections in the document.

The Navigation Pane

The Navigation pane replaces the **Find** feature of Word 2003. It provides you with multiple ways to look for information in a document and its structure by skipping directly to a section of the document or to a page using the thumbnail image. The **Browse the headings in your document** view gives the outline of the structure of the document based on the headings and subheadings of the document. The **Browse the pages in your document** view gives the thumbnail images of pages in the document. The **Browse the results of your current search** view gives the results of searched text. The pane also contains improved search features to find particular text, whether it is in the headings, body, or other components of the document.

Figure 2-1: *The Navigation pane used to navigate through a document and restructure it.*

How to Use the Navigation Pane

Procedure Reference: Display the Navigation Pane

To display the Navigation pane:
1. Open a Word document.
2. Select the **View** tab.
3. In the **Show** section, check the **Navigation Pane** check box.
4. If necessary, click the second tab in the pane to view thumbnail images of pages of the document.

Procedure Reference: Modify a Document Using the Navigation Pane

To modify a document using the Navigation pane:
1. Display the Navigation pane.
2. If necessary, click the first tab to switch to the **Browse the headings in your document** view.
3. Right-click the required heading and modify the structure of the document.
   - Choose **Promote** or **Demote** to modify the heading levels.
   - Choose **New Heading Before** or **New Heading After** to insert a new heading at the desired location.
   - Choose **New Subheading** to insert a new subheading.
   - Choose **Delete** to delete the heading.

Procedure Reference: Search for and Replace Text Using the Navigation Pane

To search for and replace text using the Navigation pane:
1. In the **Search Document** text box, click and type the search keyword.
2. Beside the **Search Document** text box, click the drop-down arrow and choose **Find.**
3. If necessary, in the **Find and Replace** dialog box, click **More.**
4. Select the **Replace** tab.
5. In the **Replace with** text box, click and type the correct word.
6. Click **Find Next** to display the next instance of the search word and then click **Replace** or **Replace All.**

ACTIVITY 2-1
Using the Navigation Pane

Data Files:

Annual Report.docx

Before You Begin:

Navigate to the C:\084574\Modifying Documents Using Microsoft Word 2010 folder and open the Annual Report.docx file.

Scenario:

You are working on a lengthy report with content structured using headings and subheadings. Within the limited time alloted, you are asked to quickly navigate through the document and modify its structure by manipulating the outlines and headings.

1. Navigate to make corrections to the content under the "National Affiliate Program" subheading.

    a. Verify that the Navigation pane is displayed.

    > On the **View** tab, in the **Show** section, check the **Navigation Pane** check box.

    b. In the Navigation pane, under the "Long Term Strategy" heading, right-click the "National Affiliate Program" subheading.

    c. Observe that the **Show Heading 3** option is checked indicating that it is a level 3 heading.

    d. Choose **Promote** to change the heading level to level 2.

    e. Click the **National Affiliate Program** subheading to navigate to and view the content under the heading.

    f. Toward the end of the third sentence, double-click **17** and type **19**

2. Search for the word "Company" and change it to sentence case in all instances.

    a. Press **Ctrl+Home**.

    b. In the Navigation pane, in the **Search Document** text box, click and type **Company**

    c. Beside the **Search Document** text box, click the drop-down arrow and choose **Find**.

    d. In the **Find and Replace** dialog box, click **More**.

    e. Check the **Match case** check box.

f. Select the **Replace** tab.

g. In the **Replace with** text box, click and type *company*

h. Click **Find Next** and then click **Replace.**

i. Click **Replace All** to replace all instances of the search word.

j. Click **OK** in the **Microsoft Word** message box.

k. Close the **Find and Replace** dialog box.

l. Save the document as *My Annual Report.docx*

m. From the Quick Access toolbar click **Close.**

TOPIC B
Apply Text Styles

You used the Navigation pane to navigate to a document and modify its the structure. You are now ready to begin authoring content. In the course of your work, you may want to make a word, line, or paragraph stand out from the surrounding text. If your documents have to meet some style requirements, you may need to apply appropriate styles. In this topic, you will apply styles to a document.

When you create a document, you may want to apply a specific set of font styles to text, modify the shape of an object, or change the colors within a table. Instead of accessing each of these options from different dialog boxes, Word 2010 makes it convenient for you to select the desired output from the selections in the preset style galleries. Word 2010 styles help you quickly achieve consistent and customized design and formatting effects.

The Styles Command

The *Styles command* contains sets of styles packaged together to apply design and formatting changes to a document. You can select a text style from the **Quick Styles** gallery on the **Home** tab, or from the corresponding galleries for other style commands on the **Design** or **Format** contextual tab. You can also modify an existing style or build a new style and add it to the **Quick Styles** gallery.

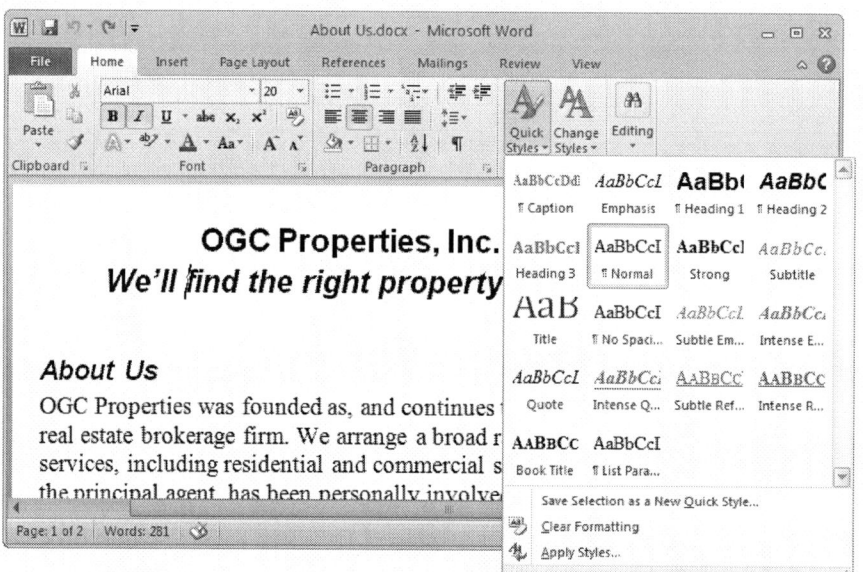

Figure 2-2: Various text styles displayed in a Word Quick Styles gallery.

Font Styles and Typography

Word 2010 fonts are designed to improve readability by ensuring that words displayed on screen appear as sharp and clear as those on paper. Calibri, which is a Sans-Serif font with soft rounded corners, is the default font in Word 2010. Gabriola is a new font style introduced in Word 2010. OpenType typography introduced in Word 2010 provides scalable font options to create content in many languages by using typography features such as *ligatures* and *stylistic sets*.

Ligatures are characters containing two letters combined into one by connecting them. Stylistic sets are used to display the same font with a slightly different look in a document. Ligatures are available for some fonts, and are not enabled by default. You can change the settings for ligatures by using the **Advanced** tab in the **Font** dialog box.

How to Apply Text Quick Styles

Procedure Reference: Create a New Quick Style

To create a new Quick style:

1. Select the desired text.
2. Apply the desired formatting to the text.
3. Save the formatting as a new style.
   - Right-click the selection and choose **Styles→Save Selection as a New Quick Style.**
   - On the **Home** tab, from the **Styles** group, click the **More** button, and from the displayed gallery, select **Save Selection as a New Quick Style.**
4. In the **Create New Style from Formatting** dialog box, in the **Name** text box, type a name.
5. Click **OK** to add the style to the **Quick Styles** gallery.
6. If necessary, in the **Styles** group, in the **Quick Styles** gallery, click the **More** button to view the new style.

Procedure Reference: Apply a Text Style from the Quick Styles Gallery

To apply a style from the Quick Styles Gallery:

1. Select the text to which you want to apply a style.
2. Apply the desired style.
   a. Press **Alt+Ctrl+Shift+S** to open the **Styles** task pane and select the desired style.
   b. On the **Home** tab, in the **Styles** group, click the **More** button and select the desired style from the **Quick Styles** gallery.

Procedure Reference: Modify an Existing Text Quick Style

To modify an existing Quick style:

1. On the **Home** tab, in the **Styles** group, from the **Quick Styles** gallery, right-click the desired style and choose **Modify.**
2. In the **Modify Style** dialog box, format the style as needed.
3. Click **OK** to close the dialog box.

4. If necessary, save the modified style.
    a. On the **Home** tab, in the **Styles** group, click **Change Styles.**
    b. From the **Style Set** submenu, choose **Save as Quick Style Set.**
    c. In the **Save Quick Style Set** dialog box, in the **File name** text box, enter a style name and click **Save.**
5. If necessary, click **Change Styles,** and from the **Style Set** submenu, choose **Reset Document Quick Styles** to restore the default styles.

ACTIVITY 2-2
Applying Text Quick Styles to a Document

Data Files:

Styles.docx

Before You Begin:

1. Navigate to the C:\084574Data\Modifying Documents Using Microsoft Word 2010 folder and open the Styles.docx file.
2. Close the Navigation pane.

Scenario:

You need to create a document to send to some of your company's new clients. Your manager has approved the content but has asked you to ensure that the company's name is displayed in a distinct style throughout the document.

---

1. Format the text "OGC Properties."

    a. In the paragraph below the heading "About Us", click before the first occurrence of the text "OGC", hold down **Shift** and click after the text "Properties."

    b. On the Mini toolbar, click the **Bold** button.

    c. On the Mini toolbar, click the **Font Color** drop-down arrow and, in the **Standard Colors** section, select the first color to apply the dark red color.

    d. On the Mini toolbar, from the **Font Size** drop-down list, select **14**.

---

2. Save the format as a quick style.

    a. Right-click the selected text and choose **Styles→Save Selection as a New Quick Style**.

    b. In the **Create New Style from Formatting** dialog box, in the **Name** text box, type *ogc_prop* and click **OK**.

    c. On the **Home** tab, in the **Styles** group, click the **More** button.

d. Verify that the **ogc_prop** style is added to the **Styles** gallery.

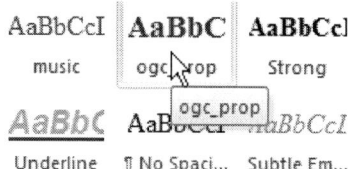

e. Click away from the **Styles** list to close the **Styles** gallery.

3. Apply the **ogc_prop** quick style to all other occurrences of the text "OGC Properties."

   a. In the second paragraph, click before the text "OGC," hold down **Shift,** and click after the text "Properties."

   b. On the **Home** tab, in the **Styles** group, click the **More** button and select the **ogc_prop** style.

   c. Observe that the quick style is applied to the text.

   d. Similarly, apply the **ogc_prop** quick style to all the other occurrences of the text "OGC Properties."

4. Save and close the document.

   a. Select the **File** tab and choose **Save As.**

   b. In the **Save As** dialog box, in the **File name** text box, type *My Styles* and click **Save.**

   c. From the Quick Access toolbar, click **Close.**

ACTIVITY 2-3
Modifying an Existing Style

Data Files:

Modify Style.docx

Before You Begin:

Navigate to the C:\084574Data\Modifying Documents using Microsoft Word folder and open the Modify Style.docx file.

Scenario:

You have highlighted your company's name with a distinct and consistent look. Having explored and implemented the Quick Style feature, you find that one Quick Style option, which you use frequently, comes in handy except that you need to make a couple of changes to it to suit your needs. You want to modify the existing style so that you can use it in the future.

1. Select the **Distinctive** style and set it as the default.

    a. On the **Home** tab, in the **Styles** group, from **Change Styles** drop down list select **Style Set.**

    b. From the **Style Set** submenu, choose **Distinctive.**

    c. Observe that the appearance of the document as well as the **Styles** gallery changes.

    d. Click **Change Styles** and choose **Set as Default.**

2. Modify the attributes of the **Distinctive** style.

    a. On the **Home** tab, in the **Styles** group, right-click the **Body** style and choose **Modify.**

    b. In the **Modify Style** dialog box, in the **Formatting** section, from the **Font** drop-down list, select **Agency FB.**

    c. From the **Font Size** drop-down list, select **14.**

    d. From the **Font Color** drop-down list, in the **Standard Colors** section, select the eighth color to apply the blue color.

    e. Click **OK** to view the changes to the document and the gallery.

3. Save the modified style and then save and close the document.

    a. On the **Home** tab, in the **Styles** group, click **Change Styles→Style Set.**

    b. From the **Style Set** submenu, choose **Save as Quick Style Set.**

    c. In the **Save Quick Style Set** dialog box, in the **File name** text box, type *My Style*

    d. Observe that the QuickStyle is save as a **Word Template (*.dotx)** format.

    e. Click **Save** to save the document.

f. In the **Styles** group, click **Change Styles** and choose **Style Set.**

g. Observe that the modified style, **My Style,** is added to the **Style Set** submenu.

h. On the **Home** tab, in the **Styles** group, click **Change Styles** to close the menu.

i. Save the document as *My Modify Style* in the DOCX format.

j. Close the file.

TOPIC C
Work with SmartArt Graphics

You applied various text styles to enhance the visual appeal of text. In a similar way, some content is conveyed more effectively by using appropriate visual elements such as SmartArt graphics, which also lend a professional look to the document. In this topic, you will add SmartArt graphics to a document.

Readers are increasingly bombarded with information from magazines, newspapers, websites, and other sources. With a variety of media vying for a target group's attention, you want to make every effort to ensure that your content stands out. With Office 2010, you can break the monotony found in pages and pages of text by including supporting graphics, charts, and shapes.

SmartArt Graphics

SmartArt graphics are layouts used to depict a time line or developmental progression, or the sequential steps in a process or workflow. The **SmartArt** button located in the **Illustrations** group of the **Insert** tab is used to insert SmartArt graphics. You can select a layout from the gallery of existing layouts, where they are categorized on the basis of whether they represent a **List, Process, Cycle, Hierarchy, Relationship, Matrix,** or **Pyramid.** These layouts can either be used as they are, or you can incorporate design and formatting changes into them by using commands on their respective contextual tabs.

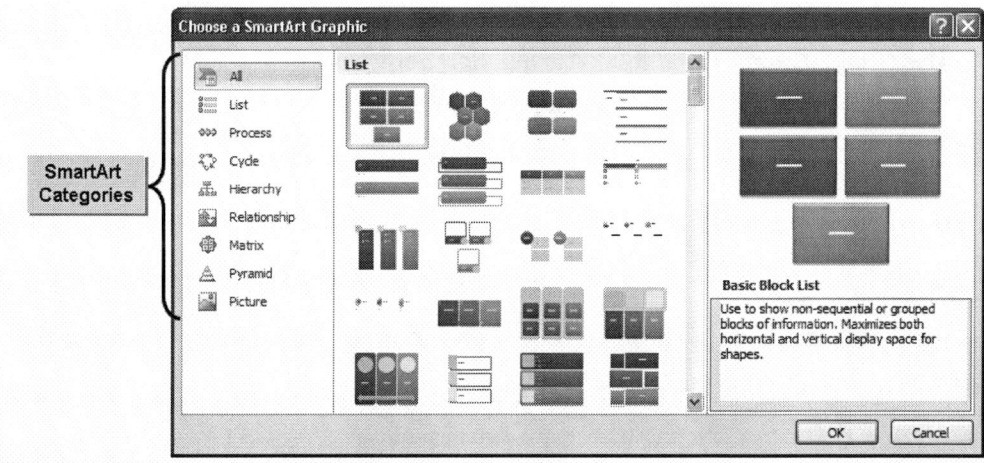

Figure 2-3: The SmartArt Graphics dialog box displaying the different types of layouts.

Categories of SmartArt Graphics

The items in the **Choose a SmartArt Graphic** dialog box are classified into nine categories. The categories are described in the table.

SmartArt Category	Content
All	Graphics that are a combination of all functional categories.
List	Graphics to display a list of items.

SmartArt Category	Content
Process	Graphics to illustrate process flows.
Cycle	Graphics to demonstrate process cycles.
Hierarchy	Graphics to represent hierarchical structures.
Relationship	Graphics to illustrate the relationship between entities.
Matrix	Graphics to illustrate the relationship of four quadrants to a single entity.
Pyramid	Graphics to illustrate a hierarchical relationship.
Picture	Graphics to display a series of pictures with corresponding captions.

Reset Graphic

The **Reset Graphic** button enables you to remove all the formatting changes made to a diagram or a SmartArt graphic and helps to restore the original version of the graphic.

How to Work with SmartArt Graphics

Procedure Reference: Insert a SmartArt Graphic

To insert a SmartArt graphic:

1. Open a file.
2. Place the insertion point where you would like to insert the SmartArt graphic.
3. On the **Insert** tab, in the **Illustrations** group, click **SmartArt.**
4. In the **Choose A SmartArt Graphic** dialog box, in the left pane, select a diagram type.
5. In the center pane, select the desired layout. A preview of the selected layout is displayed in the right pane.
6. Click **OK** to insert the selected layout in the document. Observe that the **Design** and **Format** contextual tabs appear on the Ribbon.
7. Add text to the graphic.
   - Use the **Type Your Text Here** text pane to insert text.
     a. In the **Type Your Text Here** text pane, type the text.
     b. Press **Enter** to enter the text in the next level.
     c. Close the **Type Your Text Here** text pane.
   - Or, click **[Text]** to enter text.

Procedure Reference: Apply Graphic and 3D Effects to SmartArt Graphics

To apply graphic and 3D effects to SmartArt graphics:

1. Select the desired SmartArt graphic.
2. If necessary, using the options on the **Design** contextual tab, change the layouts and styles of the SmartArt graphic.
3. If necessary, click a shape in the SmartArt graphic and, from the **Create Graphic** group, from the **Add Shape** drop-down list, select the desired option to add another shape to the graphic layout.

4. Apply the desired quick style to modify the SmartArt graphics.
   - In the **SmartArt Styles** group, click **Change Colors** and then select the desired color to apply to the graphic layout.
   - In the **SmartArt Styles** group, select the desired graphic style to apply to the graphic layout and click the **More** button to view additional graphic styles.
5. In the SmartArt graphic, select the desired shape to apply shape and style effects.
6. Select the **Format** contextual tab, and in the **Shape Styles** group, select the desired option to apply the desired shape style and effects.
7. If necessary, add a bullet list within a shape.
   a. Select the desired shape.
   b. In the **SmartArt Tools** section, select the **Design** contextual tab.
   c. In the **Create Graphic** group, click **Add Bullet.**

ACTIVITY 2-4
Creating an Organizational Chart Using SmartArt Graphics

Data Files:

Graphic.docx

Before You Begin:

Navigate to the C:\084574Data\Modifying Documents Using Microsoft Word 2010 folder and open the Graphic.docx file.

Scenario:

Your company has recently hired several marketing executives at both the senior and junior levels. As the marketing manager, you need to create a document representing the organizational hierarchy and distribute it to the new employees as part of their orientation program. The organizational structure details are listed below.

1. First level - Marketing Manager – J. Rivera
2. Second level - Associate Manager – M. Muller and R. Moore
3. Third level - Marketing Executives – J. Dillon, R. Michael, and J. Jackson
4. J. Dillon and R. Michael report to M. Muller, while J. Jackson reports to R. Moore

1. Insert a SmartArt graphic.

    a. Click at the end of second paragraph and press **Enter.**

    b. Select the **Insert** tab.

    c. In the **Illustrations** group, click **SmartArt.**

    d. In the **Choose a SmartArt Graphic** dialog box, in the left pane, select **Hierarchy.**

    e. In the center pane, in the second row, first column, select **Hierarchy.**

    f. In the right pane, click **OK.**

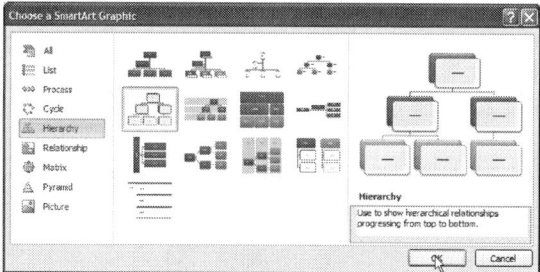

An enlarged preview of the selected layout is displayed showing greater detail.

2. Enter the organizational details.

   a. Close the text pane.

   b. At the top level, click in the first box, type **Marketing Manager** and then press **Enter.**

   c. Type **J. Rivera**

   d. Similarly, enter the associate managers' names and the marketing executives' names in the boxes provided at the appropriate levels based on the details provided in the scenario.

3. Format the SmartArt graphic and then save and close the document.

   a. Verify the **Design** contextual tab is selected.

   b. In the **SmartArt Styles** group, click **Change Colors.**

   c. Scroll down, and in the **Accent 5** section, select the third option to apply **Gradient Range - Accent 5.**

   d. In the **SmartArt Styles** gallery, click **More** and, in the second row, first column, select **Moderate Effect.**

   e. Click away from the graphic.

   f. In the first box, click before the text "Marketing" and Shift-click after the text "J. Rivera."

   g. On the **Home** tab, in the **Font** group, click the **Font Color** drop-down arrow.

   h. In the **Theme Colors** section, in the fifth row, fourth column, select **Dark Blue, Text 2, Darker 25%.**

   i. Similarly, apply the same formatting to all the text in the various levels.

   j. Click beside the diagram to select the entire organizational chart.

   k. Select the **Format** contextual tab.

   l. In the **Shape Styles** group, click **Shape Fill,** and in the **Theme Colors** section, in the second row, ninth column, select **Aqua, Accent 5, Lighter 80%.**

m. Notice that the fill color of the organizational chart has changed.

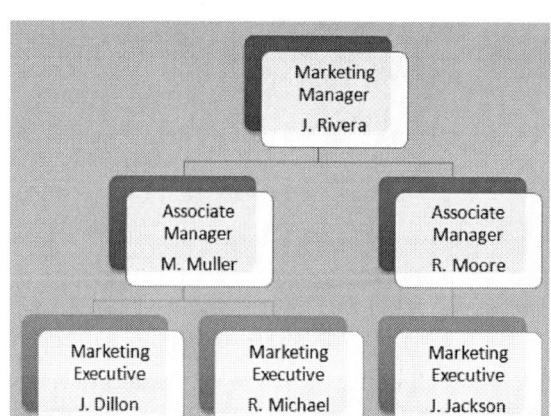

n. Save the document as **My Graphic.docx**

o. Close the file.

TOPIC D
Insert Screenshots in a Document

You added SmartArt objects to a document. In addition to this, you may also need to insert screenshots of images in a document. In this topic, you will insert images as a visual supplement to a Word document.

When working on documents, you often need to add images to supplement and enhance text in them. You may need to capture an image of an application window and insert it into the document that you are creating. Office 2010 provides you with built-in tools to capture and modify images, without the need to use any external software. This simplifies capturing and editing images, and also reduces the time taken for this process.

The Screencapture Tool

The **Screenshot** tool is a new feature in Microsoft Office 2010 that allows you to capture screens of any available windows automatically or clip a certain portion of your screen manually. The captured screen is automatically inserted in a document.

The Background Removal Tool

Background Removal is a new feature in Microsoft Office 2010 that allows you to easily remove the background of an image. When you apply this tool to an image, the background area gets highlighted in purple. You can then mark the areas to be removed and retain some parts of the background.

The Background Removal Tab

When you use the **Background Removal** tool, the **Background Removal** tab is displayed on the Ribbon. This tab provides you with different options to define areas that need to be retained in an image and the areas that are to be removed from it.

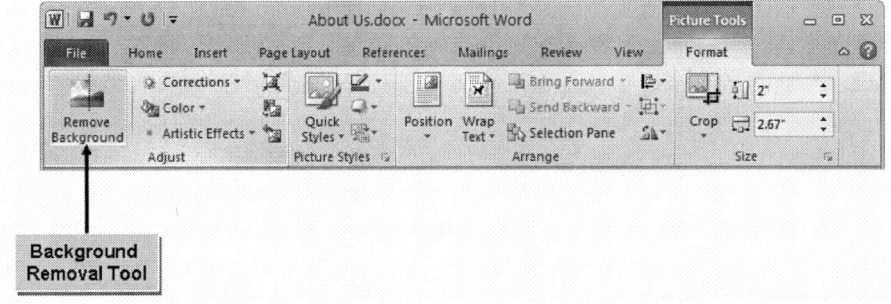

Figure 2-4: The Remove Background tool available in the Picture Tools contextual tab.

How to Screencapture Images

Procedure Reference: Capture Screenshots

To capture screenshots:

1. Place the insertion point at the desired location in the document.
2. Select the **Insert** tab.
3. Capture the screenshot.
   - In the **Illustrations** group, click **Screenshot** and, from the gallery, select the window that you want to capture a screenshot of.
   - In the **Illustrations** group, click **Screenshot** and, from the gallery, select **Screen Clipping** to capture a region of the window.
4. If necessary, click and drag to mark the area of the window that you need to capture.
5. The screenshot gets inserted into the Word document. If necessary, drag the image placeholder to reposition it.

ACTIVITY 2-5
Capturing Images

Data Files:

Cofee Makers.docx

Before You Begin:

1. Open Internet Explorer and, in the Address bar, type **www.everythingforcoffee.com** to launch the website.
2. Close the popup blocker.
3. Navigate to the C:\084574Data\Modifying Documents using Microsoft Word folder and open the Coffee Makers.docx file.

Scenario:

In your document discussing the different types of coffee beans and coffee makers, you want to display a list of products available in your company. The product list is found on your company's website. You decide to capture an image of the product list details and add it to your document. Also, you decide to edit the image to suit your company's presentation standards.

Choose your blend from the array of finest gourmet beans in our store and enjoy the exhilarating gourmet experience.

1. Display the image to be captured.

    a. Place the insertion point at the end of the third paragraph under the heading "Gourmet Beans" and press **Enter.**

    b. From the Windows taskbar, switch to the Everything For Coffee - Windows Internet Explorer window.

c. On the Home page, click the **Gourmet Beans** link.

d. On the **Gourmet Beans** page, at the bottom-right corner of the page, click the **Products List** link to display the products list in a separate pop-up window.

2. Capture a screenshot of the Products List window.

　　a. Switch to the Coffee Makers.docx - Microsoft Word window.

　　b. On the **Insert** tab, in the **Illustrations** group, click **Screenshot**.

　　c. In the displayed gallery, in the **Available Windows** section, select the **Products List window** image to insert it in the document.

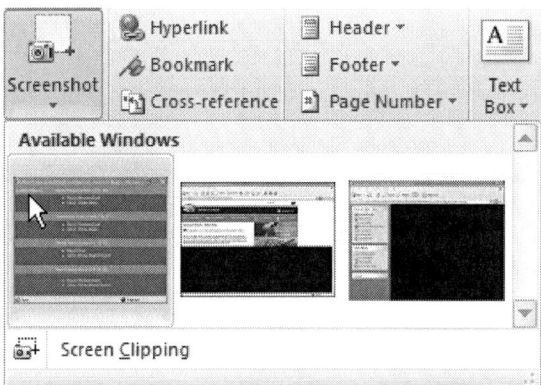

3. Edit the image.

　　a. Observe that the **Picture Tools** tool tab is displayed.

　　b. On the **Format** contextual tab, in the **Size** group, from the **Crop** drop-down list, select **Crop**.

　　c. Click and drag the top-center cropping handle downward until the border touches the gray line above the **Gourmet Beans** heading.

　　d. Place the mouse pointer over the center handle in the bottom border of the picture and drag the crop tool pointer upward until the border touches the gray line above the status bar.

　　e. Click outside the selection to view the edited picture.

　　f. Select the image and, on the **Format** contextual tab, in the **Adjust** group, click **Color** to display the **Color** gallery.

　　g. In the **Color Tone** section, select the last color tone.

　　h. Click outside the selection to view the edited picture.

　　i. Save the document as *My Coffee Makers* in the (*.docx) format and close it.

TOPIC E
Compare Reviewed Documents

You have created a document and it is now ready to be reviewed. As with most official documents sent to the client, the document might go through multiple rounds of review. Word 2010 allows for feedback from different sources to be consolidated and incorporated into documents with ease. In this topic, you will use Word 2010 to compare reviewed documents.

Sifting through multiple versions of the same document to hunt for suggested changes by reviewers can be a daunting task. In addition, you run the risk of missing crucial information and, ultimately, the integrity of your document can be threatened. With Word 2010, you can quickly and easily find all the changes that have been made to documents by using a few simple review commands.

The Compare Feature

The *Compare feature* enables you to combine or compare different versions of a document and check for information that may have been deleted, modified, moved, or replaced in the original document. This feature is available in the **Compare** group of the **Review** tab.

By clicking the **Compare** option, you can select either of the two available options to find all the suggestions and review comments placed in the document, regardless of who has made them.

Option	*Description*
Compare	Displays what has changed between the two documents being compared. Upon selecting this option, Word displays four panes. The extreme left pane displays only the changes that are made. The pane in the center displays the compared document in which changes are tracked. The panes on the right display original and revised documents.
Combine	Combines revisions from different authors into one single document. Selecting this option displays four panes. The extreme left pane displays only changes that are made. The pane in the center displays the combined document in which changes are tracked. The panes on the right display the original and revised documents.

The Tri-Pane Review Panel

The *Tri-Pane Review panel* is used to view and compare two different versions of a document along with the view that combines modifications from both versions. You can scroll simultaneously in all three views, making it easier to compare different versions of the same document. The **Tri-Pane Review** panel is displayed when you click the **Compare** command in the **Compare** group.

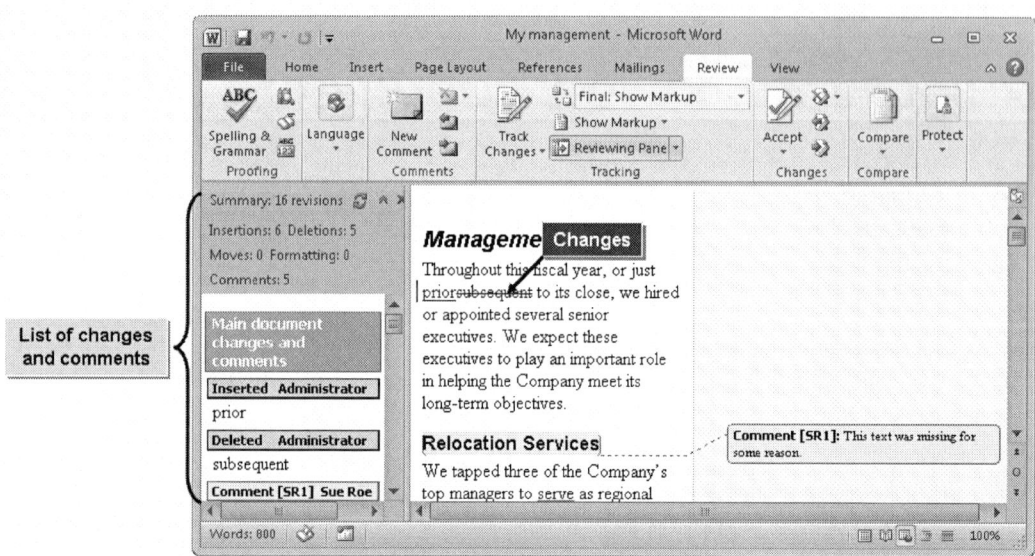

Figure 2-5: *The Review pane listing the changes and comments made by a reviewer.*

How to Compare Reviewed Documents

Procedure Reference: Compare Reviewed Documents

To compare reviewed documents:

1. Open a reviewed Word document.
2. Select the **Review** tab.
3. Compare the reviewed document with another document.
   - Compare two versions of a document.
     a. Choose **Compare.**
     b. In the **Compare Documents** dialog box, click the **Browse For Original** button and open the original document.
     c. Click the **Browse For Revised** button, open the revised document, and click **OK.**
     d. In the **Microsoft Word** message box, click **Yes.**
   - Compare revisions from multiple authors.
     a. Choose **Combine.**
     b. In the **Combine Documents** dialog box, click the **Browse For Original** button and open the original document.
     c. Click the **Browse For Revised** button and open the revised document.
     d. In the **Combine Documents** dialog box, click **OK.**

Procedure Reference: Change the Compare Options

To change the compare options:

1. Open a Word document.

2. Change the position of the **Reviewing** pane.
   a. Select the **Review** tab, and in the **Tracking** group, click **Reviewing Pane** to view the summary of changes at the side of the window.
   b. Click the **Reviewing Pane** drop-down arrow and select **Reviewing Pane Horizontal** to view the summary at the bottom of the window or select **Reviewing Pane Vertical** to view the summary in the left side of the window.
3. If necessary, in the **Tracking** group, click **Show Markup** and select the types of changes you want to review.
4. If necessary, click **Show Markup,** then click **Reviewers,** and select only the reviewers whose changes you want to view.
5. If necessary, click **Previous** or **Next** to navigate and accept or reject the changes suggested by the reviewers.
   - On the **Review** tab, in the **Changes** group, click the **Accept** drop-down list and select the required option.
   - Or, click the **Reject** drop-down list and select the required option.
6. Save and close the document.

ACTIVITY 2-6
Comparing the Changes Made to a Document

Data Files:

Management.docx, Management Reviewed.docx

Before You Begin:

Close all open windows.

Scenario:

You need to prepare a report about your management team and deliver it to a few prospective clients. You have worked on the report and sent it to your manager for review. You receive the document back with some changes tracked. Before accepting the changes, you want to compare the original and revised versions of the document.

1. Compare the original and revised documents.

    a. On the Ribbon, select the **Review** tab.

    b. In the **Compare** group, click **Compare** and choose **Compare**.

    c. In the **Compare Documents** dialog box, click the **Browse For Original** button.

    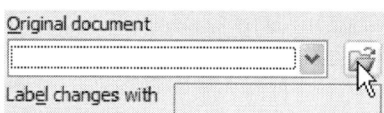

    d. Navigate to the C:\084574\Modifying Documents folder and open the Management.docx file.

    e. Click the **Browse For Revised** button, open the Management Reviewed.docx file, and click **OK**.

    f. In the **Microsoft Word** message box, click **Yes**.

    g. Observe that the **Tri-Pane Review** panel displays the original, revised, and compared documents.

2. Change the compare options and then save and close the document.

    a. On the **Review** tab, in the **Tracking** group, from the **Reviewing Pane** drop-down list, select **Reviewing Pane Horizontal**.

    b. Notice that the reviewing pane appears at the bottom of the screen, click the **Track Changes** drop-down list, and select **Change Tracking Options**.

    c. In the **Track Changes Options** dialog box, in the **Markup** section, from the **Insertions** drop-down list, select **Double underline** and click **OK**.

d. Notice that the lines inserted by the reviewer are denoted using a double underline, save the document as **My Management.docx** and close the application.

Lesson 2 Follow-up

In this lesson, you modified documents using various features available in Word 2010. Document creation and modification is easier with these features that allow users to create professional-looking documents along with various value-add elements.

1. **By using Word 2010, what changes in the document creation process do you foresee? Explain.**

2. **Which new feature in Word 2010 do you consider to be the most useful? Why?**

3 Working with Spreadsheets Using Microsoft Office Excel 2010

Lesson Time: 1 hour(s), 15 minutes

Lesson Objectives:

In this lesson, you will present spreadsheet data using Microsoft Office Excel 2010.

You will:

- Work with tables in Excel 2010.
- Apply conditional formatting to data in spreadsheets.
- Apply a formula.
- Work with charts for presenting Excel data.
- Create Sparklines
- Create PivotTables and PivotCharts.

Introduction

Now that you have used some of the latest feature enhancements in Microsoft Word, you are ready to work with the new features in Excel 2010 to create and modify spreadsheets. The latest release of this software offers various enhancements for improving the management, presentation, and distribution of spreadsheets. In this lesson, you will work with the new and enhanced features in Microsoft Office Excel 2010.

There is often a need to manipulate large volumes of data in a short period of time. The new and enhanced features in Microsoft Office Excel 2010 facilitate management of voluminous data. Another challenge lies in presenting data in a way that it is intelligible to everyone including professionals who may not be familiar with the data set, but need to understand and interpret it correctly. Excel 2010 offers visual enhancements that allow you to turn a spreadsheet filled with numbers into an interactive one, with graphs and charts to represent the numbers on the sheet. Having a working knowledge of these tools will allow you to perform complex operations and greatly expand your data-management capabilities.

TOPIC A
Work with Tables in Excel 2010

You are familiar with the common features of the Office 2010 environment and have identified various interface components. Now you are ready to effectively manage, present, and organize data in Excel 2010. In this topic, you will organize data in Excel using enhanced tables and table formats.

You may have to deal with large amounts of data that you need to process and analyze. You can use the features offered by Excel to aid you in working with data, and to enable you to efficiently organize data into a comprehensible and structured form.

Excel Table Enhancements

Excel allows you to easily insert a table in a worksheet and work with table data. The **Create Table** dialog box provides you with the option to select data to be included in a table, and also add headers to a table. The banded rows in a table help you easily associate row headers with their corresponding data. Additionally, table headers appear as column headers when you scroll down a large table. AutoFilters also appear by default in each column and are automatically moved to the column header when you scroll down a large table. An added new functionality in tables in Excel 2010 is that you can now search out data within the AutoFilter list. Using the filter option, you can also filter rows based on values and cell color.

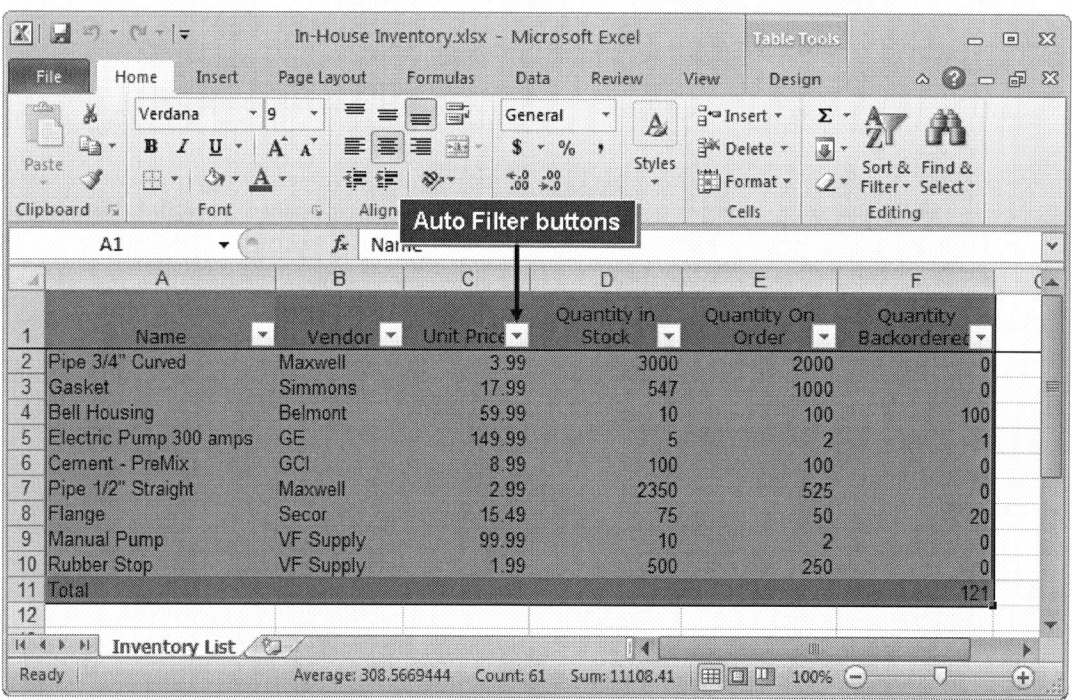

Figure 3-1: A table displaying the enhancements to Excel.

Excel Template Enhancements

Excel 2010 includes additional template categories and templates that you can use to create professional-looking spreadsheets. You can either use templates that ship with Office 2010 or download them from Microsoft Office Online. The templates in Excel 2010 are customizable and can suit specific requirements of businesses or individuals.

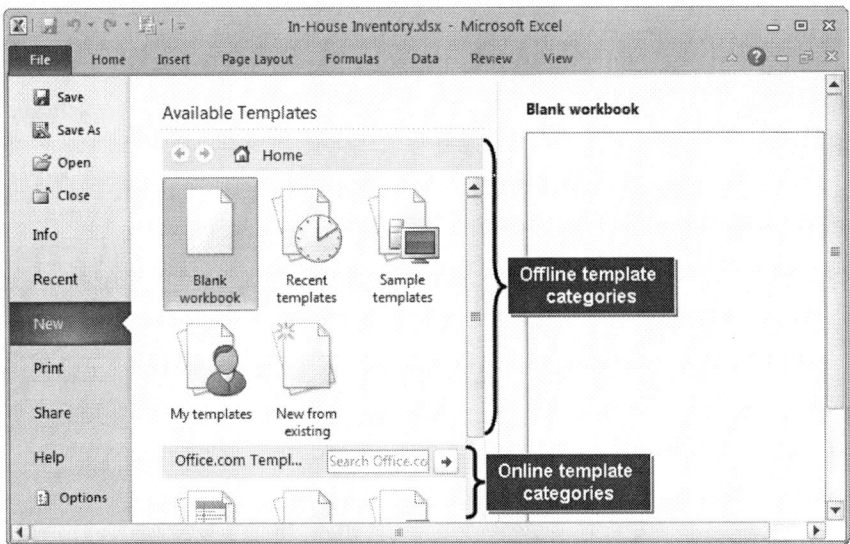

Figure 3-2: The Backstage view displaying the offline and online template categories.

How to Work with Tables in Excel 2010

Procedure Reference: Build a Table from an Existing Data Source

To build a table from an existing data source:

1. On an open Excel worksheet, select a range of cells to be displayed as a table.
2. On the **Insert** tab, in the **Tables** group, click **Table.**
3. In the **Create Table** dialog box, specify the data range for the table.
4. If necessary, check the **My table has headers** check box to specify headers for the table.

 If you do not check the **My table has headers** check box in the **Create Table** dialog box, then the table will be displayed with the default header names.

5. In the **Create Table** dialog box, click **OK.**

Procedure Reference: Convert a Table to a Data Range

To convert a table to a data range:

1. Open the Excel worksheet with a table.
2. Select the table to display contextual tabs on the Ribbon.
3. On the **Design** tab, in the **Tools** group, click **Convert to Range.**
4. In the **Microsoft Excel** message box, click **Yes** to convert the table to a normal range.

When you convert a table into a normal range of cells, contextual tabs on the Ribbon disappear.

Procedure Reference: Filter Data in a Table

To filter data in a table:

1. In the table header, click the drop-down arrow to display the **AutoFilter** drop-down list.
2. In the **AutoFilter** drop-down list, in the **Search** text box, type the search item.
3. Check the check box of the item you want to filter.
4. If necessary, in the **Search** text box, type the next search item and check **Add current selection to filter** to add the new search item to the existing filter.

Procedure Reference: View Excel Templates in Backstage View

To view Excel templates in Backstage view:

1. Select the **File** tab and choose **New** to display available templates.
2. Open a template.
   - Select a saved template.
     a. In the **Available Templates** pane, select **My templates.**
     b. In the **New** dialog box, select the desired template and click **OK.**
   - Select an existing template.
     a. In the **Available Templates** section, select **New from existing.**
     b. In the **New from Existing Workbook** dialog box, navigate to the required folder.
     c. Select the desired template and click **Create New.**
   - Select an installed template.
     a. In the **Available Templates** section, select **Sample templates.**
     b. Select the desired template and click **Create.**
   - Select an online template.
     a. In the **Office.com Templates** section, select a category.
     b. If necessary, in the middle pane, select a subcategory.
     c. Select the desired template and click **Download.**

To access online templates, your workstation must have an Internet connection.

ACTIVITY 3-1
Working with Tables

Data Files:

In-House Inventory.xlsx

Before You Begin:

From the C:\084574Data\Working with Spreadsheets folder, open the In-House Inventory.xlsx file.

Scenario:

You are using Excel 2010 to store data related to inhouse inventory. You need to effectively present data, and also discuss at the weekly meeting issues related to inventory levels. You plan to organize data so that the statistics can be easily understood by all attendees.

1. Convert data into a table.

    a. Select the **Insert** tab, and in the **Tables** group, click **Table**.

    b. In the **Create Table** dialog box, click **OK**.

    c. Observe that the selected range of cells is displayed as a table with column headers, filter drop-down arrows, and banded rows.

    d. Click any of the cells outside the table to deselect the table.

2. Use the table filter options to filter data related to rubber stops.

    a. In the Name header, click the drop-down arrow, to display the **AutoFilter** drop-down list.

    b. In the **AutoFilter** drop-down list, in the **Search** text box, click and type *ru*

    c. Observe that Rubber Stop is displayed in the filtered list and click **OK**.

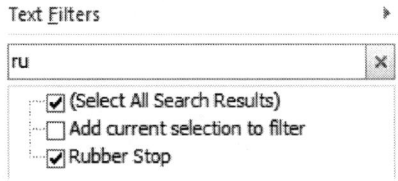

3. Add another filter item.

    a. In the Name header, click the drop-down arrow to display the **AutoFilter** drop-down list.

    b. In the **Search** text box, click and type *ti*

    c. Below the text box, check the **Add current selection to filter** check box and click **OK**.

d. Observe that the table now displays the first item that you filtered as well as the filtered results for tiles.

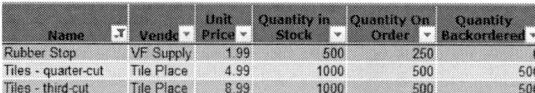

e. Save the file as **My In-House Inventory.xlsx**

f. Close the file.

TOPIC B
Apply Conditional Formatting

You identified the enhancements to Excel 2010 and formatted tables to improve their layout and appearance. In addition to adding templates and table styles, you need to present data logically and in a visually appealing manner by formatting it using the options available in Excel 2010. In this topic, you will apply conditional formatting to data.

When looking at data, you often need to identify specific information in a data range. These can be exceptions, unusual values, or variances that often do not stand out from the rest of the data, and are difficult to locate. Excel 2010 provides advanced features that enable you to effectively and attractively present data by highlighting specific information.

Enhanced Conditional Formatting Options

The *Conditional Formatting* button in the **Styles** group of the **Home** tab enables you to format values based on conditions. You can highlight key information in a sheet by formatting a data range and applying visual cues to data. The **Conditional Formatting** menu contains conditional formatting categories that each offer predefined formatting options. Some of the conditional formatting categories contain galleries that complement the **Live Preview** feature, enabling you to preview a format selection before applying it to data. In Excel 2010, you can apply conditional formatting by referencing different worksheets in the same workbook.

How to Apply Conditional Formatting
Procedure Reference: Apply Conditional Formatting

To apply conditional formatting:

1. On an open Excel worksheet, select a range of cells or a table with numerical values.
2. On the **Home** tab, in the **Styles** group, click **Conditional Formatting.**
3. Apply the desired conditional formatting.
    a. On the displayed menu, place the mouse pointer over the desired icon.
    b. On the displayed submenu, choose the desired option to launch the respective dialog box that is used to specify the formatting.
    c. In the displayed dialog box, specify formatting options and click **OK** to apply the formatting.

Procedure Reference: Create a Formatting Rule

To create a formatting rule:

1. Select the range of cells or the table to be formatted.
2. On the **Home** tab, in the **Styles** group, click **Conditional Formatting.**
3. Display the **New Formatting Rule** dialog box.
    - On the displayed menu, select **New Rule.**
    - On the displayed menu, select **Manage Rules,** and in the displayed **Conditional Formatting Rules Manager** dialog box, click **New Rule.**
    - Or, on the displayed menu, select the desired format option, and on the displayed submenu or gallery, select **More Rules.**

4. In the **New Formatting Rule** dialog box, in the **Select a Rule Type** section, select the rule type to be modified.
5. In the **Edit the Rule Description** section, format the existing rule to create a rule and click **OK**.

Clearing a Formatting Rule

You can clear a formatting rule by displaying the **Conditional Formatting** drop-down list and choosing an option from the **Clear Rules** submenu.

Procedure Reference: Manage a Formatting Rule

To manage a formatting rule:

1. Select the range of cells or the table to be formatted.
2. On the **Home** tab, in the **Styles** group, click **Conditional Formatting.**
3. On the displayed menu, select **Manage Rules.**
4. Work with the options in the **Conditional Formatting Rules Manager** dialog box to manage a formatting rule.
    - In the **Show formatting rules for** text box, select the desired option to specify the selection or sheet.
    - Click **New Rule** to create a formatting rule.
    - Select a rule, click **Edit Rule,** and in the displayed **Edit Formatting Rule** dialog box, edit an existing rule.
    - If necessary, double-click a rule to display the **Edit Formatting Rule** dialog box and edit an existing rule.
    - Select a rule and click **Delete Rule** to delete an existing rule.
    - Use the **Move Up** or **Move Down** arrow button to the right of the **Delete Rule** button to move a rule.
    - In the **Applies to** section, specify the range of cells for which formatting needs to be applied.
    - If necessary, uncheck the **Stop If True** check box against the corresponding rules.
5. Click **Apply** to apply the changes and then click **OK**.

ACTIVITY 3-2
Applying Conditional Formatting

Data Files:

Product Sales.xlsx

Before You Begin:

From the C:\084574Data\Working with Spreadsheets folder, open the Product Sales.xlsx file.

Scenario:

You have received the sales report for a few of the company's branches for the last year. You want to apply a format that will help you compare and highlight the sales trend across the branches in New York and Chicago. You also want to highlight the profit trend in the New York branch to help you make decisions on the sales strategy that you need to adopt in the future for that branch.

1. Preview conditional formatting options.

    a. On the New York worksheet, select cells **B2** to **G13**.

    b. On the **Home** tab, in the **Styles** group, click **Conditional Formatting**.

    c. On the displayed menu, place the mouse pointer over the **Data Bars** option.

    d. On the displayed gallery, in the **Gradient Fill** section, place the mouse pointer over the first data bar at the top, and on the worksheet, preview the data bar conditional formatting applied over the selected range of cells.

    e. Place the mouse pointer over the other data bars to preview them.

    f. Click **Conditional Formatting** again to close the menu.

2. Apply a conditional formatting rule by referencing the Chicago worksheet.

    a. On the New York worksheet, select cells **B2** to **B13**.

    b. On the **Home** tab, in the **Styles** group, click **Conditional Formatting**.

    c. On the displayed menu, place the mouse pointer over the **Highlight Cells Rules** option.

    d. On the **Highlight Cells Rules** submenu, click **Greater Than**.

    e. In the **Greater Than** dialog box, in the **Format cells that are GREATER THAN** text box, click the **RefEdit** button, that is displayed to the right of the text box.

    f. Switch to the Chicago worksheet and click cell **B2**.

    g. In the **Greater Than** dialog box, in the text box, click after the letter "B" and press **Delete**.

    h. Click the **RefEdit** button, again and then click **OK**.

i. Click outside the data range to view the conditional formatting. Observe that the shaded cells indicate that the sales in New York were higher than Chicago in the months of January, March, May, June, July, and September.

3. Apply a new rule to highlight the profit trend.

   a. Select cells **G2** to **G13**.

   b. On the **Home** tab, in the **Styles** group, click **Conditional Formatting**.

   c. On the displayed menu, place the mouse pointer over **Icon Sets**.

   d. On the **Icon Sets** submenu, in the **Directional** section, click the first icon set to apply the **3 Arrows (Colored)** icon set.

   e. Click any of the cells on the worksheet to deselect the range of cells.

   f. Observe that the green directional arrow indicates the months when the profit was above 67% and the red directional arrow indicates the months when the profit dipped to below 33%.

   g. Save the workbook as *My Product Sales* and close it.

TOPIC C
Apply a Formula

You applied conditional formatting for performing data analysis. In the process of analyzing data, you may have to apply a formula to perform calculations with data. In this topic, you will apply formulas and identify the associated enhancements.

When you have data whose values are interdependent, you may be faced with the need to perform numerous calculations to obtain the required information. The advancements in the use of formulas in Excel 2010 allow you to perform complex calculations with very little effort.

The Enhanced Formula Bar

The **Formula Bar,** located below the Ribbon, comprises the **Name Box** and **Insert Function** buttons. It is enhanced to provide more space to accommodate formulas with an option to expand or collapse the bar. Additionally, you can resize the **Formula Bar** to suit your preferences, and also choose to hide it when not in use.

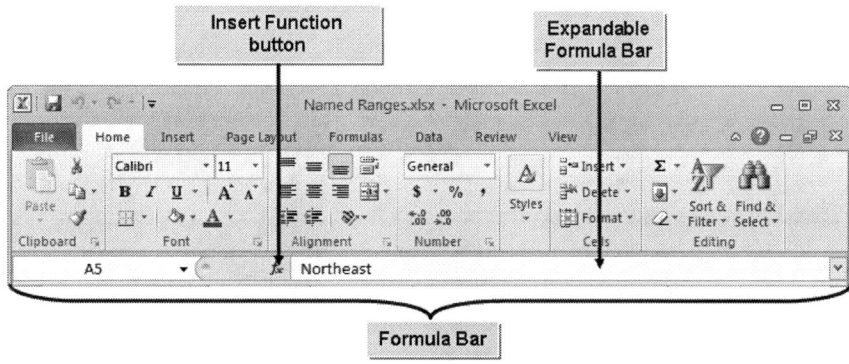

Figure 3-3: A sheet displaying the improved Formula Bar.

The Formula AutoComplete Feature

The *Formula AutoComplete feature* simplifies the process of entering a formula in the **Formula Bar.** When you type the equal sign followed by the first letter of a formula, a drop-down list with all the available function names beginning with the same character will appear. You can then select the required function from the list without having to remember lengthy function names or risk a spelling error.

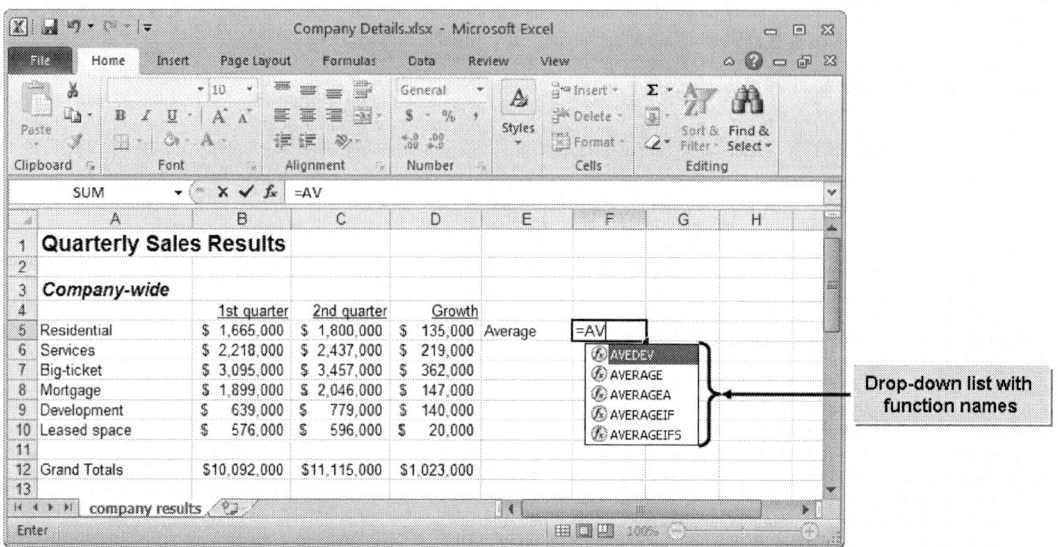

Figure 3-4: A worksheet displaying the Formula AutoComplete feature.

The Insert Function Button

The *Insert Function button* is located both on the **Formulas** tab and on the **Formula Bar.** This button displays the **Insert Function** dialog box, which holds numerous functions under several categories. There are two additions to the categories of functions: **Engineering** and **Cube.** These categories contain specialized functions for operating on data related to each category.

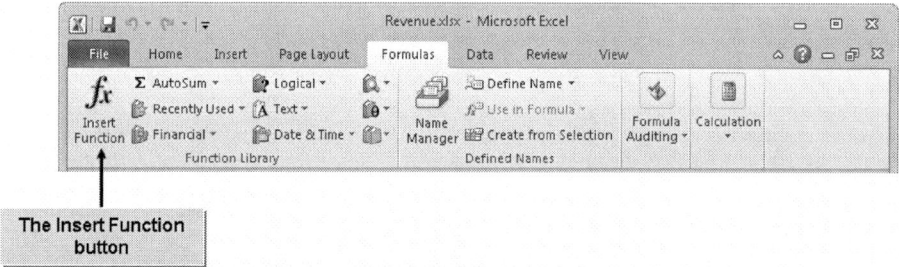

Figure 3-5: The Formulas tab displaying the Insert Function button.

How to Apply a Formula

Procedure Reference: Apply a Formula Using the Formula Bar

To apply a formula using the **Formula Bar:**
1. Open an Excel worksheet with data.
2. Select the cell that will reflect the new figure.
3. Type the formula.
   - In the **Formula Bar,** type the equal sign (=) and the beginning letters of the function you need to use or type a display trigger.
   - Or, in the cell in the worksheet, type the equal sign (=) and the beginning letters of the function you need to use or type a display trigger.
4. In the displayed **AutoComplete** drop-down list, double-click to select and enter the formula.
5. Specify appropriate values, close the parentheses, and press **Enter.**
6. If necessary, click the **Expand Formula Bar** or **Collapse Formula Bar** button to expand or collapse the **Formula Bar,** respectively.

Procedure Reference: Apply a Formula Using the Function Library

To apply a formula by using options in the **Function Library** group:
1. Open an Excel worksheet with data.
2. Select the cell that will reflect the new figure.
3. On the Ribbon, select the **Formulas** tab.
4. Apply a formula by using options in the **Function Library** group.
   - Apply a formula using the **Insert Function** dialog box.
     a. Display the **Insert Function** dialog box.
        - On the **Formulas** tab, in the **Function Library** group, click **Insert Function.**
        - On the **Formulas** tab, in the **Function Library** group, click the **AutoSum** drop-down arrow, and on the displayed menu, select **More Functions.**
        - On the **Formulas** tab, in the **Function Library** group, click any of the drop-down arrows, and on the displayed menu, select **Insert Function.**
        - On the **Formulas** tab, in the **Function Library** group, click **More Functions,** and place the mouse pointer over any option and then on the displayed submenu, select **Insert Function.**
        - Or, on the **Formula Bar,** click the **Insert Function** button.
     b. In the **Insert Function** dialog box, select the desired options and click **OK.**
   - Apply a formula using the other categories.
     - In the **Function Library** group, click the **AutoSum** arrow, and on the displayed menu, select a function.
     - Click **Recently Used,** and on the displayed menu, select the desired option.
     - Click **Financial,** and on the displayed menu, select the desired option.
     - Click **Logical,** and on the displayed menu, select the desired option.
     - Click **Text,** and on the displayed menu, select the desired option.

- Click **Date & Time,** and on the displayed menu, select the desired option.
- Click **Lookup & Reference,** and on the displayed menu, select the desired option.
- Click **Math & Trig,** and on the displayed menu, select the desired option.
• Apply an additional formula.
   a. On the **Formulas** tab, in the **Function Library** group, click **More Functions,** and, on the displayed menu, place the mouse pointer over the desired option.
   b. On the displayed submenu, select the desired option.

Procedure Reference: Name a Range of Cells

To name a range of cells:

1. Open the Excel worksheet with relevant data.
2. On the Ribbon, select the **Formulas** tab.
3. Specify a name for the range.
   a. Display the **New Name** dialog box.
      - On the **Formulas** tab, in the **Defined Names** group, click **Name Manager,** and in the **Name Manager** dialog box, click **New.**
      - Or, on the **Formulas** tab, in the **Defined Names** group, click **Define Name.**
   b. In the **New Name** dialog box, type the name, select the scope, specify the reference to cells, and then click **OK.**
   c. In the **Name Manager** dialog box, click **Close.**

Procedure Reference: Work with Named Cells

To work with named cells:

1. Open the Excel worksheet with relevant data.
2. On the Ribbon, select the **Formulas** tab.
3. Select the cell where the formula is to be applied.
4. Use options in the **Defined Names** group.
   • Use an existing named range in a formula.
      - On the **Formulas** tab, in the **Defined Names** group, click **Use in Formula** and select a named reference.
      - Paste an existing named range.
         a. On the **Formulas** tab, in the **Defined Names** group, click **Use in Formula** and select **Paste Names.**
         b. In the **Paste Name** dialog box, select the desired option and click **OK.**
   • Create names from the selection.
      a. On the **Formulas** tab, in the **Defined Names** group, click **Create from Selection.**
      b. In the **Create Names from Selection** dialog box, check the desired check boxes and click **OK.**
   • Manage named cells.
      a. On the **Formulas** tab, in the **Defined Names** group, click **Name Manager.**
      b. Use the desired option.

- Click **New** to display the **New Name** dialog box and create another named reference.
- Select a named reference and click **Edit** to display the **Edit Name** dialog box and modify a named reference.
- Select a named reference and click **Delete** to display the **Microsoft Excel** message box to delete a named reference.
- If necessary, click **Filter** to access different options for filtering named ranges.

   c. Click **Close** to return to the Excel worksheet.
5. If necessary, use the named reference in a formula.
   a. Select the cell in which the formula has to be applied.
   b. Enter the formula with the named reference and press **Enter.**

Procedure Reference: Work with Formula Auditing Options

To work with formula auditing options:
1. Open an Excel worksheet with data.
2. Select the desired cells.
3. On the Ribbon, select the **Formulas** tab.
4. Select the appropriate option in the **Formula Auditing** group.
   - Click **Trace Precedents.**
   - Click **Trace Dependents.**
   - Click **Remove Arrows,** or from the **Remove Arrows** drop-down list, select the desired option.
   - Click the **Show Formulas** button.
   - Click the **Error Checking** button, or from the **Error Checking** drop-down list, select the desired option or place the mouse pointer over the **Circular References** option, and in the displayed list, select an option.
   - Click the **Evaluate Formula** button to display the **Evaluate Formula** dialog box to evaluate.
   - Click **Watch Window** to display the respective dialog box.

Procedure Reference: Work with Calculation Options

To work with calculation options:
1. On the Ribbon, select the **Formulas** tab.
2. Select a calculation option.
   - On the **Formulas** tab, in the **Calculation** group, click **Calculation Options** and select an option.
     - Select **Automatic** to automatically recalculate interdependent formulas.
     - Select **Automatic Except for Data Tables** to automatically recalculate interdependent formulas, except for data tables.
     - Select **Manual** to enable the function to calculate values in the sheet automatically before saving the workbook.

> The **Formulas** section of the **Excel Options** dialog box consists of calculation options. Each calculation option comprises options to either automatically or manually recalculate the workbook before saving it.

- Click the **Calculate Now** button to recalculate all open worksheets.
- Click the **Calculate Sheet** button to recalculate values in the active sheet.

Named Tables

A named table can be referenced within a formula. The name of the table should be specified in the **Table Name** text box available in the **Properties** group of the table **Design** tab before referencing.

ACTIVITY 3-3
Working with Formulas

Data Files:

Named Ranges.xlsx

Before You Begin:

From the C:\084574Data\Working with Spreadsheets folder, open the Named Ranges.xlsx file.

Scenario:

Your manager has asked you to organize the Named Ranges worksheet so that it can be used at a presentation. You decide to rename cells, calculate total sales, or rearrange cells in the worksheet as required so that the formulas are easier to understand and less complicated when writing additional formulas.

1. Name a range "Quarter 1."

    a. Select the range **B5:B8**.

    b. On the **Formula Bar,** click the **Name Box,** type *Quarter1* and then press **Enter** to name the selected range.

2. Create named ranges for Quarter 2 through Quarter 4 by using labels from the worksheet and then create named ranges for the Sales Group regions.

    a. Select the range **C4:E8**.

    b. On the **Formulas** tab, in the **Defined Names** group, click **Create from Selection.**

    c. In the **Create Names from Selection** dialog box, verify that the **Top row** check box is checked and click **OK.**

    d. From the **Name Box** drop-down list, select **Quarter 1.**

    e. Observe that the data range for Quarter1 is selected.

Our Global Company		
Sales Performance, Prior Fiscal Year		
Sales Group:	Quarter1	Quarter2
Northeast	$ 1,259	$ 1,345
Southeast	$ 1,536	$ 2,301
Northwest	$ 1,945	$ 3,012
Southwest	$ 1,385	$ 1,945
TOTAL	$ 6,125	$ 8,603

    f. From the **Name Box** drop-down list, select **Quarter 4.**

    g. Select cells A5:E8, and on the **Formulas** tab, in the **Defined Names** group, click **Create from Selection.**

h. In the **Create Names from Selection** dialog box, verify that the **Left column** check box is checked and click **OK**.

i. From the **Name Box** drop-down list, select **Northeast.**

3. Use the **Name Manager** dialog box to rename the Sales groups.

    a. On the **Formulas** tab, in the **Defined Names** group, click **Name Manager.**

    b. In the **Name Manager** dialog box, verify that **Northeast** is selected and click **Edit.**

    c. In the **Edit Name** dialog box, in the **Name** text box, type *NE* and then click **OK**.

    d. Similarly, rename Northwest, Southeast, and Southwest to NW, SE, and SW respectively.

    e. Close the **Name Manager** dialog box.

    f. In the **Name Box** observe that the Northeast name range has been changed to NE.

4. Calculate the total sales for East Coast and West Coast.

    a. Select cell **B11.**

    b. On the **Formulas** tab, in the **Function Library** group, click **AutoSum.**

    c. In the **Defined Names** group, click **Use in Formula.**

    d. Select **NE** and then type a comma.

    e. From the **Use in Formula** drop-down list, select **SE** and press **Enter.**

    f. Similarly, enter the formula in A12 to total West Coast Sales.

    g. Observe that the total sales has been added for East Coast and West Coast.

East Coast Sales:	$ 15,562.00
West Coast Sales:	$ 19,323.00

    h. Save the file as *My Named Ranges.xlsx* and close it.

TOPIC D
Work with Charts

You analyzed data using various features in Excel 2010. You can also allow others to view and analyze data by graphically presenting it to them. In this topic, you will create a chart using enhanced chart tools.

The monotony of reading large amounts of text can cause a reader to lose interest and attention to a subject. A balanced use of text and graphics can help resolve this problem. Moreover, text content backed up by graphical representation enables easier understanding of the subject. Microsoft Excel 2010 provides various options to represent data in an organized and easy-to-understand method.

Chart Enhancements

Charts in Excel have been greatly enhanced with graphic elements and chart styles that allow for effective presentation of data. Improvements include finer textures, better lighting effects, and more predefined styles and layouts. Tools to create charts never had been more easily accessible and the process of creating a chart has also been simplified. In addition, several chart formatting tools have been grouped under the **Design**, **Layout**, and **Format** contextual tabs so that you can access the relevant formatting tools quickly, without having to perform an extensive search.

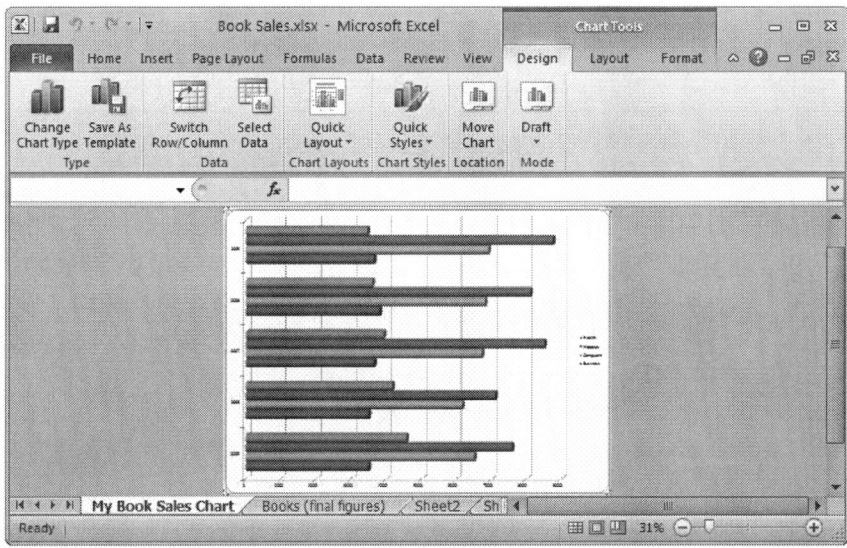

Figure 3-6: The Design contextual tab displaying options for a bar chart.

Enhanced Chart Tools

Enhanced chart tools are a group of contextual tabs that are displayed when a chart is selected. The commands on these tabs enable you to manipulate the appearance and layout of charts.

Contextual Tab	Description
Design	Provides options to modify the style, layout, data source, and type of chart. The groups on the tab are: • Type – Provides options to change the type of chart and to save it as a template. • Data – Provides options to switch between row and column data, as well as to edit the data source. • Chart Layouts – Provides options to modify the layout of the chart. • Chart Styles – Provides options to change the appearance of the chart to one of the preset styles in the **Quick Styles** gallery. • Location – Provides options to move the chart to another worksheet or as another chart. • Draft Mode – Provides the option to draft a chart with simple formatting.
Layout	Provides options for further customizing chart elements. The groups on the tab are: • Current Selection – Provides options to format the selected chart element. • Insert – Provides options to include shapes from the **Shapes** gallery or import pictures from a file. • Labels – Provides options to manage labels on various locations of a chart. • Axes – Provides options to manage the formatting of axes and gridlines. • Background – Provides options to modify the background elements of a chart. • Analysis – Provides options to add elements that aid analysis. • Properties — Provides an option to specify a chart name.
Format	Provides options to format the chart and chart elements. The groups on the tab are: • Current Selection – Allows a chart element to be selected and formatted. • Shape Styles – Provides options to modify the color, style, and effects applied to a shape. • WordArt Styles – Provides options to preview WordArt styles, and modify the fill color, line color, and effects. • Arrange – Provides options to arrange, align, and rotate shapes, WordArt, or text boxes. • Size – Provides options to modify the width and height of the selected graphical object.

Chart Templates

In Excel 2010, you can save charts that you created and formatted as templates so that you can use them in the future without having to design a chart all over again. The **Save As Template** button located on the **Design** contextual tab allows you to access this feature. Charts that are saved as templates are automatically assigned the .crtx filename extension.

How to Work with Charts

Procedure Reference: Create a Chart

To create a chart:

1. Open an Excel workbook with data.
2. If necessary, arrange the data according to the chart to be created.
3. Select the desired data.

> When you select a single cell with data, all the adjacent cells with data around the selected cell are automatically selected for chart creation.

4. On the Ribbon, select the **Insert** tab.
5. In the **Charts** group, select the desired chart type.
   - Click a chart type to display the chart gallery and select a chart type from the gallery.
   - Or, click the **Dialog Box Launcher** to display the **Insert Chart** dialog box and select a chart type from the gallery and click **OK.**
6. With the chart selected, on the Ribbon, select a contextual tab and use the commands on it to format the chart.
   - Select the **Design** contextual tab to display options to change the chart type and chart layout, apply chart styles, and move a chart.
   - Select the **Layout** contextual tab to display options to modify chart properties and elements.
   - Select the **Format** contextual tab to display options to apply styles to the chart, arrange the chart as desired, or resize the chart.

Procedure Reference: Save a Chart as a Chart Template

To save a chart as a chart template:

1. In an Excel worksheet, select a chart.
2. Select the **Design** contextual tab.
3. In the **Type** group, click **Change Chart Type.**
4. In the **Change Chart Type** dialog box, in the left pane, select a chart type.
5. In the right pane, select a chart and click **OK.**
6. Format the chart using the **Design, Layout,** and **Format** contextual tabs.
7. If necessary, on the Ribbon, select the **Design** contextual tab.
8. In the **Type** group, click **Save As Template.**
9. In the **Save Chart Template** dialog box, in the **File name** text box, type a name for the template.

10. Click **Save**.
11. View the saved template.
    - View the template in the **Insert Chart** dialog box.
        a. Display the **Insert Chart** dialog box.
        b. In the **Insert Chart** dialog box, in the left pane, select **Templates**.
        c. In the right pane, view the saved template.
        d. Close the **Insert Chart** dialog box.
    - View the template in the **Change Chart Type** dialog box.
        a. Display the **Change Chart Type** dialog box.
        b. In the **Change Chart Type** dialog box, in the left pane, select **Templates**.
        c. In the right pane, view the saved template.
        d. Close the **Change Chart Type** dialog box.
    - View the template in Windows Explorer.
        a. Display either the **Insert Chart** or **Change Chart Type** dialog box.
        b. Click **Manage Templates**.
        c. In the displayed Windows Explorer window, view the saved template.
        d. Close Windows Explorer.
        e. Close the dialog box.

ACTIVITY 3-4
Creating a Chart

Data Files:

Book Sales.xlsx

Before You Begin:

From the C:\084574Data\Working with Spreadsheets folder, open the Book Sales.xlsx file.

Scenario:

You are doing a comparative analysis of sales figures over the last five years in the Books department of your company. The information in your workbook does not provide a clear picture of the sales trend. So, you decide to present this information in a visual.

1. Create a chart.

   a. In the Books (final figures) worksheet, select cells **A1** to **F5** to select the sales figures for the years 2005 to 2009.

   b. Select the **Insert** tab, and in the **Charts** group, click **Bar**.

   c. On the displayed gallery, in the **Cylinder** section, select the first chart to create a **Clustered Horizontal Cylinder** chart.

   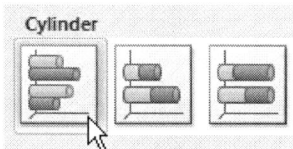

   d. Observe that the selected data is presented as a chart.

   e. Observe that the **Design, Layout,** and **Format** contextual tabs are displayed on the Ribbon.

2. Modify chart legend data to display the year on the vertical axis.

   a. On the **Design** contextual tab, in the **Data** group, click **Select Data**.

   b. In the **Select Data Source** dialog box, in the **Legend Entries (Series)** list box, verify that **Year** is selected and click **Remove**.

   c. In the **Horizontal (Category) Axis Labels** pane, click **Edit**.

   d. In the table data, select cells **B1:F1**.

e. Observe that the label range is populated in the **Axis Labels** dialog box and click **OK**.

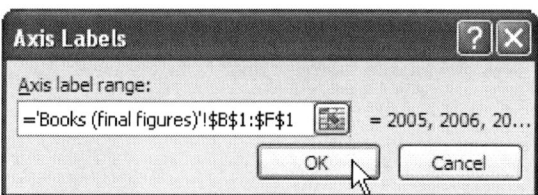

f. In the **Select Data Source** dialog box, click **OK**.

g. Observe that the legend data reflects the year on the vertical axis and the chart displays the sales generated in each book category for each of the last five years.

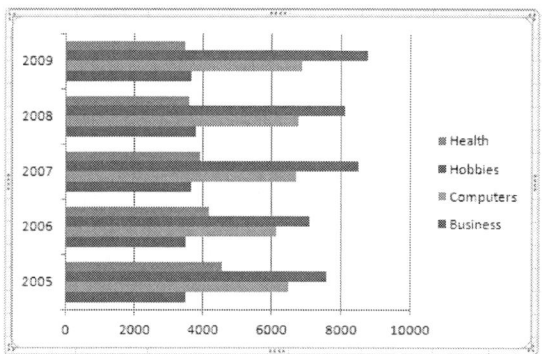

3. Move the chart to a new worksheet.

   a. On the **Design** contextual tab, in the **Location** group, click **Move Chart**.

   b. In the **Move Chart** dialog box, in the **New sheet** text box, double-click and type *My Book Sales Chart* and then click **OK**.

   c. Observe that the chart is displayed in a new worksheet.

   d. Save the workbook as *My Book Sales.xlsx*

ACTIVITY 3-5
Formatting a Chart

Scenario:
You have created a chart to represent the sales data of your company. You want to add a title and then make this chart a standard chart format for your company.

1. Change the chart type.

   a. Verify that the My Book Sales Chart worksheet is selected.

   b. On the **Design** contextual tab, in the **Type** group, click **Change Chart Type**.

   c. In the **Change Chart Type** dialog box, in the left pane, select **Line**.

   d. In the right pane, in the **Line** section, verify that the fourth chart is selected and click **OK**.

2. Apply a chart style.

   a. In the **Chart Styles** group, click the **More** button.

   b. On the displayed gallery, select a chart style.

3. Enter the chart title.

   a. Select the **Layout** contextual tab, and in the **Labels** group, click **Chart Title** and select **Above Chart**.

   b. Observe that the **Chart Title** text box appears on top of the chart.

   c. On the chart, select the text in the **Chart Title** text box and type *Sales Data (2009 - 2010)*

4. Enter a title for the horizontal axis.

   a. In the **Labels** group, click **Axis Titles**.

   b. On the displayed menu, place the mouse pointer over the **Primary Horizontal Axis Title** and choose **Title Below Axis**.

   c. If necessary, scroll down in the worksheet.

d. Observe that the horizontal category **Axis Title** text box appears in the chart area below the horizontal axis.

e. Select the text in the **Axis Title** text box and type *Years*

5. Enter a title for the vertical axis.

    a. In the **Labels** group, click **Axis Titles.**

    b. On the displayed menu, place the mouse pointer over **Primary Vertical Axis Title** and choose **Horizontal Title.**

    c. Observe that in the chart area, to the left of the vertical axis, the vertical **Axis Title** text box appears.

    d. Select the text in the **Axis Title** text box and type *Total Sales*

6. Save the chart as a template and then save and close the workbook.

    a. Select the **Design** contextual tab, and in the **Type** group, click **Save As Template.**

    b. In the **Save Chart Template** dialog box, in the **File name** text box, type *My Chart* and click **Save.**

    c. On the **Design** contextual tab, in the **Type** group, click **Change Chart Type.**

    d. In the **Change Chart Type** dialog box, in the left pane, select **Templates.**

    e. Observe that the saved chart template is displayed in the right pane.

    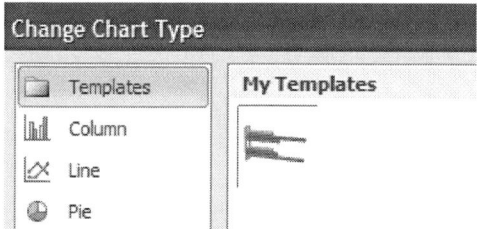

    f. Click **Cancel** to close the **Change Chart Type** dialog box.

    g. If necessary, in the worksheet, click a blank area to deselect the chart.

    h. Save the workbook as *My Product Details* and close it.

TOPIC E
Create Sparklines

You worked with charts. You may now want to analyze data in cells graphically. In this topic, you will create Sparklines.

Though you can have large amounts of data structured and organized within tables, graphically presenting the data is a way to help your audience understand complex information and make decisions based on the graphical representation.

Sparklines

Sparklines are miniature graphical representations of data in a worksheet table. They are small, cell-sized charts that appear within the worksheet, depicting the numbers in the worksheet. Excel 2010 allows you to create three types of Sparklines—**Line** Sparklines that show trends and changes in values over time; **Column** Sparklines that compare values; and **Win/loss** Sparklines that analyze values in relation to a norm.

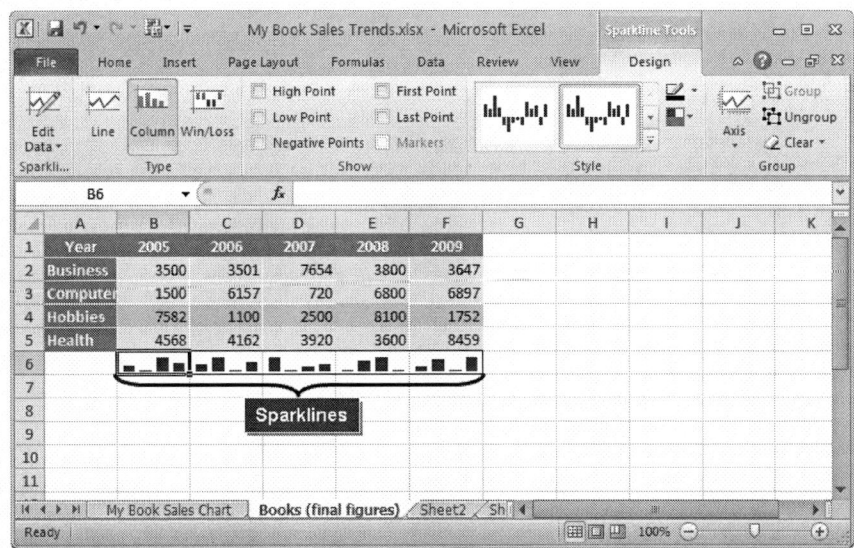

Figure 3-7: *A workbook displaying the sales trend by using Sparklines.*

How to Create Sparklines

Procedure Reference: Create Sparklines for Cell Data

To create a Sparkline for cell data:

1. Open an Excel workbook with data.
2. Select the cells that you want to display in the Sparkline.
3. On the Ribbon, on the **Insert** tab, select the Sparkline type you want to create.
4. In the **Create Sparklines** dialog box, in the top data field, verify the range of cells you selected.
5. In the **Location Range** field, click the cell on the worksheet where you want the Sparkline to appear and then click **OK.**

ACTIVITY 3-6
Present Data by Using Sparklines

Data Files:

Book Sales.xlsx

Before You Begin:

From the C:\084574Data\Working with Spreadsheets folder, open the Book Sales.xlsx file.

Scenario:

The Books department in your company has given you the sales figures for each of their best selling book categories. You created a chart to display this information, but you are unable to view the sales trends by comparing their numbers. You decide to use the new features in Excel to highlight trend data in each cell.

1. Insert a Sparkline.

    a. On the Books (final figures) worksheet, and on the **Insert** tab, in the **Sparklines** group, click **Line**.

    b. In the **Create Sparklines** dialog box, in the **Data Range** text box, type *B2:B5* and press **Tab**.

    c. Click cell **B6**.

    d. Observe that in the **Create Sparklines** dialog box, in the **Location Range** text box, the location range is automatically populated and click **OK**.

    e. Observe that a Line Sparkline is created in cell B6.

    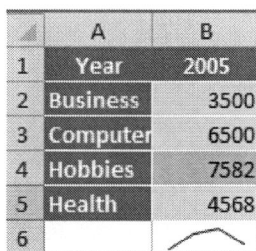

2. Add Sparklines to the other book categories.

    a. Place the mouse pointer at the right edge of cell B6 until the mouse pointer changes to a four-headed arrow and drag the mouse pointer to cell F6.

b. Observe that Sparklines are applied for the remaining book categories.

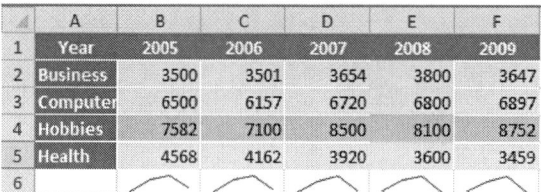

c. Save the workbook as *My Book Sales Trends* and close it.

TOPIC F
Work with PivotTables and PivotCharts

You worked with illustrations for improving the presentation and comprehension of data. To selectively analyze the data that has been presented, you need to be able to manually select the information for analysis. In this topic, you will create PivotTables and PivotCharts for selectively displaying the required information.

When you have large amounts of data to analyze, it may not be easy to compare the data manually. Excel 2010 provides enhanced PivotChart and PivotTable features that enable you to focus only on the elements that you wish to analyze.

Enhanced PivotTables

The *PivotTable button* located in the **Tables** group on the **Insert** tab allows you to insert a PivotTable for selected data. PivotTables are now more dynamic and efficient with the enhancement of the **PivotTable Field List** pane. The list now includes drop zones that allow you to not only drag and drop fields into each of them but also reorient and rearrange data and calculated values in multiple formats, enabling you to set the data for quick analysis.

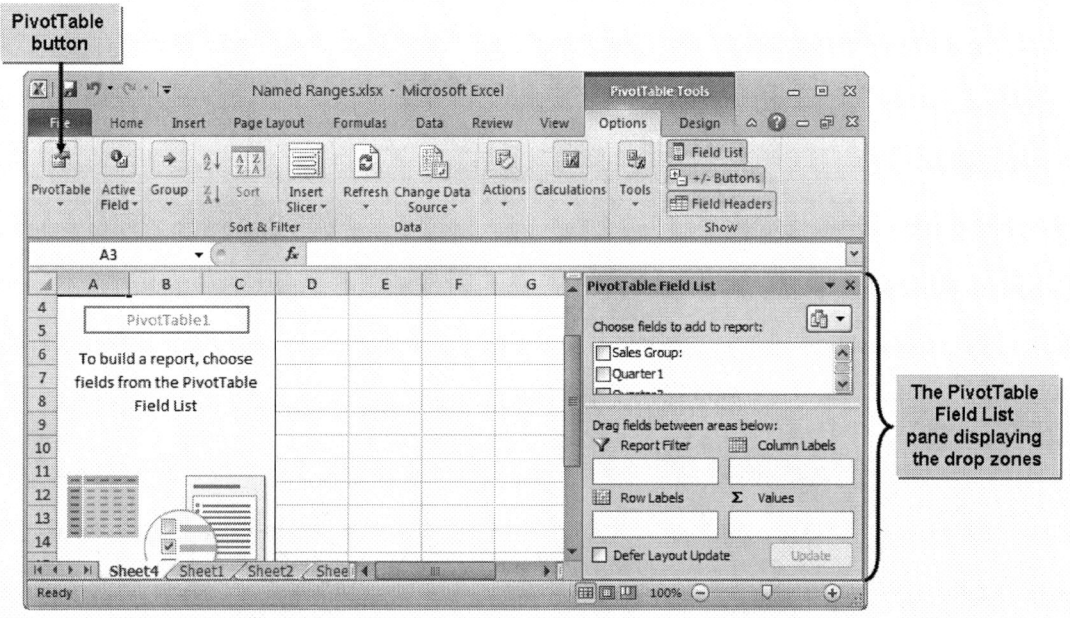

Figure 3-8: The PivotTable field List pane displaying the drop zones to drag and drop fields.

Excel 2010 also includes a **Show Values As** context menu, which displays calculations that can be applied to fields in a PivotTable. There are six new calculation options including **% of Parent Row Total, % of Parent Column Total, % of Parent Total, % Running Total In, Rank Smallest to Largest,** and **Rank Largest to Smallest.** Additionally, you can use the What-If-Analysis feature to modify values in PivotTable cells.

PowerPivot

PowerPivot is the latest add-in in Excel 2010 that supports worksheets as large as 2 gigabytes (GBs) in size. PowerPivot enables you to model and analyze data on worksheets so you can sort, filter, and use table lookup functions on multiple tables. You can manipulate large data sets and integrate data from multiple sources seamlessly. PowerPivot needs to be downloaded and installed separately. The URL to download PowerPivot is **www.powerpivot.com**.

Enhanced PivotCharts

You can access *PivotChart options* from the **PivotTable** drop-down list of the **Tables** group. When you create a PivotChart, a PivotTable is automatically created for the chart. In Excel 2010, the context menu allows you to change the position of fields on the PivotChart. You can also filter data on the chart by using the drop-down lists displayed on the PivotChart and remove them by choosing the **Show/Hide Field** buttons on the **Analyze** tab. Once you have manipulated the fields of the PivotTable, you can view its dynamic output on the PivotChart.

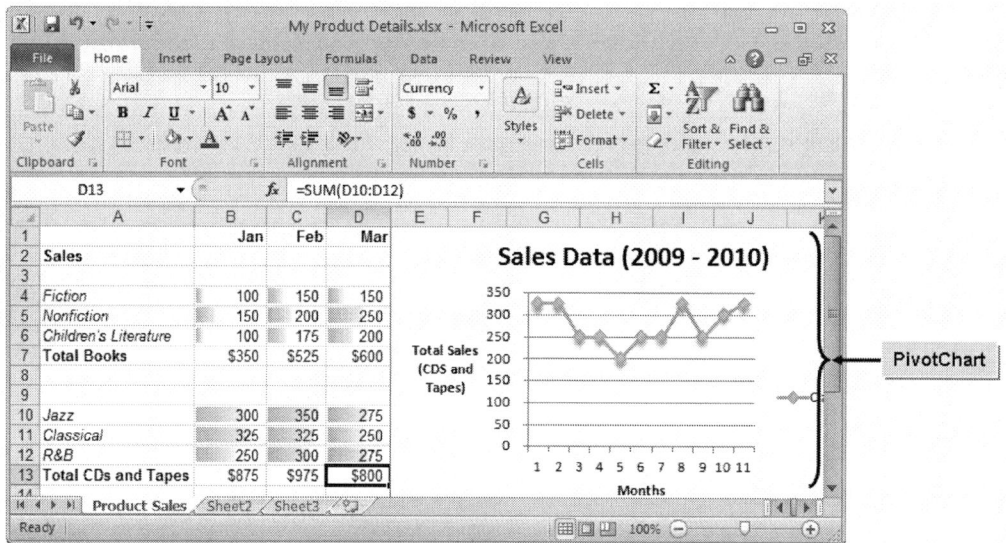

Figure 3-9: A PivotChart displaying PivotTable data.

Slicers

The *Slicers* feature enables you to slice data and include only the elements you want in Pivot-Tables and PivotCharts. It allows you to add and remove elements from the table display so that you can compare and evaluate data from different perspectives. You can also use Slicers with multiple PivotTables and PivotCharts to showcase your data consistently in a variety of scenarios.

How to Work with PivotTables and PivotCharts

Procedure Reference: Create a PivotTable

To create a PivotTable:

1. Open an Excel workbook with data.
2. In the workbook, select a cell with data.
3. On the Ribbon, select the **Insert** tab.
4. In the **Tables** group, click **PivotTable.**
5. In the **Create PivotTable** dialog box, specify the data range and the location for the PivotTable, and then click **OK.**
6. Specify appropriate settings in the **PivotTable Field List** pane.
   - In the **Choose fields to add to report** section, check the desired check boxes to be displayed in the PivotTable.
   - If necessary, place the mouse pointer over the desired field name and click the displayed arrow to sort and filter data.
   - Drag the desired fields to the desired boxes in the **Drag fields between areas below** section.
   - If necessary, check the **Defer Layout Update** check box.
7. Close the **PivotTable Field List** pane.

Procedure Reference: Format a PivotTable

To format a PivotTable:

1. In the worksheet, select the PivotTable.
2. On the Ribbon, select a **PivotTable Tools** tool tab to format the PivotTable.
   - Select the **Options** contextual tab to format the options in the PivotTable.
   - Select the **Design** contextual tab to design the layout and apply **PivotTable Styles** to the PivotTable.

The Field List and Filter Panes

PivotTables and PivotCharts can be modified using options in the **PivotTable Field List** and **PivotChart Filter** panes, respectively. The options used to display or hide a **PivotTable Field List** pane are available on the **Options** or **Analyze** tab. The **Options** tab is displayed when a PivotTable is selected, and the **Analyze** tab when a **PivotChart** tab is selected. The option used to display or hide a **PivotTable Field List** pane is also available in a **PivotChart Filter** pane. When you deselect a PivotTable, the pane disappears. The option used to display the **PivotChart Filter** pane is available on the **Analyze** tab.

Procedure Reference: Create a PivotChart

To create a PivotChart:

1. Open an Excel workbook with data.
2. In the workbook, select the required cells with data.
3. On the Ribbon, select the **Insert** tab.
4. On the **Insert** tab, in the **Tables** group, click the **PivotTable** drop-down arrow.
5. Select **PivotChart.**

6. In the **Create PivotTable with PivotChart** dialog box, specify the data range, and the location for the PivotChart and PivotTable, and then click **OK.**
7. Specify the appropriate settings in the **PivotTable Field List** pane.
8. In the worksheet, in the PivotTable, click the **All, Column Labels, Row Labels** filter drop-down arrow and, on the displayed menu, select the desired filter option.

Procedure Reference: Format a PivotChart

To format a PivotChart:

1. In the worksheet, select the PivotChart.
2. On the Ribbon, select the desired **PivotChart Tools** tool tab to format the PivotChart.
    - Select the **Design** contextual tab to design the PivotChart.
    - Select the **Layout** contextual tab to format the layout of the PivotChart.
    - Select the **Format** contextual tab to modify the styles of the PivotChart.
    - Select the **Analyze** contextual tab to analyze the data in the PivotChart.
3. On the selected contextual tab, in the desired group, select the appropriate command to format the PivotChart.

Procedure Reference: Insert a Slicer

To insert a Slicer:

1. Open a workbook with a PivotTable.
2. Click the PivotTable, and in the **PivotTable Field List** pane, select an item.
3. On the **Insert** tab, in the **Filter** section, click **Slicer.**
4. In the **Insert Slicers** dialog box, select an item and click **OK.**
5. In the Slicer that appears, click each item to observe the change in the corresponding item.

ACTIVITY 3-7
Presenting Data by Using a PivotTable and PivotChart

Data Files:

Journal Sales.xlsx

Before You Begin:

From the C:\084574Data\Working with Spreadsheets folder, open the Journal Sales.xlsx file.

Scenario:

You are analyzing the sales revenue of your company's journals for the years 2007 to 2009. You want to create a report that will help your manager navigate the data randomly using different criteria such as sales figures for a year or a month in a year. Your manager also needs the data represented in a graphical format.

---

1. Create a PivotChart along with a PivotTable.

    a. In the Journal Sales worksheet, click cell **A4.**

    b. Select the **Insert** tab, and in the **Tables** group, click the PivotTable drop-down arrow and select **PivotChart.**

    c. In the **Create PivotTable with PivotChart** dialog box, view the default options and click **OK.**

    d. In the **PivotTable Field List** pane, in the **Choose fields to add to report** section, click and drag the **Year** field to the **Legend Fields (Series)** box in the **Drag fields between areas below** section to display the legend in the PivotChart area.

    e. Drag the **Month** field to the **Axis Fields (Categories)** box to display the **Month** in the X-axis field of the PivotChart.

    f. Drag the **Copies** field to the **Values** box to display the **Sum of Copies** in the Y-axis field of the PivotChart.

    g. Drag the **Income** field to the **Report Filter** box.

    h. Observe that the PivotChart and PivotTable have been created.

    i. Close the **PivotTable Field List** pane.

2. Sort the PivotTable data.

    a. In the worksheet, on the table, click the **Row Labels** filter drop-down arrow.

    b. In the drop-down list, uncheck the **Select All** check box.

    c. Check the **Jan** and **Feb** check boxes and click **OK.**

    d. Click the **Column Labels** filter drop-down arrow.

    e. In the drop-down list, uncheck the **Select All** check box.

    f. Check the **2009** check box and click **OK.**

g. Observe that the PivotTable reflects the total sales figures for the months of January and February in 2009.

3. Format the PivotChart.

   a. In the worksheet, click the chart area to select the PivotChart.

   b. Observe that the **PivotChart Tools** contextual tabs appear on the Ribbon.

   c. Select the **Design** contextual tab, and in the **Type** group, click **Change Chart Type**.

   d. In the **Change Chart Type** dialog box, in the right pane, in the **Column** section, in the second row, select the second chart type to select the **Stacked Cylinder** chart, and click **OK.**

   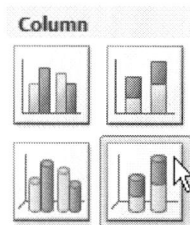

   e. In the **Chart Styles** group, click the **More** button.

   f. On the displayed gallery, in the third row, select the fifth chart style which is **Style 21.**

   g. Observe that the chart appears with the applied chart style.

4. Format the PivotTable.

   a. In the worksheet, click a cell in the table to activate the PivotTable contextual tabs.

   b. Select the **Design** contextual tab, and in the **PivotTable Styles** group, click the **More** button.

   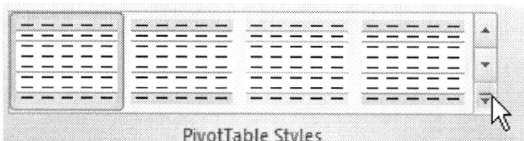

   c. On the displayed gallery, scroll down and, in the **Dark** section, in the first row, select the sixth PivotTable style which is **Pivot Style Dark 6.**

d. Observe that the PivotTable style has been applied to the PivotTable.

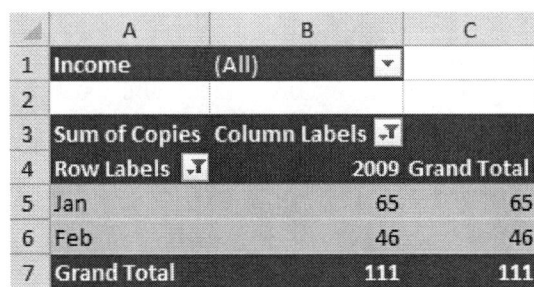

5. Insert a Slicer in the PivotTable.

   a. In the worksheet, on the table, click the **Row Labels** filter drop-down arrow.

   b. In the drop-down list, check the **Select All** check box and click **OK**.

   c. Click the **Column Labels** filter drop-down arrow.

   d. In the drop-down list, check the **Select All** check box and click **OK**.

   e. Select the **Insert** tab, and in the **Filter** group, click **Slicer.**

   f. In the **Insert Slicers** dialog box, check the **Product** check box, and click **OK.**

   g. In the **Product** Slicer, select each product to verify that the sum of copies in the PivotTable changes to the corresponding income on that product.

   h. Save the workbook as *My Journal Sales* and close it.

   i. Close the Microsoft Excel application.

Lesson 3 Follow-up

In this lesson, you worked with the new and enhanced features available in Microsoft Office Excel 2010. Using the enhanced conditional formatting features, PivotTables and PivotCharts, and so on enables you to improve the management and presentation of your spreadsheets, along with improved sharing features.

1. **How do you think the enhanced spreadsheet features in Excel 2010 will improve the organization and presentation of data?**

2. **When would you use conditional formatting options at your workplace?**

4 Creating Dynamic Presentations Using Microsoft PowerPoint 2010

Lesson Time: 45 minutes

Lesson Objectives:

In this lesson, you will create Microsoft Office PowerPoint 2010 presentations.

You will:

- Create a custom theme for a presentation.
- Apply picture effects to a presentation.
- Apply animation effects to objects on a PowerPoint slide.
- Add videos to a presentation.
- Divide a presentation into sections.

Introduction

You worked with Microsoft Office PowerPoint 2003 (or earlier) to create presentations. PowerPoint 2010, with its redesigned interface, enhanced features, and result-oriented authoring tools, improves the process of creating dynamic presentations. In this lesson, you will create dynamic presentations.

Just as you need to create a blueprint for a house before you begin to construct it, you must decide on the various factors that impact a presentation, such as the layout, theme, effects, and so on. All of these factors need to be taken into consideration for a presentation prior to creating it. PowerPoint 2010 offers options that help you create an effective presentation.

TOPIC A
Apply Themes

You worked with the earlier versions of Microsoft® PowerPoint to create presentations. PowerPoint 2010 provides numerous options to create effective layouts which are complemented by suitable themes and backgrounds. In this topic, you will create and apply themes and backgrounds.

When faced with the task of creating a complex document in a short time, you will find that experimenting with different styles, selecting a specific format or layout, and applying it to the document on a trial and error basis requires a lot of time and effort. Wouldn't it be nice if you could have the option of seeing how an effect looks like on the file just by a click or a mouseover without really applying the effect? Office 2010 provides features that help you achieve just that.

Themes

Definition:

Themes are design templates that provide a consistent visual look and feel for presentations. They affect not just the background color of a slide but also the color of the diagram, table, or any other component present in the presentation. Themes enable you to create a professional-looking presentation and can be applied using the options displayed in the **Themes** gallery. You can choose to apply a theme either to all of the slides or only to selected slides.

Example:

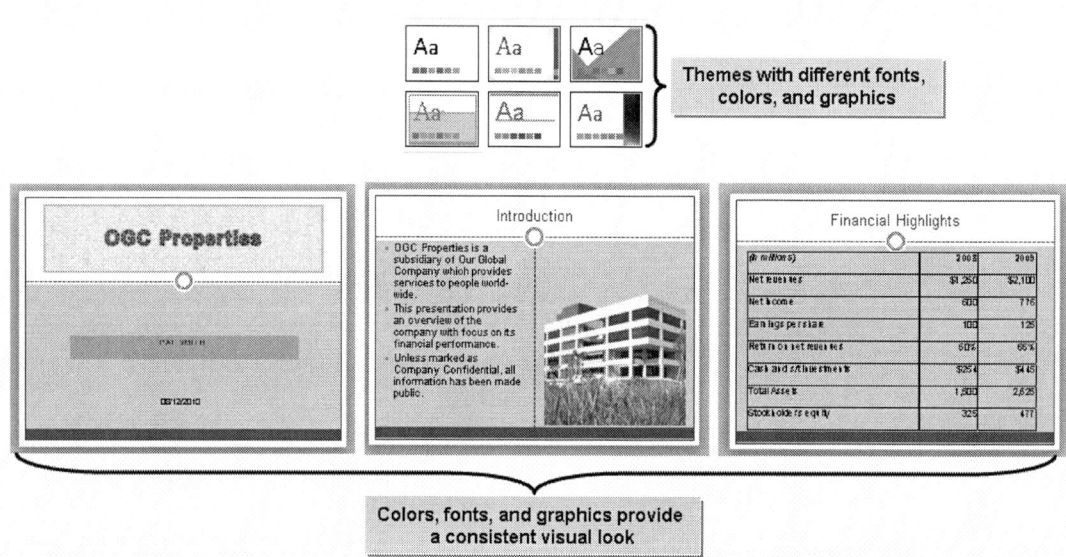

Figure 4-1: Display of themes used in different pages to give a consistent look.

Types of Themes

A theme encompasses three critical formatting components: **Theme Colors, Theme Fonts,** and **Theme Effects.**

Theme Type	Enables You To
Theme Colors	Apply a color theme to a presentation. You can also create, name, and save new theme colors to suit specific requirements.
Theme Fonts	Customize and modify the fonts used in a presentation theme. It consists of two different font types: one for the heading and one for the body text.
Theme Effects	Change the visual effects in a built-in theme.

How to Apply Themes

Procedure Reference: Apply a Background Style

To apply a background style:

1. Open an existing PowerPoint presentation.
2. On the Ribbon, select the **Design** tab.
3. In the **Background** group, click **Background Styles** and select the desired background style.
4. If necessary, check the **Hide Background Graphics** check box to keep any background graphics from being displayed on the slide.

Procedure Reference: Create a Custom Theme Color and Font

To create a custom theme color and font:

1. Open an existing PowerPoint presentation.
2. On the Ribbon, select the **Design** tab.
3. In the **Themes** group, select the desired option.
   - Click **Colors** and, from the drop-down list, select **Create New Theme Colors.**
     a. In the **Create New Theme Colors** dialog box, in the **Theme colors** section, set the desired color options.
     b. If necessary, in the **Sample** section, preview the custom color theme.
     c. In the **Name** text box, enter the desired name for the custom color theme.
     d. If necessary, click **Reset** to reset the color theme to the default theme.
     e. Click **Save.**
   - Click **Fonts** and, from the drop-down list, select **Create New Theme Fonts.**
     a. In the **Create New Theme Fonts** dialog box, from the **Heading font** drop-down list, select the desired heading font type.
     b. From the **Body font** drop-down list, select the desired body font type.
     c. If necessary, in the **Sample** section, preview the custom font theme.
     d. In the **Name** text box, enter the desired name for the custom font theme and click **Save.**

Procedure Reference: Create a Custom Theme

To create a custom theme:

1. Open an existing PowerPoint presentation.

2. On the Ribbon, select the **Design** tab.
3. In the **Themes** group, select the desired colors, fonts, effects, and background styles to create a custom theme.
4. Save the custom theme.
   a. In the **Themes** group, click the **More** button.
   b. Select **Save Current Theme.**
   c. In the **Save Current Theme** dialog box, in the **File name** text box, enter the desired file name for the custom theme and click **Save.**

Procedure Reference: Format a Theme

To format a theme:

1. Open a file.
2. Display the **Themes** group.
3. In the **Themes** group, in the **Built-In** gallery, select a theme to apply it.
4. If necessary, browse for more themes.
   a. In the Themes gallery, choose **Browse For Themes** or **Enable Content Updates from Office.com.**

 You need to be connected to the Internet in order to use this option.

   b. Select the theme and click **Open.**
5. If necessary, save the current theme.
   a. In the **Themes** group, display the **Themes** gallery.
   b. Choose **Save Current Theme** to save the theme.
   c. In the **Save Current Theme** dialog box, in the **File name** text box, type a desired name and click **Save.**
6. In the **Themes** group, from the corresponding gallery, select a theme color, theme font, or theme effect that you want to apply.

ACTIVITY 4-1
Creating a Custom Theme

Data Files:

Company Overview.pptx

Before You Begin:

1. Launch the Microsoft PowerPoint application.
2. From the C:\084574Data\Creating Dynamic Presentation folder, open the Company Overview.pptx file.

Scenario:

Your colleague has asked you to review a PowerPoint presentation and make any necessary changes before finalizing it. You find that the presentation is designed with different font types, font sizes, and color combinations. You want to enhance the presentation so that the fonts and color schemes have a consistent look across all the slides. You also want to ensure that the presentation is visually appealing.

1. Add a prebuilt theme.

    a. On the Ribbon, select the **Design** tab.

    b. In the **Themes** group, click the **More** button.

    c. Position the mouse pointer over each theme to see a live preview of it.

    d. In the **Built-In** section, in the third row, in the seventh column, select the **Median** theme.

    e. Observe that the theme is applied to all the slides.

2. Create a custom color theme.

    a. In the **Themes** group, click **Colors** and select **Create New Theme Colors**.

    b. In the **Create New Theme Colors** dialog box, from the **Text/Background - Dark 2** drop-down list, in the **Theme Colors** section, in the fifth row, third column, select the **Brown, Background 2, Darker 25%** color.

    c. From the **Accent 1** drop-down list, in the **Theme Colors** section, in the sixth row, second column, select the **White, Text 1, Darker 50%** color.

    d. From the **Accent 2** drop-down list, in the **Theme Colors** section, in the first row, eighth column, select the **Gold Accent 4** color.

    e. In the **Sample** section, observe that a preview of the color theme is displayed.

    f. In the **Name** text box, triple-click the text "Custom 1," type *My Color Theme* and click **Save**.

    g. Observe that the changes reflect on all slides.

3. Define a custom theme font.

   a. In the **Themes** group, click **Fonts** and select **Create New Theme Fonts**.

   b. In the **Create New Theme Fonts** dialog box, in the **Heading font** drop-down list, scroll down and select **Verdana**.

   c. In the **Body font** drop-down list, scroll up and select **Arial**.

   d. In the **Sample** section, observe that a preview of the theme font is displayed.

   e. In the **Name** text box, triple-click the text, "Custom 1," type **My Font Theme** and click **Save**.

   f. Observe the change is visible on the current slide.

   g. Click **Save** to save the changes.

4. Save the custom theme.

   a. In the **Themes** group, click the **More** button and select **Save Current Theme**.

   b. In the **Save Current Theme** dialog box, in the **File name** text box, type **My Office Theme** and click **Save**.

5. Verify the custom theme.

   a. In the **Themes** group, click the **More** button.

   b. In the Themes gallery, in the **Custom** section, observe that the newly saved theme is displayed.

   c. Click away from the gallery to close the gallery.

   d. On the Quick Access toolbar, click the **Save** button to save the changes and close the presentation.

TOPIC B
Apply Picture Effects to Presentations

You created custom themes to enhance your presentations. Including graphics, process diagrams, and graphical effects to objects in your presentation will help to add emphasis and visual appeal. In this topic, you will work with graphical elements in your presentation.

A presentation is not just a series of slides with textual information. Flow charts, process related diagrams, and pictures have always been an integral part of slide shows. Enhancing the graphic objects on your slides helps add a visual effect. PowerPoint 2010 has enhanced features that help create complex diagrams and apply graphical effects to your presentation.

The Picture Tools Format Contextual Tab

The *Picture Tools Format contextual tab* includes commands to modify and enhance a picture. The **Adjust, Picture Styles, Arrange,** and **Size** groups enable you to adjust the picture color and effects, add new picture styles, format picture layouts, and arrange and resize pictures on a slide.

How to Apply Picture Effects to Presentations
Procedure Reference: Modify a Picture

To modify a picture:

1. Open an existing file with the picture to be modified.
2. Select the desired picture and observe that the sizing handles appear on the selected object.
3. On the **Home** tab, in the **Editing** group, from the **Select** drop-down list, select an object.
4. If necessary, on the **Format** contextual tab, choose Remove background to make the background of the image transparent.
5. On the **Picture Tools** contextual tab that is enabled, select the **Format** tab.
6. Apply the desired picture styles and effects.
   - In the **Adjust** group, select the desired option to adjust the brightness, contrast, or recolor.
   - In the **Picture Styles** group, select the desired picture style, shape, border, and effects.
   - Using the options provided in the **Arrange** group, set the position of the image.
   - In the **Size** group, set the desired picture size.

Procedure Reference: Create a Photo Album

To create a photo album:

1. Open a blank or existing PowerPoint presentation.
2. On the Ribbon, select the **Insert** tab.
3. In the **Images** group, click the **Photo Album** button.
4. In the **Photo Album** dialog box, in the **Insert picture from** section, click **File/Disk**.
5. If necessary, in the **Insert New Pictures** dialog box, navigate to the desired folder.

6. Select the images to add and click **Insert**.
7. If necessary, click **New Text Box** to add a text box to the next slide.
8. If necessary, rearrange the order of pictures in the album.
    a. In the **Pictures in album** section, select the desired picture or text box.
    b. Click **Up, Down,** or **Remove** to rearrange the order of pictures or text boxes.
9. If necessary, in the **Picture Options** section, specify picture options.
10. If necessary, in the **Album Layout** section, specify options to modify the album layout.
11. If desired, in the **Preview** section, click the appropriate button to modify the picture.
12. Click **Create**.

The PowerPoint Show (*.ppsx) Format

Saving a presentation in the .ppsx format allows you to view the presentation as a slide show.

ACTIVITY 4-2
Applying Picture Styles and Effects

Data Files:

OGC Properties.pptx

Before You Begin:

Navigate to the C:\084374Data\Creating Dynamic Presentations folder and open the OGC Properties.pptx file.

Scenario:

In one of the slides of the presentation that you are working on, you inserted a picture to complement content. However, you feel that you need to apply more effects and change the style so that the picture blends well with the presentation layout.

---

1. Remove the background.

    a. In the left pane, on the **Slides** tab, select slide 2.

    b. Select the picture to activate the **Picture Tools Format** contextual tab.

    c. On the **Picture Tools Format** contextual tab, in the **Adjust** group, click **Remove Background.**

    d. Observe that portions of the picture are shaded in pink and that a background marquee is displayed on the picture.

    e. Drag the top-center handle of the background marquee to the top edge of the image.

    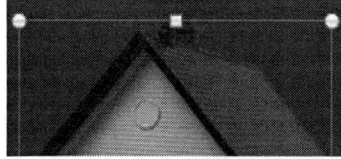

    f. On the **Background Removal** tab, in the **Refine** group, click **Mark Areas to Remove.**

    g. Click above the top-left corner of the house to select the background.

h. On the **Background Removal** tab, in the **Close** group, click **Keep Changes** to remove the background.

2. Apply a picture style.

   a. In the **Picture Styles** group, click the **More** button.

   b. In the Picture Styles gallery, in the first row, second column, select the **Beveled Matte, White** option.

3. Apply picture effects.

   a. In the **Picture Styles** group, click **Picture Effects** and position the mouse pointer over the **3-D Rotation** option.

   b. In the 3-D Rotation gallery, in the **Perspective** section, in the first row, second column, select the **Perspective Left** option.

   c. Save the presentation as *My OGC Properties*

TOPIC C
Applying Animation Effects

You have applied picture effects to a presentation. After enhancing pictures, you may want to animate the objects displayed on the slides to increase the visual interest in the presentation. In this topic, you will apply an animation effect.

When you present slides that contain just static objects and text, your audience may lose interest in the content being presented. Animating the objects on a slide and adding special effects will help you capture the attention of the audience.

Enhanced Animation Effects

PowerPoint 2010 allows you to add animations to objects by using the commands on the **Animations** tab. You can select an Entrance, Emphasis, Exit, or Motion Paths animation effect from the Animations gallery or choose other animation effects from the options at the bottom of the gallery. You can also add more than one custom animation to a slide, and manage them using the **Animation Pane.** PowerPoint 2010 also includes a new **Trigger** command to set a trigger to start an animation. You can also apply variations to animation effects, set the timing and duration of the effects, reorder the animations, and finally preview the animations as you are applying them.

The Trigger Command
The **Trigger** command is used to start an animation when a certain event, such as the clicking of a shape, a title placeholder, or a bookmark, occurs.

The Add Animations Gallery
You can also add variations to animations by using the effects in the **Add Animations** gallery. These effects are applied in addition to the existing animation effects.

The Animation Painter Command

The *Animation Painter command* provides you with an easy way to animate objects. You can use the **Animation Painter** button to copy the existing animation of objects on a slide and apply it to other objects. You can also apply the desired animation effect to multiple objects not only in one presentation but also across different presentations.

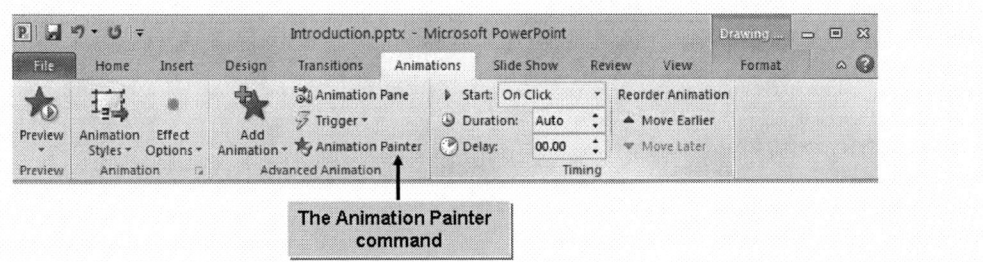

Figure 4-2: The Animation Painter command displayed in the Advanced Animation group.

How to Apply Animation Effects

Procedure Reference: Apply an Animation Effect to an Object or Text

To apply built-in animations to an object or text on a slide:

1. Select the object or text.
2. On the Ribbon, select the **Animations** tab.
3. In the **Animations** group, from the **More** drop-down list, select an animation.
4. If necessary, run the presentation to view the animation that you have selected.

Procedure Reference: Animate Objects by Using the Animation Painter Command

To animate objects by using the **Animation Painter** command:

1. Select the object that has the animation effect you want to copy.
2. On the **Animations** tab, in the **Advanced Animation** group, click **Animation Painter** to copy the existing object's animation.
3. Click the object to which you want to apply the copied animation effect.
4. If necessary, apply the same animation to objects located in multiple places within the presentation.
5. Click outside the slide to deactivate the **Animation Painter.**

ACTIVITY 4-3
Applying an Animation Effect

Scenario:
While reviewing a presentation that you recently created, you observe that all the slides are static and not lively and interactive. You realize that by using a variety of ways to introduce the content in the slides, such as by adding animation effects, you can draw the audience's attention. You decide to animate the first slide to begin the presentation on an interactive note.

1. Apply the **Fade** animation to the title placeholder.

    a. In the left pane, on the **Slides** tab, select slide 1.

    b. On slide 1, click before the text, "Our" to display the title placeholder.

    c. Select the **Animations** tab and, in the **Animation** group, select **Fade.**

2. Apply the **Split** animation to the subtitle placeholder.

    a. On slide 1, click before the text, "J. Rivera" to display the subtitle placeholder.

    b. On the **Animations** tab, in the **Animation** group, click the **More** button and, in the Animation Styles gallery, in the **Entrance** section, select **Split.**

3. Preview the animation effects that are applied to slide 1.

    a. On the **Animations** tab, in the **Preview** section, click **Preview.**

    b. Observe the animation effects that have been applied to the slide.

4. Apply the subtitle's animation effect to slide 22.

    a. On slide 1, click before the text, "J. Rivera" to display the subtitle text placeholder.

    b. On the **Animations** tab, in the **Advanced Animation** section, click **Animation Painter.**

    c. On the **Slides** tab, scroll down and select slide 22.

    d. Click before the text "Questions?" to apply the subtitle's animation effect to the slide.

    e. Save the presentation.

TOPIC D
Add Videos to a Presentation

You have added animation effects to your presentation. You may also want to add visually appealing content such as video clips. In this topic, you will add videos to a presentation.

The video capabilities of PowerPoint 2010 give you the advantage of not only adding videos to your presentation, but also effectively editing them without having to rely on any external applications or add-ins. The new video editing tools in PowerPoint 2010 allow you to manage and control the quality and effectiveness of your videos and create professional-looking presentations.

Video Tools Commands

The *Video Tools* tool tab comprises tabs with commands that enable you to edit, modify, and format videos. The video formatting commands are distributed within the following two contextual tabs: **Format** and **Playback.** The contextual tabs provide you with various options to adjust the brightness and color tone, apply video styles and effects, arrange and resize videos, add or remove bookmarks, edit and trim videos, and apply other options such as **Play Full Screen** and **Rewind after Playing.**

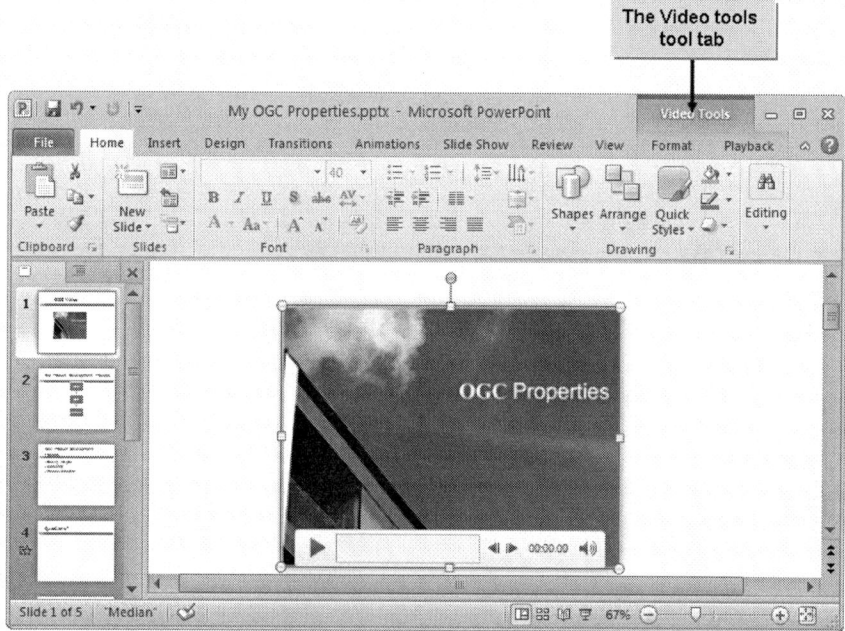

Figure 4-3: *The Video Tools Format contextual tab displaying the commands used to format a video.*

Video Styles and Effects

PowerPoint 2010 includes options to add styles and effects to the videos in a presentation. The **Video Styles** group on the contextual **Video Tools Format** tab provides options to add subtle, moderate, or intense styles, modify the shape of videos, add borders and outlines using colors, and apply video effects such as **Shadow, Reflection,** and **Glow,** among others.

How to Add Videos to a Presentation

Procedure Reference: Insert a Video

To insert a video:

1. Open a new blank PowerPoint presentation.
2. On the Ribbon, select the **Insert** tab.
3. In the **Media** group, click **Video** and, from the drop-down list, select **Video from File.**
4. In the **Insert Video** dialog box, select a video file and click **Insert** to insert the video in the slide.

Procedure Reference: Make Adjustments to a Video

To make adjustments to a video:

1. Open an existing PowerPoint presentation.
2. Select the desired video.
3. In the **Video Tools** section, select the **Format** contextual tab.
4. In the **Adjust** group, select the desired option to adjust brightness and color settings.
5. In the **Video Styles** group, apply the desired video style and video effects.
6. In the **Size** group, adjust the size of the video to get the desired size.

Procedure Reference: Modify Playback Settings

To modify playback settings:

1. Open an existing PowerPoint presentation.
2. Select the desired video.
3. In the **Video Tools** section, select the **Playback** contextual tab.
4. In the **Editing** group, click **Trim Video.**
5. In the **Trim Video** dialog box, specify the start and end times to trim the video and click **OK.**
6. In the **Editing** group, specify the desired **Fade In** and **Fade out** time.
7. In the **Video Options** group, check the check boxes for the desired playback settings.

ACTIVITY 4-4
Adding Videos to a Presentation

Scenario:
Your manager has asked to highlight your company's activities using videos. You decide to use one of the company's promotional videos in the presentation but you need to apply video styles and effects and trim a section of the video so that it does not display a blank screen.

1. Insert a new video.

   a. On the **Slides** tab, scroll down and select slide 19.

   b. On the **Home** tab, in the **Slides** group, from the **New Slide** drop-down list, select **Title and Content.**

   c. In the **Click to add title** placeholder, click and type *OGC Video*

   d. On the displayed slide, click in the **Click to add text** placeholder.

   e. On the **Insert** tab, in the **Media** group, from the **Video** drop-down list, select **Video from File.**

   f. In the **Insert Video** dialog box, navigate to the C:\084574Data\Creating Dynamic Presentations folder.

   g. Select the **OGC Properties.avi** file and click **Insert** to insert the video.

2. Edit the video.

   a. On the **Video Tools Format** contextual tab, in the **Adjust** group, click **Corrections** to display the Corrections gallery.

   b. In the Corrections gallery, in the **Brightness and Contrast** section, in the fourth row, third column, select the **Brightness: 0% (Normal) Contrast: +20%** option.

   c. In the **Video Styles** group, in the **Picture Styles** group, select the **Center Shadow Rectangle** video style.

   d. In the **Video Styles** group, click **Video Effects,** position the mouse pointer over **Soft Edges,** and then select the **2.5 Point** option.

3. Preview and trim the video.

   a. Select the **Video Tools Playback** contextual tab and, in the **Preview** section, click **Play.**

   b. Observe that the last few seconds of the video are blank. Therefore, you need to delete that part.

   c. On the **Video Tools Playback** contextual tab, in the **Editing** group, click **Trim Video.**

   d. In the **Trim Video** dialog box, verify that the **Start Time** text box displays the start time as **00:00.**

   e. In the **End Time** text box, triple-click, type *00:08* and press **Tab.**

f. Click **OK** to trim the video.

g. On the **Video Tools Playback** contextual tab, in the **Preview** section, click **Play.**

h. Observe that the video has now been trimmed to 00:08 seconds.

i. Save and close the presentation.

TOPIC E
Divide a Presentation into Sections

You added video elements to your presentation. You may now want to apply further customizing options to slides so that you can organize your presentation. In this topic, you will divide a presentation into sections.

Imagine a situation where you had to prepare a presentation which included half a dozen subjects or more. All the slides in your presentation are displayed randomly, and you want to find a particular slide so that you can edit it. It can be a time consuming effort if you had to rummage through all the slides to find the one you want to fix. This is particularly annoying when you do not have too much time at your disposal. PowerPoint 2010 gives you the advantage of grouping related slides into sections, so that you can quickly and easily identify the slides that you need to work on.

The Slide Section Option

The **Section** feature enables you to organize slides for a presentation. You can name sections in presentations to keep track of groups of slides. Using the **Section** feature, you can add a section, rename a section, move a section up or down in a list of slides, and remove a section. The **Section** feature can be accessed from the **Slides** group on the **Home** tab.

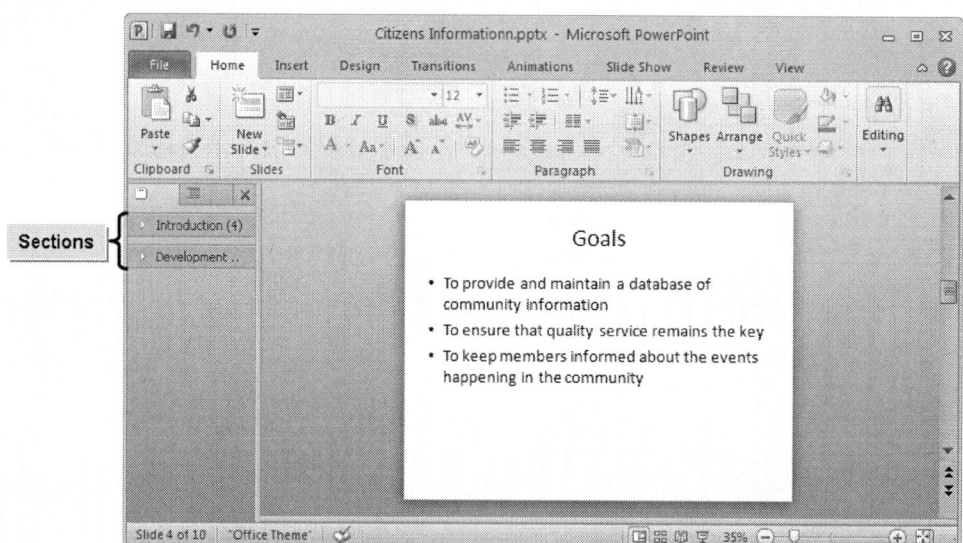

Figure 4-4: Sections in a presentation.

How to Divide a Presentation into Sections

Procedure Reference: Create a Section in an Existing Presentation

To create a section in an existing presentation:

1. Open an existing PowerPoint presentation.
2. Add a section.
   - On the **Home** tab, in the **Slides** group, from the **Section** drop-down list, select **Add Section.**
   - Or, right-click between the two slides where you want to add a section and choose **Add Section.**
3. Rename a section.
   a. Display the **Rename Section** dialog box.
      - On the **Home** tab, in the **Slides** group, from the **Section** drop-down list, select **Rename Section.**
      - Or, right-click the **Untitled Section** bar, and choose **Rename Section.**
   b. In the **Rename Section** dialog box, in the **Section name** text box, enter a section name and click **Rename.**

Procedure Reference: Rearrange the Sections in a Presentation

To rearrange the sections in a presentation:

1. If necessary, open a presentation with multiple sections.
2. Right-click a section title bar and choose **Move Section Down** to move a section to below another section.
3. Right-click the section title bar and choose **Move Section Up** to move a section to above another section.

The **Move Section Up** and **Move Section Down** options are enabled only if there are two or more sections.

ACTIVITY 4-5
Dividing a Presentation

Data Files:

OGC Properties Overview.pptx

Before You Begin:

From the C:\084574Data\Creating Dynamic Presentation folder, open the OGC Properties Overview.pptx file.

Scenario:

You are preparing a presentation on the company's achievements. There are multiple slides in the presentation and your manager wants to highlight the financial results of the company, followed by the performances of the company's meritorious staff. She wants you to organize the slides in such a manner that the slides related to the financial aspects of the company can be easily distinguished from the slides that contain information about the performance of the employees.

1. Create sections for the "Financial Overview" and "Awards" slides.

    a. In the left pane, on the **Slides** tab, scroll down and select slide 13, and on the **Home** tab, in the **Slides** group, from the **Section** drop-down list, select **Add Section.**

    b. On the **Slides** tab, observe that an **Untitled Section** title bar is displayed and that the slides below it are included in that section.

    c. From the **Section** drop-down list, select **Rename Section,** and in the **Rename Section** dialog box, in the **Section name** text box, type *Financial Overview* and click **Rename.**

    d. On the **Slides** tab, select slide 10 and, on the **Home** tab, in the **Slides** group, from the **Section** drop-down list, select **Add Section.**

    e. In the **Slides** group, from the **Section** drop-down list, select **Rename Section.**

    f. In the **Rename Section** dialog box, in the **Section name** text box, type *Awards* and click **Rename.**

2. Reorder the sections.

    a. Right-click the **Awards** section title bar and choose **Move Section Down** to move the Awards section to below the **Financial Overview** section.

    b. Observe that the sections have been reordered.

    c. Click and drag slide 19 to below slide 22.

    d. Save the presentation as *My OGC Properties Overview* and close it.

    e. Close the application.

Lesson 4 Follow-up

In this lesson, you explored the redesigned user interface and designed the framework for building your presentation. You also added visual elements to slides. These skills will enable you to create interactive and visually appealing presentations that will help you deliver information to a wider audience.

1. **How do you think applying themes to a presentation will add value to it?**

2. **How do you think applying picture effects will enhance the effectiveness of a presentation?**

5 Working with Databases Using Microsoft Office Access 2010

Lesson Time: 1 hour(s), 45 minutes

Lesson Objectives:

In this lesson, you will work with databases using Microsoft Office Access 2010.

You will:

- Work with tables in Access 2010.
- Work with forms.
- Work with macros.
- Work with reports.
- Work with external data.
- Design a database for the web.

Introduction

You worked with Microsoft Office Access 2003 and you now need to be aware of additional features in the latest release of the software for improving the management, presentation, and distribution of your databases. In this lesson, you will be introduced to the new features available in Microsoft Office Access 2010.

By using the new and enhanced features in Microsoft Office Access 2010, you will be able to create a robust and highly functional database that will help you manage large amounts of data efficiently, and thereby increase productivity. Access 2010, with its enhanced user interface, will help you to quickly develop and deploy database applications, with minimal effort.

TOPIC A
Work with Tables

You have used Access 2003 or the earlier versions to store data. Although Access 2010, like all database applications, uses tables to store data, it provides certain features that enable you to easily store, access, and modify data in a table. In this topic, you will create a table in Access 2010.

Storing data in text files requires careful considerations of file size as the amount of data you can store in a text file is limited. Moreover, accessing and manipulating data in a text document can at times be cumbersome and may lead to errors or data loss. Databases enable you to store large and complex data that can be easily retrieved and manipulated without any considerations for file size. The redesigned Access table has several features that enable you to store and manipulate data effortlessly.

The Field Insertion Feature

The *field insertion feature* in Access 2010 allows you to easily insert a new field by just typing the field name in the first row of a new column in the Datasheet view. This feature eliminates the cumbersome process of using the Design view to insert a new field as in the earlier versions of Access. This feature also enables you to quickly create a table structure even if you are not familiar with the intricacies of a database.

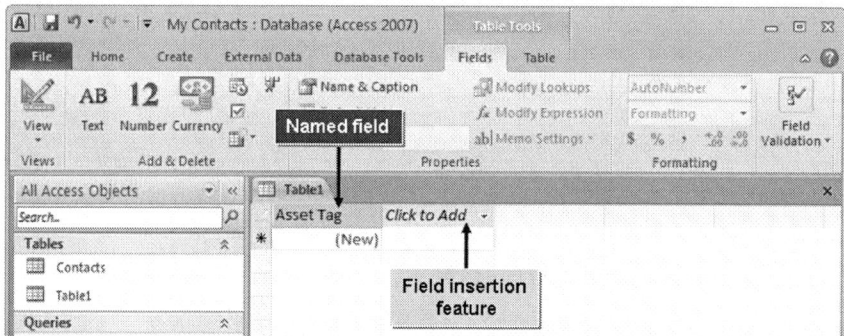

Figure 5-1: The tabbed table window displaying the option to add a field by using the field insertion feature.

Data Types

A *data type* is a categorization of data associated with a particular field based on certain predefined characteristics. In addition to supporting the data types of earlier versions, Access now supports the *Attachment* data type. This feature enables you to store external documents and binary files in a record, and attach multiple files to a single record. Some of the attachments are compressed by Access, leading to optimization of space.

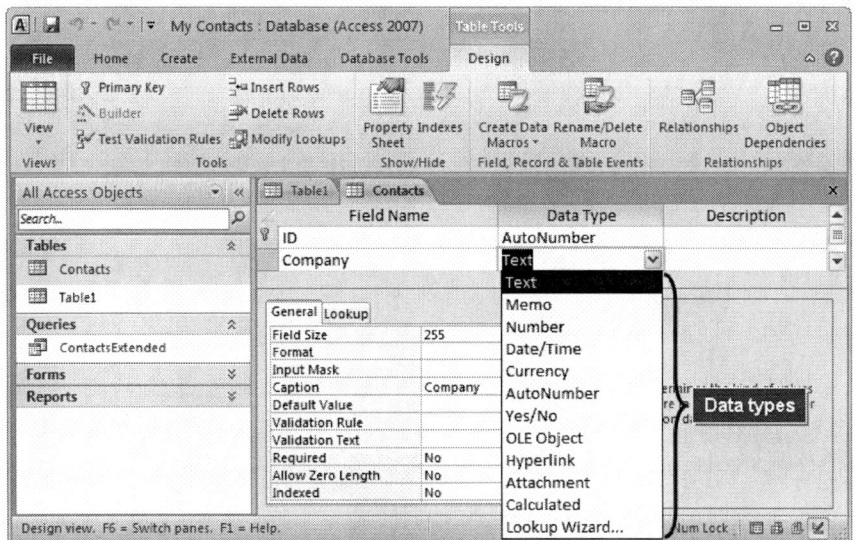

Figure 5-2: The Data Type drop-down list displaying the various data types.

The Rich Text Memo Field

The *rich text memo field* enables you to format data in tables, forms, or reports. You can apply text formatting such as boldface, italics, and font color to individual characters or words in a rich text enabled memo field in the Datasheet view. To enable the rich text feature, you need to open a table in the Design view, and under the memo field's **Field Properties**, set the **Text Format** property to **Rich Text.** Alternatively, you can use the **Memo Settings** option in the **Properties** group on the **Fields** tab to set the properties for a Memo field. The Memo field also has an **Append Only** property which when set enables you to append data to a memo field, but not modify the existing data in the field.

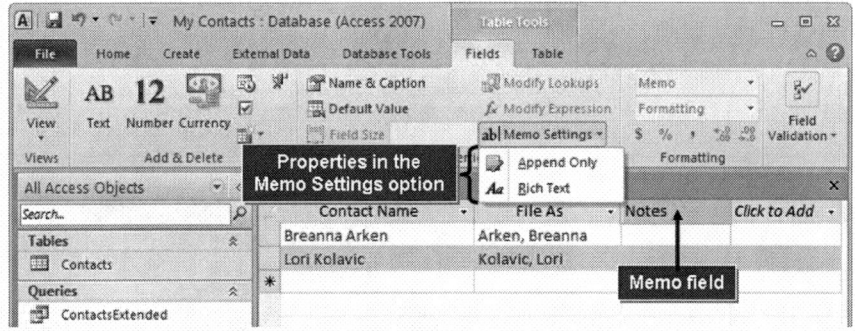

Figure 5-3: Rich Text Memo field options.

The Data Type Gallery

The *Data Type gallery* in Access 2010 allows you to add common field types such as Attachment and Currency to a table. It contains predefined fields that are organized into various sections. You can insert either one field at a time or a group of fields at a click, using **Quick Start** options. You can also add custom fields to predefined sections and save them as new data types.

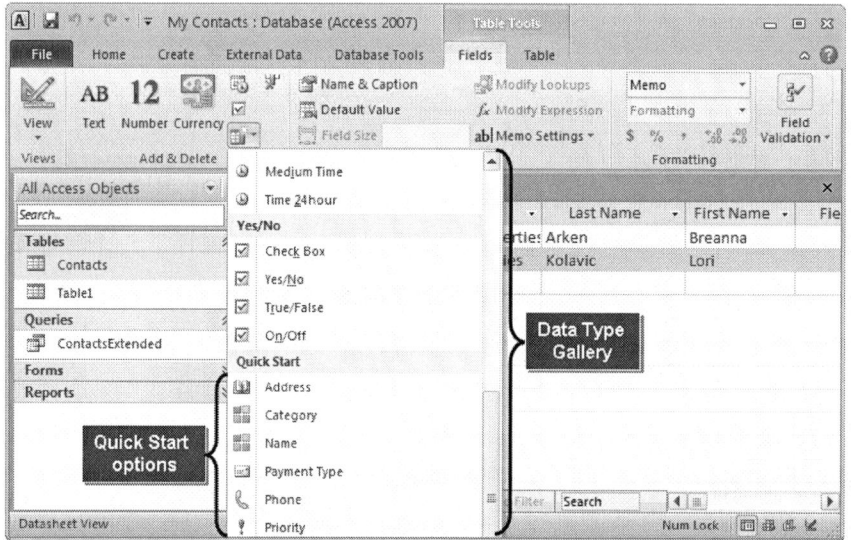

Figure 5-4: The Data Type gallery displaying the common fields arranged in sections.

The Auto Calendar

The *Auto Calendar* is an icon that is displayed to the right of the **Date/Time** data type cell when you select the cell. Clicking this icon displays a calendar from which you can choose a date.

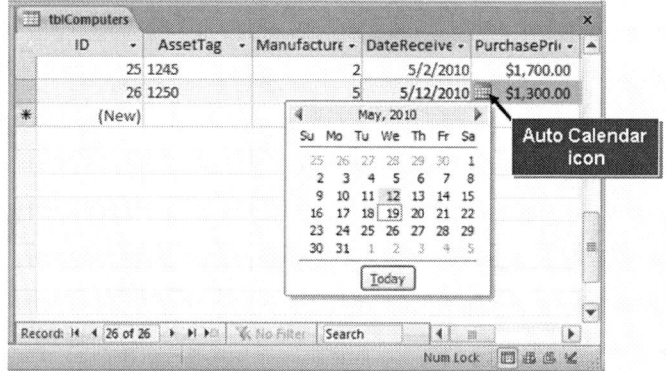

Figure 5-5: The Auto Calendar icon that displays a calendar.

Displaying the Auto Calendar Icon

To display the **Auto Calendar** icon, you need to enable the Auto Calendar feature by using the **Show Date Picker** property in the **Field Properties** section of the Design view. You can turn off the Auto Calendar feature by setting the **Show Date Picker** property to **Never**.

Multivalued Fields

A *multivalued field* enables you to store multiple values in a field. You can create a multivalued field by using the **Lookup Wizard**. In the wizard, you can either type a required value or use a value from a table or query. The **Allow Multiple Values** check box in the wizard allows you to store multiple values for the lookup.

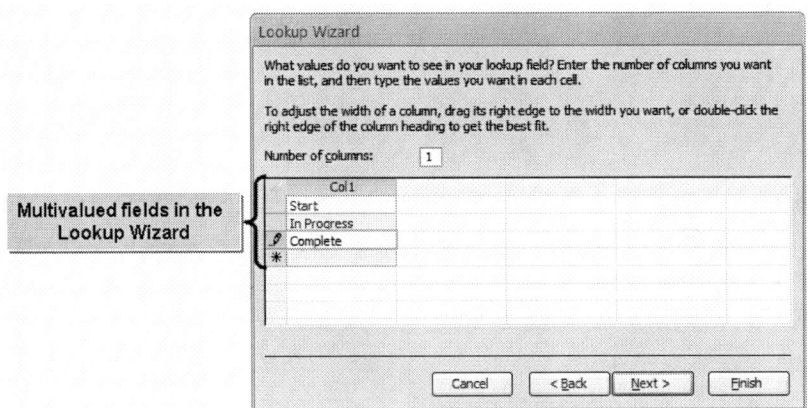

Figure 5-6: A table displaying options to add multivalued fields.

Alternate Background Color

Access supports the *alternate background color feature* which you can use to set a specific color for every other row in a table. You can use this feature in the Datasheet view, and for tables in continuous forms and reports, so that rows in tables are banded and more readable. You can access this feature from the **Text Formatting** group on the **Home** tab.

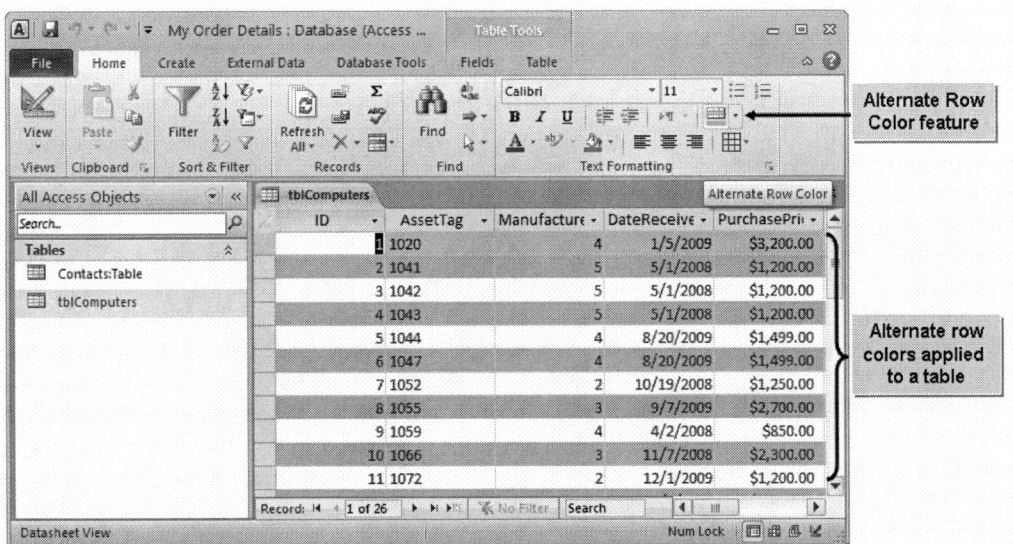

Figure 5-7: Alternate rows in a table displayed with different background colors.

How to Work with Tables

Procedure Reference: Create a Table in a Blank Database

To create a table in a blank database:

1. If necessary, launch the Microsoft Office Access 2010 application.
2. Create a database.
   - In the Backstage view, in the **Available Templates** pane, click **Blank database** and then click **Create.**
   - Or, in the Backstage view, in the **Available Templates** pane, double-click **Blank database.**
3. In the **Blank database** pane, in the **File name** text box, type a file name.
4. If necessary, click the **Browse** button and navigate to the location where you want to create the database.
5. If necessary, in the **File New Database** dialog box, click **OK.**
6. In the **Blank database** pane, click **Create** to display a blank table.

Procedure Reference: Work with a Table

To work with a table:

1. Create a table.
2. Save the table.
3. In the **Save As** dialog box, in the **Table Name** text box, type a name and click **OK.**
4. Add fields to a table.
   - Add a field manually.
     a. In the table tabbed window, from the **Click to Add** drop-down list, select a data type and enter a field name.
     b. If necessary, press **Enter** to add another field.
   - Add a field by using the **More Fields** option.
     a. On the Ribbon, select the **Fields** contextual tab.
     b. In the **Add & Delete** group, select the **More Fields** option to display the Data Type gallery.
     c. In the Data Type gallery, from the desired section, double-click the values for the table.
5. Set the data type.
   a. Select the **Home** tab.
   b. Switch to the Design view.
   c. In the table, click the **Data Type** column next to the desired field, and from the **Data Type** drop-down list, select a data type.
6. Insert a record.
   - In the Datasheet view, in the table, specify the desired values in each row.
   - On the **Home** tab, in the **Records** group, click **New** to create a new record.

Procedure Reference: Create a Multivalued Field Manually

To create a multivalued field manually:

1. In the Design view, click the **Data Type** column next to the desired field, and from the **Data Type** drop-down list, select **Lookup Wizard.**
2. Select the **I will type in the values that I want** option and click **Next.**
3. If necessary, in the **Number of columns** text box, specify the required number of columns.
4. In the list box, specify the necessary values and click **Next.**
5. In the **What label would you like for your lookup field** text box, specify a name.
6. Check **Allow Multiple Values** and click **Finish.**
7. Save the changes.
8. If necessary, in the **Microsoft Office Access** message box, click **Yes** to change the data type field to store multiple values.

Procedure Reference: Create a Multivalued Field by Using Values from Another Table

To create a multivalued field by using values from another table:

1. In the Design view of the table, click the **Data Type** column next to the desired field, and from the **Data Type** drop-down list, select **Lookup Wizard.**
2. Verify that the **I want the lookup field to get the values from another table or query** option is selected and click **Next.**
3. In the **View** section, select a view.
   - Select **Tables** to view a list of all the tables in the database.
   - Select **Queries** to view a list of all the queries in the database.
   - Select **Both** to view a list of both the tables and queries in the database.
4. From the displayed view, select a table or query option and click **Next.**
5. Add fields to be included in the lookup column.
   - Add a single field.
     a. In the **Available Fields** list box, select a field.
     b. Click the **Greater Than** button to add the field to the **Selected Fields** list box.
   - Click the **Double Greater Than** button to add all the fields in the **Available Fields** list box to the **Selected Fields** list box.
6. If necessary, remove fields from the **Selected Fields** list box.
   - Remove a single field.
     a. In the **Available Fields** list box, select a field.
     b. Click the **Less Than** button to remove the field from the **Selected Fields** list box.
   - Click the **Double Less Than** button to remove all the fields from the **Selected Fields** list box.
7. Click **Next.**
8. On the **What sort order do you want for the items in your list box** page, from the **Ascending** drop-down list, select a field, click the toggle button to select a sort order and then click **Next.**

9. If necessary, on the **How would you like the columns in your lookup field** page, double-click the right edge of the column heading to adjust the width of the column and click **Next.**
10. In the **What label would you like for your lookup field** text box, specify the desired name.
11. Check **Allow Multiple Values** and click **Finish.**
12. Save the changes.
13. If necessary, in the **Microsoft Office Access** message box, click **Yes** to change the data type field to store multiple values.

ACTIVITY 5-1
Creating a Table

Scenario:
Your client, Claire Connor, from Eastern Connection, just called in to inform you that you are assigned a $20,000 project. However, this is only a prototype, and further decisions will be made depending on the quality of the project. Because this is a high priority project, you want to allocate multiple resources for it. You decide to collate all information in one sheet so that it is available at a glance. You also want to create a database of projects that could be referenced later.

1. Create a table.

   a. Launch the Microsoft Access 2010 (Beta) application.

   b. In the Backstage view, verify that **New** is selected and, in the **Available Templates** pane, verify that **Blank database** is selected.

   c. In the **Blank database** pane, in the **File Name** text box, click and type *Project Details*

   d. Click the **Browse** button that is displayed to the right of the **File Name** text box.

   e. Navigate to the C:\084574Data\Working with Databases Using Microsoft Office Access 2010 folder.

   f. In the **File New Database** dialog box, click **OK.**

   g. In the **Blank database** pane, click **Create.**

   h. Observe that a database is created and a blank table displayed.

   i. On the Quick Access toolbar, click **Save.**

   j. In the **Save As** dialog box, in the **Table Name** text box, type *Project* and click **OK.**

2. Create field headers in a table.

   a. In the Project table tabbed window, from the **Click to Add** drop-down list, select **Text.**

   b. In the **Field1** header, type *Project Name* and press **Tab.**

   c. From the **Click to Add** drop-down list, select **Text** to add another field header.

   d. Type *Employee Name* and press **Tab.**

   e. Similarly, add fields with the names *Date of Completion, Details,* and *Home Page.*

3. Add another field to the header row.

   a. On the **Fields** contextual tab, in the **Add & Delete** group, click **More Fields** to display the Data Type gallery.

   b. From the Data Type gallery, in the **Number** section, click **Currency.**

c. Double-click **Field1,** and type *Current Value* and then press **Enter.**

d. Click away to close the drop-down list.

e. On the Quick Access toolbar, click **Save.**

4. Set a data type for all fields.

    a. On the Ribbon, select the **Home** tab.

    b. In the **Views** group, from the **View** drop-down list, select **Design View.**

    c. In the Project table, click the **Data Type** column next to Date of Completion, and from the **Data Type** drop-down list, select **Date/Time.**

    d. Click the **Data Type** column next to Details, and from the **Data Type** drop-down list, select **Memo.**

    e. Click the **Data Type** column next to Home Page, and from the **Data Type** drop-down list, select **Hyperlink.**

5. Create a multivalued field.

    a. Click the **Data Type** column next to Employee Name, and from the **Data Type** drop-down list, select **Lookup Wizard.**

    b. In the **Lookup Wizard,** select **I will type in the values that I want** and click **Next.**

    c. In **Col1,** in the first cell, click and type *Josephine Riggs*

    d. In the second cell in the same column, click and type *Mike Allen*

    e. Similarly, in the third and fourth cells of the same column, enter the names *Julia Barret* and *Beth Robinson,* respectively.

    f. Click **Next.**

    g. Check **Allow Multiple Values** and click **Finish.**

    h. In the **Microsoft Access** message box, click **Yes** to allow the lookup column to store multiple values.

    i. On the Quick Access toolbar, click **Save.**

6. Insert a record.

    a. In the **Views** group, from the **View** drop-down list, select **Datasheet View.**

    b. In the Project table, in the Project Name column, in the first cell, click and type *Eastern Connection*

c. In the Employee Name column, click the first cell, and from the drop-down list, check **Mike Allen** and **Julia Barret** and then click **OK**.

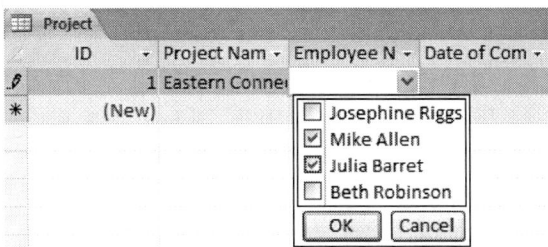

d. Place the mouse pointer on the separator line between the Employee Name and Date of Completion headers, and when the mouse pointer changes to a double-headed arrow, double-click to expand the Employee Name column.

e. Observe that the Employee Name column now contains multiple resources.

f. Press **Tab,** and next to the Date of Completion column, click the **Auto Calendar** icon.

g. Navigate to and select a date six months from today.

h. Similarly, enter the information given below in the appropriate fields.
   - Details: This is a prototype.
   - Home Page: http://eastern.example
   - Current Value: 20000

7. Save and close the table and the database.

   a. On the Quick Access toolbar, click **Save.**

   b. Close the Project tabbed window.

   c. Save the database as *My Project Details* in the C:\084574Data\Working with Databases Using Microsoft Office Access 2010 folder.

   d. Choose **File→Close Database** to close the database.

TOPIC B
Work with Forms

You created tables and are now ready to enter and edit data in tables. You can use forms to efficiently accomplish this. In this topic, you will create a form using the new features in Access 2010.

If you are working with a reasonably large database, you may need to input thousands of records, and this could prove to be a cumbersome process. However, by using forms in Access, you can streamline the data entry process, thereby increasing productivity.

Form Creation Tools

You can create forms by using the form creation tools in the **Forms** group on the **Create** tab.

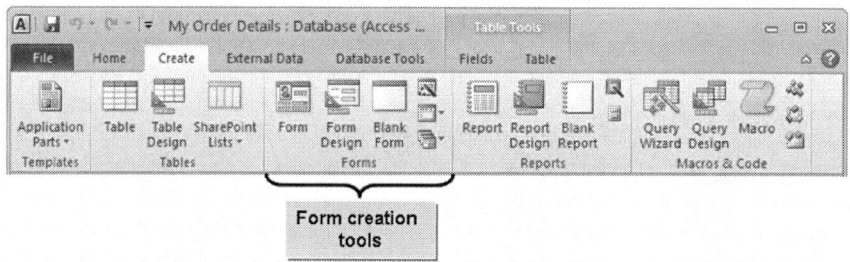

Figure 5-8: *The form creation tools displayed in the Forms group.*

The following table describes the form creation tools.

Form Creation Tool	Enables You To
Form	Use all the fields in the table. The form will be displayed in the Layout view. Also, it consists of a subform that is dependent on the related table or query if the table has a one-to-many relationship with another table or query. A subform, however, can be deleted. If the table has a one-to-many relationship with more than one table, the subform will not be created.
Form Design	Create a form in the Design view.
Blank Form	Create a blank form from which you can build a form from the beginning.
More Forms	Create additional forms such as: • **Multiple Items:** Allows you to generate a form that displays all the records in the table. • **Datasheet:** Allows you to create a form in the Datasheet view. • **Split Form:** Allows you to view the form simultaneously in the Form and Datasheet views. • **Modal Dialog:** Allows you to create a modal form with the **OK** and **Cancel** buttons enabled. • **PivotChart:** Allows you to create a form in the PivotChart view. • **PivotTable:** Allows you to create a form in the PivotTable view.

The WYSIWYG Interface

The *What You See Is What You Get (WYSIWYG) interface* enables you to modify design layouts in a form even as you are working in it. In the Layout view, you can use this interface to modify layouts, saving you the need to switch to the Design view each time you want to modify them, reducing the time and effort required to design and format a form or report.

Layouts

Definition:

Layouts are groups of controls that enable you to make design changes to an interface element. In Access, you can set layouts for forms you create by using the **Arrange** contextual tab. Each layout consists of control margins, such as **Narrow**, **Medium**, and **Wide**, that you can use to point out the location of information displayed within a control. Layouts also incorporate control padding, which is used to set spacing between gridlines on the form. Access consists of two types of layouts: Tabular and Stacked. *Tabular layouts* display controls in a horizontal table format with one row per record, whereas *Stacked layouts* display controls vertically.

Example:

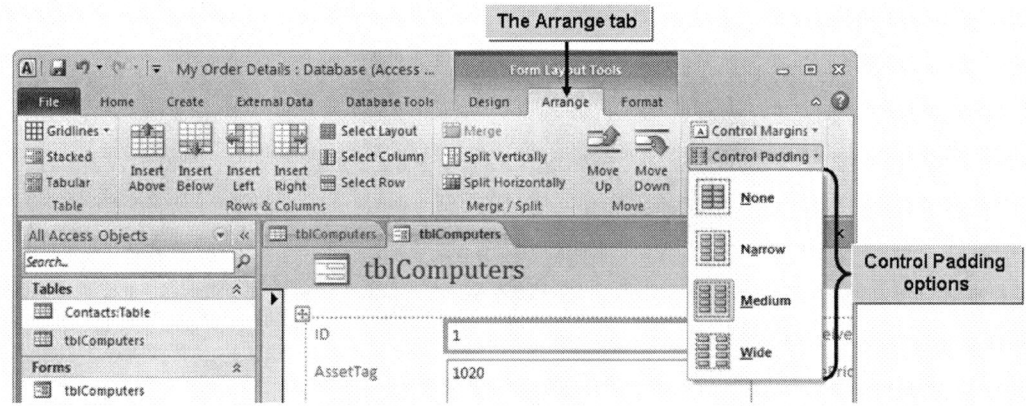

Figure 5-9: The control padding options used to make design changes to a form.

Anchoring

Anchoring enables you to tie a control or a section of a control to another control so that you can move and resize them simultaneously. There are various anchoring options available, such as **Top Left, Stretch Down,** and **Bottom Left.** You can access this feature in the Layout view from the **Position** group on the **Arrange** contextual tab. In the Design view, you can access this feature from the **Position** group on the **Arrange** contextual tab.

The Property Sheet

The *Property Sheet* is a collection of tools that enable you to set properties for the controls in a form, such as a text box, an image, a label, or a combo box. You can access the **Property Sheet** from the **Arrange** contextual tab. The tools in the **Property Sheet** pane are grouped into five functional tabs. The contents of each of the tabs are described in the table.

Tab	Allows You To
Format	Set properties for font, color, line spacing, and text alignment.

Tab	Allows You To
Data	Set properties for text validations, the text format, and input mask.
Event	Set properties for events such as mouse up and key press.
Other	Set properties for tabs, AutoCorrect, and the status bar.
All	Set properties for a control.

The Application Parts Gallery

The *Application Parts gallery* lists database objects such as tables, queries, reports, and forms as templates. You can select a template from the **Blank Forms** section to add a specific form to the database or you can use the **Quick Start** section to add tables such as comments, contacts, issues, tasks, or users. The **Contacts, Issues, Tasks,** and **Users** templates allow you to create a relationship with one or more parts of an existing database by importing such data into the newly created database.

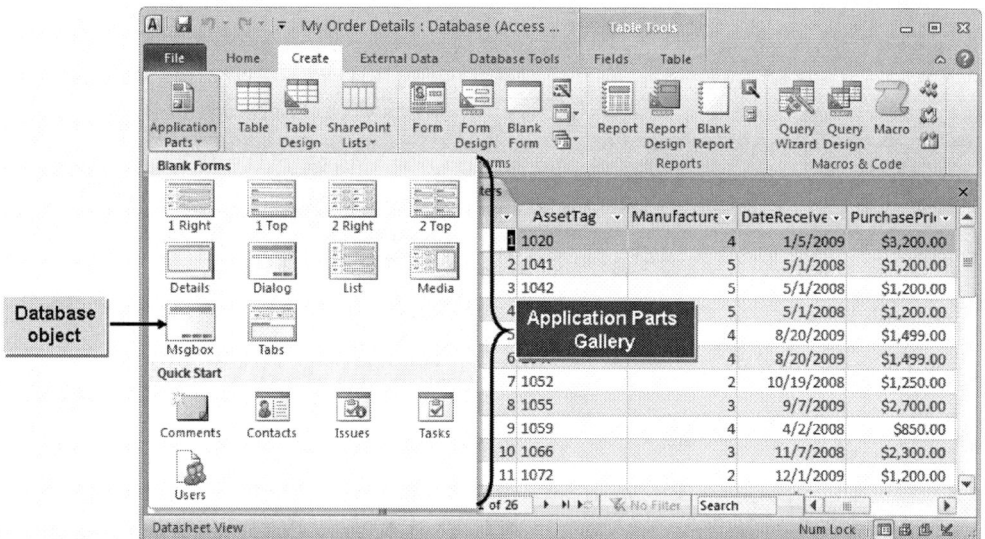

Figure 5-10: The Application Parts gallery displaying the application templates available in Access 2010.

How to Work with Forms

Procedure Reference: Build a Form from Existing Table Data

To build a form from existing table data:

1. Open a table.
2. On the Ribbon, select the **Create** tab.
3. Generate a form by using the options in the **Forms** group on the **Create** tab.
4. If necessary, switch to the Form view.
5. Work with the form.
   - In the form, navigate to a record and update the desired fields.
   - Insert a new record.
     - On the **Home** tab, in the **Records** group, click **New** and fill in the necessary fields.
     - Or, on the **Record** navigation bar, click the **New (blank) record** button and fill in the necessary fields.
6. On the Quick Access toolbar, click **Save**.
7. In the **Save As** dialog box, in the **Form Name** text box, specify a name and click **OK**.
8. If necessary, close the database.

Procedure Reference: Build a Database Object by Using the Application Parts Gallery

To build a database object by using the Application Parts gallery:

1. Open a blank database and, on the **Create** tab, in the **Templates** group, click **Application Parts.**
2. From the Application Parts gallery, select an application part.
   - In the **Blank Forms** section, select a form to add to the database.
   - In the **Quick Start** section, select an application part template and, in the **Create Relationship** wizard, specify the relationship to include in the database object.
3. Open the database object that is added and insert records and fields as required.
4. Save and close the database.

Procedure Reference: Design a Form Layout

To design a form layout:

1. Open a form.
2. Switch to the Layout view.
3. In the form, select the desired fields.
4. Arrange the form controls by selecting the control you want to move and dragging it to the desired location.
5. If necessary, add a background image.
   a. On the **Format** tab, in the **Background** group, from the **Background Image** drop-down list, select **Browse**.
   b. In the **Insert Picture** dialog box, navigate to a folder, select the desired background image, and click **OK**.

6. If necessary, format the controls by selecting options from the **Design, Arrange,** and **Format** contextual tabs.
7. Save the form.

ACTIVITY 5-2
Creating a Form Using Application Parts

Scenario:
You want to build a database of your contacts. You do not have the time to create tables and forms from scratch. So, you decide to use application parts to simplify this job.

1. Add the **Contacts** application part to a database.

   a. Open a blank database.

   b. Select the **Create** tab and, in the **Templates** group, from the **Application Parts** drop-down list, in the **Quick Start** section, click **Contacts** to add the **Contacts** template.

   c. In the **Microsoft Access** message box, click **Yes** to close all open objects.

   d. If necessary, on the **Security Warning** bar, click **Enable Content.**

   e. Observe that the **Contacts** template is displayed and also observe that a related table, query, forms, and reports are displayed in the Navigation Pane.

2. Enter the name and email address of a customer.

   a. Double-click the **Contacts** table to open it.

   b. In the **Company** column, in the first row, click and type *New World Properties* and then press **Tab.**

   c. In the **Last Name** column, in the first row, type *Arken* and press **Tab.**

   d. In the **First Name** column, in the first row, type *Breanna* and press **Tab.**

   e. In the **E-mail Address** column, in the first row, type *barken@ogc.com* and press **Tab.**

3. Enter other contact information.

   a. In the **Job Title** column, in the first row, type *Sales Rep* and press **Tab.**

   b. In the **Business Phone** column, in the first row, type *617–555–3698*

   c. Similarly, type the information appended below in the respective fields.
      - Address: 145 Windsor Drive
      - City: Alexandria
      - State/Province: VA
      - Zip/Postal Code: 22314

   d. On the Quick Access toolbar, click **Save.**

4. Check whether the contact information is displayed in other database objects.

a. In the Navigation Pane, double-click the **ContactDetails** form to open it.

b. Observe that the details entered in the table are auto populated in the form.

c. Double-click the **ContactList** report to view the updated details.

d. Right-click the **ContactList** tabbed window and choose **Close All** to close all the open windows.

5. Insert a record into a form.

   a. Double-click the **ContactDetails** form to open it.

   b. Click the **New (blank) record** button to open a new record.

   c. In the form tabbed window, enter the information furnished below.
      - First Name: Lori
      - Last Name: Kolavic
      - Title: Sales Manager
      - Company: Tri-mark Properties
      - Business Phone: 617–555–3699
      - Address: 15 Milestrip Road
      - City: Fairfield
      - State/Province: CT
      - Zip/Postal Code: 16430

   d. On the Quick Access toolbar, click **Save.**

6. Check for the contact details in the table and report.

   a. In the Navigation Pane, double-click the **Contacts** table to open it.

   b. Observe that the details entered in the form are auto populated in the table.

   c. Double-click the **ContactList** report to view the updated details.

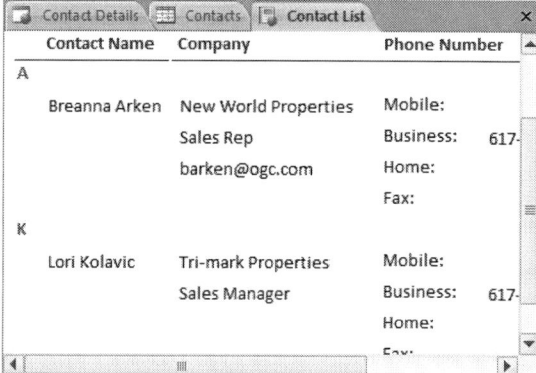

7. Save and close the database.

   a. Close all the open windows.

b. Save the database as **My Contacts** in the C:\084574Data\Working with Databases Using Microsoft Office Access 2010 folder and close it.

TOPIC C
Work with Macros

You created a form and designed its layout. You can simplify working with forms and tables by automating certain tasks using macros. In this topic, you will work with macros.

When working in a database, you may need to perform repetitive tasks such as inserting data into forms or tables, creating tables, opening forms, or generating reports. This may be time consuming and require additional effort. By creating and using macros, you can automate these tasks and save valuable time and effort. Access 2010 has a new redesigned macro interface that helps you create smart macros and accomplish common tasks quickly and efficiently.

The Macro Designer

The *Macro Designer* is a tool that enables you to create macros. The designer interface displays the **Add New Action** drop-down list, which helps build code blocks to add conditional statements and arguments. You can add a conditional statement or an argument by clicking the **Add New Action** drop-down list and selecting an action, or by double-clicking or dragging an action from the **Action Catalog.** With Access 2010, you can use additional conditional statements such as **Add Else** and **Add Else If.** You can also perform other functions such as deleting an action or moving an action up or down one level in the Macro Designer. The **Expand Actions** and **Collapse Actions** buttons in the **Collapse/Expand** group enable you to view a compact view of the macro.

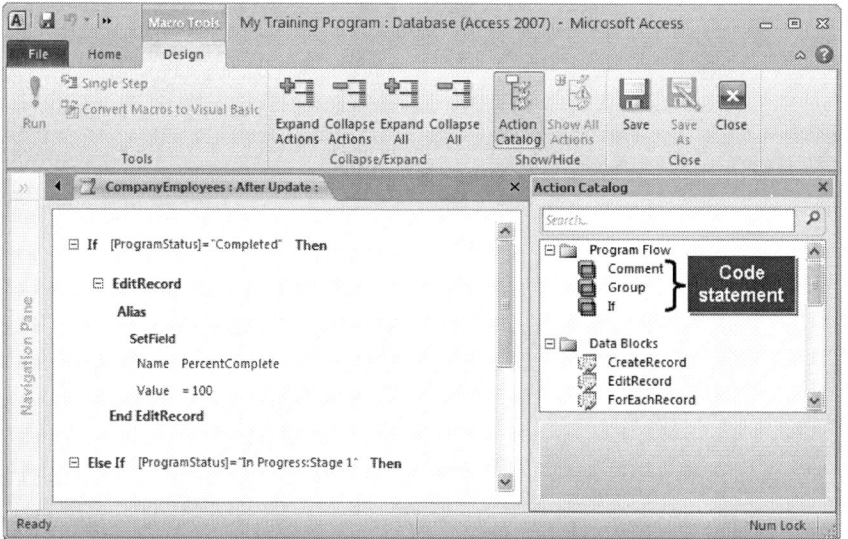

Figure 5-11: The Macro Designer displaying the area where you will build macros.

Data Macros

A *data macro* is a feature that allows you to attach macros to table data. You can create data macros using the Macro Designer. When you attach logic to fields in a table or record, any changes made to the table will automatically execute that logic. The advantage of using data macros is that when you attach a data macro to a field, you can execute the same logic in other Access objects, such as forms and reports, that share that field, saving you from having to re-create the logic. However, data macros cannot process multivalued or attachment data types.

Embedded Macros

Embedded macros are macros that are part of the property attached to an event, and they can be accessed from the **Event** tab on the **Property Sheet.** They can be referenced only from the event property of the object they are attached to and not from the Navigation Pane like regular macros. Using the embedded macro feature, you can embed macros in events associated with a form, report, or control.

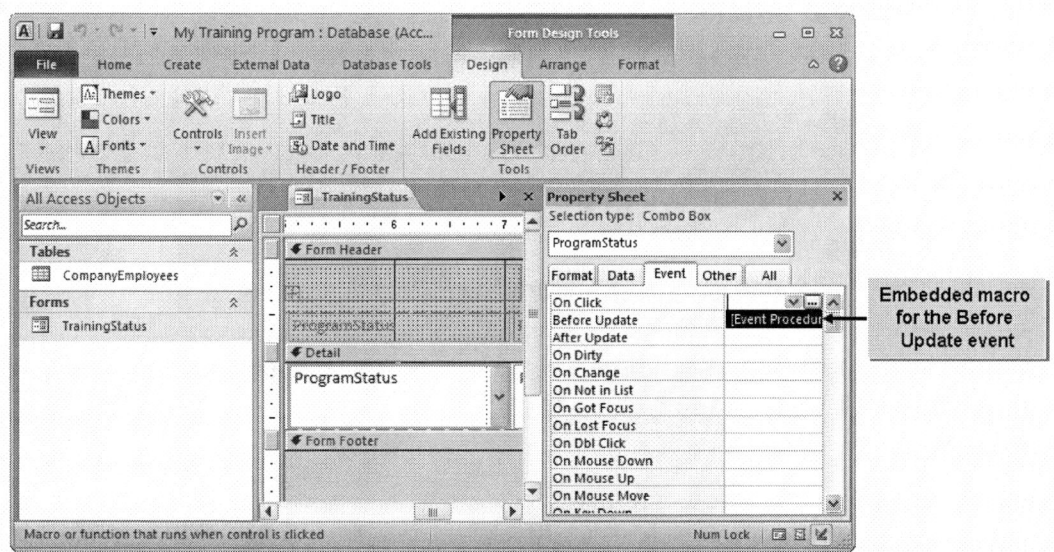

Figure 5-12: The Property Sheet displaying an event property.

IntelliSense

The *IntelliSense feature* in Access 2010 allows you to effortlessly build expressions that you want to use in a given context by automatically displaying the expression as you type. As you build expressions, the IntelliSense feature displays a drop-down list from which you can select the expression you want to use. It also displays the complete declaration for the expression and a screen tip providing additional information about the selected item. This feature is also available in tables, queries, forms, and reports where expressions are used. The advantage of this feature is that it will help you minimize errors that may arise when working with long expressions and field names.

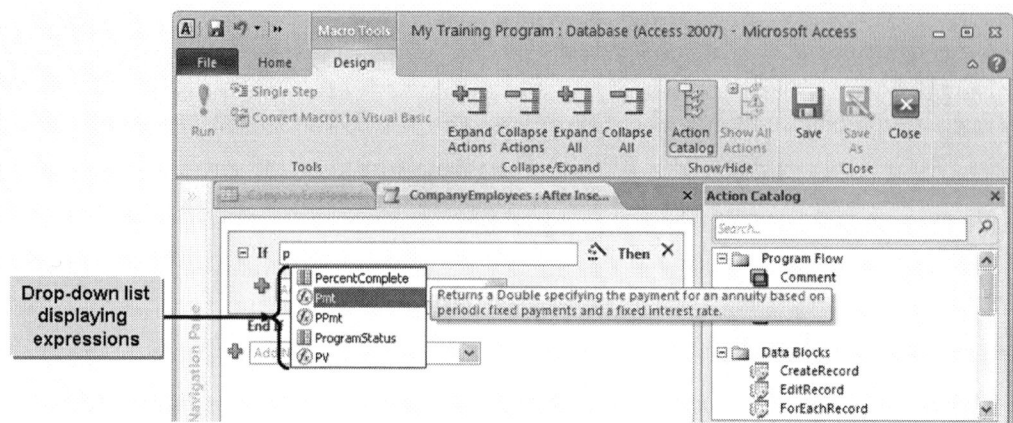

Figure 5-13: Expressions displayed by the IntelliSense feature of a macro.

How to Work with Macros

Procedure Reference: Create and Run a Macro

To create and run a macro:

1. Open the database and display the table which you want to update.
2. On the **Table** contextual tab, in the **After Events** group, click **After Update.**
3. Add an If statement.
   - In the **Action Catalog,** in the **Program Flow** section, double-click **If** to add an If conditional statement block.
   - Or, in the **Action Catalog,** in the **Program Flow** section, drag the **If** condition onto the **Add New Action** text box.
4. In the Macro Designer, in the **If** text box, type the condition statement.
5. Set a field value.
   a. In the **Action Catalog,** in the **Data Blocks** section, double-click **EditRecord** to add an **EditRecord** block to the Macro Designer.
   b. In the **Action Catalog,** in the **Data Actions** section, double-click **SetField** to add a **SetField** block to the Macro Designer.
   c. In the **Name** text box, type the desired name and, in the **Value** text box, type a value.
6. Add an Else If statement.
   a. Click the **If** statement to activate the **If** block and click the **Add Else If** link to add an Else If block.
   b. In the **Else If** text box, type the desired expression.
   c. Add the **EditRecord** action to add an EditRecord block.
7. If necessary, add other action blocks as required.
8. On the **Design** contextual tab, click **Save** and then click **Close** to save the changes and close the Macro Designer.
9. Navigate to the table and update the records as desired to execute the macro logic.

10. If necessary, run the macro in a form.

    a. On the **Create** tab, in the **Forms** group, from the **More Forms** drop-down list, select **Multiple Items.**

    b. On the **Design** contextual tab, in the **Views** group, from the **View** drop-down list, select **Form View.**

    c. Update the form record to run the macro.

ACTIVITY 5-3
Creating a Macro

Data Files:
TrainingProgram.accdb

Before You Begin:
From the C:\084574Data\Working with Databases Using Microsoft Office Access 2010 folder, open the Training Program.accdb database.

Scenario:
As the Human Resources manager of your organization, you need to keep track of the training programs that are assigned to your employees and update the completion status of the programs assigned. You have the employee records listed in a table. You don't want to manually update the percentage of completion, as this would be a time-consuming and tedious task. You decide to create a macro to automate the process.

1. Display the Macro Designer.

   a. Double-click the **CompanyEmployees** table to open it.

   b. Select the **Table** contextual tab and, in the **After Events** group, click **After Update**.

   c. Observe that the Macro Designer is displayed along with the **Action Catalog.**

2. Add an If statement to a macro to perform an action.

   a. In the **Action Catalog,** in the **Program Flow** section, double-click **If** to add an If conditional statement block.

   b. In the **If** text box, type *P*

   c. Observe that the IntelliSense feature, which lists all the possible field names that you may add as the criteria for the If statement, is activated.

   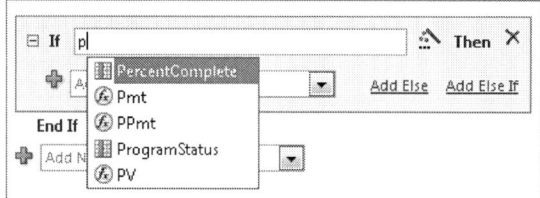

   d. In the **AutoComplete** list, double-click **ProgramStatus** to add it to the **If** text box and type *= "Completed"*

3. Set a field value for the PercentComplete field.

   a. In the **Action Catalog,** in the **Data Blocks** section, double-click **EditRecord** to add an **EditRecord** block to the Macro Designer.

b. In the **Action Catalog,** in the **Data Actions** section, double-click **SetField** to add a **SetField** block.

c. In the **SetField** block, in the **Name** text box, type *PercentComplete* and press **Tab.**

d. In the **Value** text box, type *100*

4. Set a field value for the ProgramStatus field.

   a. In the Macro Designer, click the **If** statement to activate the block.

   b. Click the **Add Else If** link to add an Else If block.

   c. In the **Else If** text box, type *P*

   d. From the options displayed in the drop-down list, double-click **ProgramStatus** to add it to the **Else If** text box and type *= "In Progress:Stage 1"*

   e. In the **Action Catalog,** in the **Data Blocks** section, double-click **EditRecord** to add an **EditRecord** block within the **Else If** block.

   f. In the **Data Actions** section, double-click **SetField** to add a **SetField** block.

   g. In the **SetField** block, in the **Name** text box, type *PercentComplete* and press **Tab.**

   h. In the **Value** text box, type *25*

   i. On the **Design** contextual tab, in the **Close** group, click **Save** and then click **Close** to save the changes and close the Macro Designer.

5. Run the macro.

   a. In the CompanyEmployees table tabbed window, in the ProgramStatus column, click the first row, and from the **ProgramStatus** drop-down list, select **Completed** and then press **Tab** twice.

   b. Observe that in the PercentComplete column, in the first row, the macro automatically updates the record.

   c. Similarly, make changes to the next two rows and verify that the updates are automated to reflect the current status.

   d. On the Quick Access toolbar, click **Save** to save the changes to the table.

6. Run the macro on a form.

   a. Select the **Create** tab and, in the **Forms** group, from the **More Forms** drop-down list, select **Multiple Items.**

   b. Switch to the Form view.

   c. In the CompanyEmployees form tabbed window, in the ProgramStatus column, in the fourth row, from the **ProgramStatus** drop-down list, select **Completed** and press **Tab** twice.

   d. Observe that in the PercentComplete column, fourth row, the macro automatically updates the record.

7. Save and close the database.

   a. Save the form as *TrainingStatus*

b. Right-click the **TrainingStatus** form tabbed window and, from the context menu, choose **Close All.**

c. Save the database as *My Training Program* and close it.

TOPIC D
Work with Reports

You created macros to automate repetitive tasks and increase productivity. Although macros can be used to extract data from tables, you may at times require to extract selective data and present it in an easy to read format. In this topic, you will generate a report.

You may have to share information in the database with your clients. However, in the interest of the company, you may not be willing to share confidential information contained in the database, or you may want to specify the data display in particular ways. Such tasks are made easier with the redesigned report creation tools in Access 2010.

Advanced Querying Options

Advanced querying options such as macros, modules, and class modules can be accessed from the **Macros & Code** group on the **Create** tab. When you select the **Macro** option, the **Design** contextual tab is displayed, which contains various commands such as **Run, Expand Actions,** and **Action Catalog** under the groups **Tools, Collapse/Expand,** and **Show/Hide** for manipulating a macro. When you select the **Module** or **Class Module** option, the enhanced Microsoft Visual Basic for Applications opens, where you can write code blocks for the module or class.

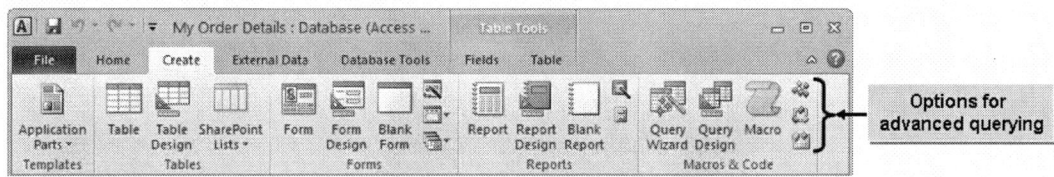

Figure 5-14: The advanced querying options available in the Macros & Code group.

The Report Command

The *Report command,* available on the **Create** tab, enables you to create a simple report using data from the current table or query. You can manipulate the properties of a simple report by using the **Property Sheet** in the **Tools** group on the **Design** contextual tab. While fields in a report can be grouped and sorted by using the **Group, Sort, and Total** pane on the **Design** contextual tab, the formatting and layout of a report can be changed by using the **Format** and **Arrange** contextual tabs. You can also set page layouts by using the **Page Setup** contextual tab.

The Grouping Feature

The *Grouping feature* enables you to organize large data sets into smaller groups and subgroups. It provides you with a clear view of data groupings as you preview changes and apply them in a report. You can display the **Group, Sort, and Total** pane by using the **Group & Sort** option on the **Design** contextual tab. You can then make the grouping by using the **Add a group** button. You can also group by column name, specify the grouping expression, and create nested groups.

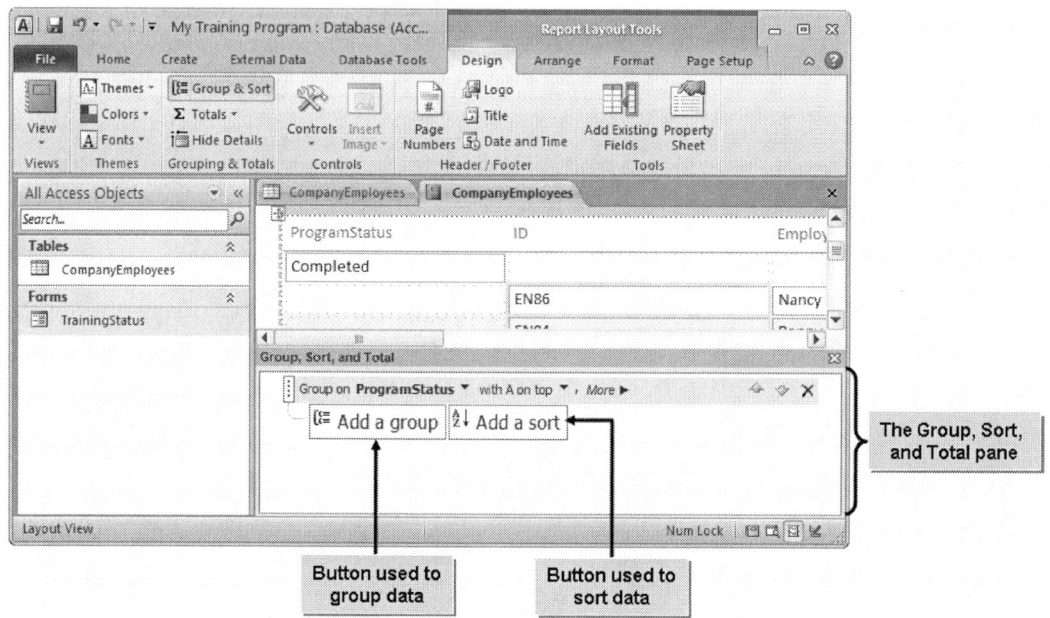

Figure 5-15: Data being sorted based on the program status.

Enhanced Sorting and Filtering Options

Data in reports can be sorted in either ascending or descending order, based on the numeric or alphabetic information. You can also sort data ranging from the smallest to the largest and from the oldest to the newest records by launching the **Group, Sort, and Total** pane or by using the right-click contextual menu. Moreover, you can *filter* data based on the data type in a column. Filters are available in all of the views that display data. You can filter data to display only the records that match your criteria. You can apply filters such as text filters for the text data type, number filters for the number data type, and date filters for the date data type.

The Totals Feature

The *Totals command* is used to add a totals row to a report. This command can be accessed from the **Grouping & Totals** group on the **Design** contextual tab. It provides options for summation, average, count of records, count of values, maximum, minimum, standard deviation, and variance.

The Rich Text Support Feature

The *rich text support feature* provides you with enhanced formatting capabilities such as boldface, underline, text alignment, font color, and indentation of text in a report. After generating a report, you can enable this feature for a memo field by using the **Property Sheet.**

Enhanced Conditional Formatting Options

Conditional formatting is a formatting technique that applies a specified format to a cell or a range of cells based on a set of predefined criteria. The **Conditional Formatting Rules Manager** dialog box allows you to set the condition for formatting by using the default rules or user defined rules, and preview the effects of your changes before applying them. Conditional formatting in Access 2010 supports data bars, which enable you to visually depict data.

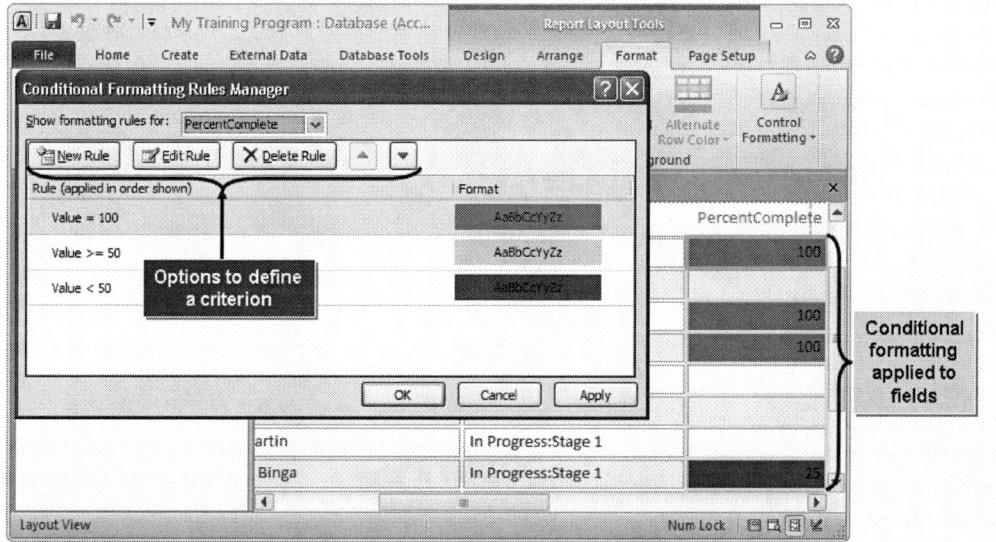

Figure 5-16: The Conditional Formatting Rules Manager dialog box displaying options to apply conditional formatting rules.

Printing Reports with Conditional Formatting

You may want to print reports that have conditional formatting applied to them. To get the best results out of a report, ensure that you apply a formatting style that will highlight the information you want displayed in print. For example, if you have a color printer, you can highlight key information by using color formatting rules, but its effect will be lost if you use a black and white printer.

Data Bars

Data bars, a new conditional formatting technique introduced in Access 2010, enables you to view trends in data as a shaded bar. You can format data using numbers, percent, or values. When you apply data bar settings, the longest bar displays cells with the highest values and the shortest bar displays cells with the lowest values. All the other data bars are sized in proportion to the highest and lowest values. You can also choose the color you want the data bar to display.

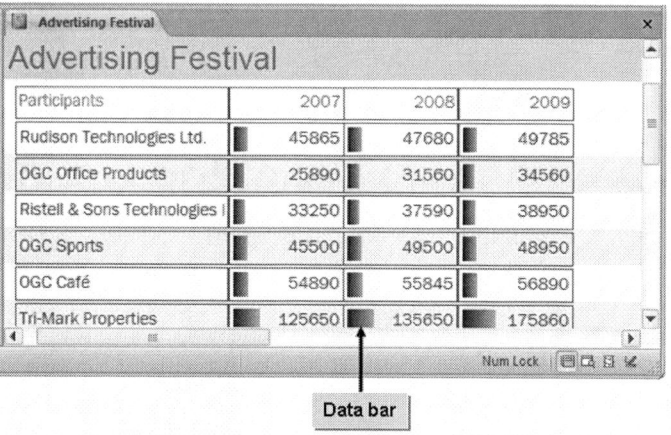

Figure 5-17: A report displaying data visually by using data bars.

The Expression Builder Dialog Box

The *Expression Builder dialog box* allows you to select database objects. It also allows you to build formulas and calculations that are used with queries and reports by using the application's built-in operators and functions. The improved **Expression Builder** interface in Access 2010 includes three columns that display expression elements, expression categories, and expression values. Creating expressions is now easier because the builder incorporates the IntelliSense functionality, which displays context-specific information when you type.

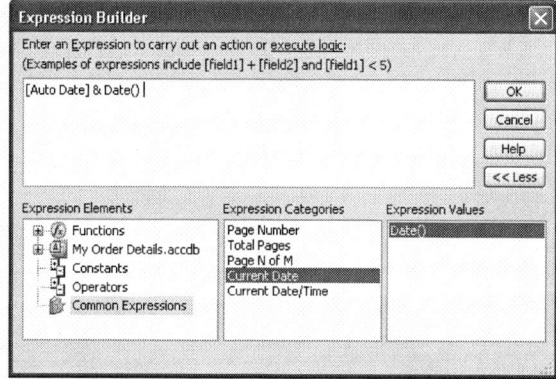

Figure 5-18: The Expression Builder dialog box that holds expressions in visually improved columns.

How to Work with Reports

Procedure Reference: Generate a Report by Using the Report Wizard

To generate a report by using the **Report Wizard:**

1. Select the table, form, or query that you want to display as a report.
2. On the **Create** tab, in the **Reports** group, click **Report Wizard.**
3. On the **Which fields do you want on your report** page, in the **Available Fields** list box, double-click the desired fields to add them to the **Selected Fields** list box and click **Next.**
4. On the **Do you want to add any grouping levels** page, choose a grouping option and click **Next** to add the fields by grouping them.
5. On the **What sort order do you want for your records** page, select the order in which the fields will be displayed in your report and click **Next.**
6. On the **How would you like to lay out your report** page, select a layout option and click **Next.**
7. On the **What title do you want for your report** page, enter a report name and click **Finish.**
8. If necessary, close the **Print Preview** page.

Procedure Reference: Group Data in a Report

To group data in a report:

1. Open a report and switch to the Layout view.
2. If necessary, on the **Format** contextual tab, in the **Grouping & Totals** group, select the **Group & Sort** option.
3. In the **Group, Sort, and Total** pane, click **Add a Group.**
4. From the **Group On Select Field** drop-down list, select the field on which data has to be grouped.
5. If necessary, print the report.
6. If necessary, save and close the report and the database.

Procedure Reference: Sort Data in a Report

To sort data in a report:

1. Open a report and switch to the Layout view.
2. If necessary, on the **Design** contextual tab, in the **Grouping & Totals** group, select the **Group & Sort** option.
3. In the **Group, Sort, and Total** pane, click **Add a Sort.**
4. From the **Sort by select field** drop-down list, select the field on which data has to be sorted.
5. In the **Sort by** pane, from the drop-down list that appears next to the item to be sorted, select a sort option to sort in either ascending or descending order, or from the smallest to the largest value.
6. If necessary, print the report.
7. If necessary, save and close the report and the database.

Procedure Reference: Add a Total by Using the Totals Command

To add a total by using the Totals command:
1. Open a report and switch to the Layout view.
2. If necessary, select the **Format** contextual tab.
3. In the report window, select a column.
4. In the **Grouping & Totals** group, click **Totals** and select an option.
5. If necessary, print the report.
6. If necessary, save and close the report and the database.

Procedure Reference: Filter Data in a Report

To filter data in a report:
1. Open a report and switch to the Layout view.
2. In the report window, select the column in which data is to be filtered.
3. On the Ribbon, select the **Home** tab.
4. In the **Sort & Filter** group, click **Filter.**
5. On the context menu that appears, uncheck the options that are not required and click **OK.**
6. If necessary, print the report.
7. If necessary, save and close the report and the database.

Procedure Reference: Apply Conditional Formatting to a Report

To apply conditional formatting to a report:
1. Open a report in the Layout view.
2. On the **Format** contextual tab, in the **Control Formatting** group, click **Conditional Formatting.**
3. In the **Conditional Formatting Rules Manager** dialog box, click **New Rule** to add a new rule.
4. In the **New Formatting Rule** dialog box, select a rule type.
   - Select **Check values in the current record or use an expression** and, in the **Format only cells where the** section, choose an appropriate rule.
   - Or, select **Compare to other records** and, in the **Data bar format settings** section, choose an appropriate rule.
5. In the **New Formatting Rule** dialog box, click **OK** to close it.
6. If necessary, in the **Conditional Formatting Rules Manager** dialog box, click the **Edit Rule** button to edit the rule that you created.
7. If necessary, in the **Conditional Formatting Rules Manager** dialog box, click the **Delete Rule** button to delete the rule that you created.
8. Click **OK** to close the **New Formatting Rule** dialog box.
9. Click **Apply** and then click **OK** to apply conditional formatting to the report and close the dialog box.

Procedure Reference: Apply Conditional Formatting to a Report by Using Data Bars

To apply conditional formatting to a report by using data bars:

1. Display the **New Formatting Rule** dialog box.
2. In the **Select a rule type** section, select the **Compare to other records** option.
3. In the **Data bar format settings** section, choose an appropriate rule.
   - From the **Type** drop-down list, select a data bar type.
   - If necessary, from the **Value** drop-down list, select a data bar value.
   - From the **Bar color** drop-down list, select a data bar color.
4. Click **OK** to close the **New Formatting Rule** dialog box and then click **OK** again to close the **Conditional Formatting Rules Manager** dialog box.

ACTIVITY 5-4
Working with Reports

Data Files:

Employee Benefits.accdb

Before You Begin:

From the C:\084574Data\Working with Databases Using Microsoft Office Access 2010 folder, open the Employee Benefits.accdb database.

Scenario:

One of the highlights of your company's corporate programs is the Annual Advertising Festival that is held every year. You want to determine the popularity of each participant booth by examining the sales leads generated at each booth. You decide to display this information in a visually appealing manner by using data bars.

1. Enter the details of the report in the **Report Wizard**.

   a. Double-click the **AdvertisingFest** table to open it.

   b. On the Ribbon, select the **Create** tab.

   c. In the **Reports** group, click **Report Wizard**.

   d. In the **Report Wizard,** on the **Which fields do you want on your report** page, from the **Tables/Queries** drop-down list, verify that the **Table: AdvertisingFest** is selected.

   e. In the **Available Fields** list box, double-click **Participants** to add it to the **Selected Fields** list box.

   f. Similarly, add the fields mentioned below to the **Selected Fields** list box.
   - 2007
   - 2008
   - 2009

   g. Click **Next**.

   h. On the **Do you want to add any grouping levels** page, click **Next** to add the fields without grouping them.

   i. On the **What sort order do you want for your records** page, click **Next** to create the report in the order in which you selected the fields.

   j. On the **How would you like to lay out your report** page, click **Next** to create the report in a tabular layout.

   k. On the **What title do you want for your report** page, double-click the existing text, type *Advertising Festival* and click **Finish**.

l. Observe that the report displays the selected fields.

Advertising Festival			
Participants	2007	2008	2009
Rudison Technologies Ltd.	45865	47680	49785
OGC Office Products	25890	31560	34560
Ristell & Sons Technologies Ltd	33250	37590	38950
OGC Sports	45500	49500	48950
OGC Café	54890	55845	56890
Tri-Mark Properties	125650	135650	175860

m. On the **Print Preview** tab, in the **Close Preview** group, click the **Close Print Preview** button.

2. Apply gridlines to the report.

    a. Switch to the Layout view.

    b. Select the table by clicking the selection handle.

    c. Select the **Arrange** contextual tab and, in the **Table** group, from the **Gridlines** drop-down list, on the **Border** menu, choose the second option to select the **Solid** border.

    d. From the **Gridlines** drop-down list, on the **Width** menu, choose the first option to select the **Hairline** width.

    e. From the **Gridlines** drop-down list, on the **Color** menu, in the **Standard Colors** section, in the sixth row, third column, select the **Medium Gray 5** color.

3. Format the data in the report.

    a. Click the **Advertising Festival** title to select it.

    b. Select the **Format** contextual tab and, in the **Font** group, in the **Font** drop-down list, select **Arial**.

    c. From the **Font Color** drop-down list, in the **Standard Colors** section, in the first row, sixth column, select the color **Maroon**.

    d. Click the **Participants** column header, and then click the **Arrange** contextual tab and in the **Rows & Columns** group, click **Select Row**.

    e. On the **Format** contextual tab, in the **Font** group, click the **Font Color** button to apply the **Maroon** color font.

4. Format the page layout.

    a. Select the **Page Setup** contextual tab.

    b. In the **Page Size** group, click **Size**.

    c. Observe that **Letter** is selected and click **Legal**.

    d. Click **Margins** and select **Normal**.

5. Preview a formatted report.

a. Select the **File** tab and choose **Print**.

b. In the right pane, click **Print Preview** to preview the report.

c. Observe that the report reflects the formatting changes made.

d. On the **Print Preview** contextual tab, click **Close Print Preview**.

6. Display the **Conditional Formatting Rules Manager** dialog box.

   a. In the second row, second column, click the cell containing the value 45865.

   b. Select the **Format** contextual tab and, in the **Control Formatting** group, click **Conditional Formatting**.

7. Apply data bar settings.

   a. In the **Conditional Formatting Rules Manager** dialog box, click **New Rule** to add a new rule.

   b. In the **New Formatting Rule** dialog box, in the **Select a rule type** section, select the **Compare to other records** option and click **OK**.

   c. From the **Show formatting rules for** drop-down list, select **2008**.

   d. In the **Microsoft Access** message box, click **Continue and Apply Changes** to continue applying the rules.

   e. In the **Conditional Formatting Rules Manager** dialog box, click **New Rule**.

   f. In the **New Formatting Rule** dialog box, in the **Select a rule type** section, select the **Compare to other records** option and click **OK**.

   g. Similarly, add the data bar rule for the years 2008 and 2009.

   h. In the **Conditional Formatting Rules Manager** dialog box, click **Apply** and then click **OK** to apply data bar settings for the year 2009.

   i. Scroll down to view the data bars that represent the sales leads generated by the booths over the last three years.

Advertising Festival			
Participants	2007	2008	2009
Rudison Technologies Ltd.	45865	47680	49785
OGC Office Products	25890	31560	34560
Ristell & Sons Technologies Ltd	33250	37590	38950
OGC Sports	45500	49500	48950
OGC Café	54890	55845	56890
Tri-Mark Properties	125650	135650	175860

8. Save and close the database.

   a. On the Quick Access toolbar, click **Save**.

   b. Right-click the Advertising Festival report and choose **Close All**.

   c. Save the database as *My Employee Benefits* and close it.

TOPIC E
Work with External Data

You generated reports to present data in an easy to read format. Now, you want to export the report to other file formats, or import the data contained in other applications into Access. In this topic, you will work with external data.

Most companies use a wide variety of applications and file formats in their work environment. However, some users may not have the Office suite installed on their systems. In such circumstances, you should be able to convert Access data into other file formats and integrate external data into your Access databases. This is easy to do using the enhanced features in Access 2010.

Options for Importing Data

Access provides you with options for importing data from various data sources such as Excel spreadsheets, Access databases, ODBC databases, text files, XML files, SharePoint lists, data services, HTML documents, Outlook folders, or dBASE files. The commands in the **Import & Link** group on the **External Data** tab enable you to import data with the help of several user-friendly wizards.

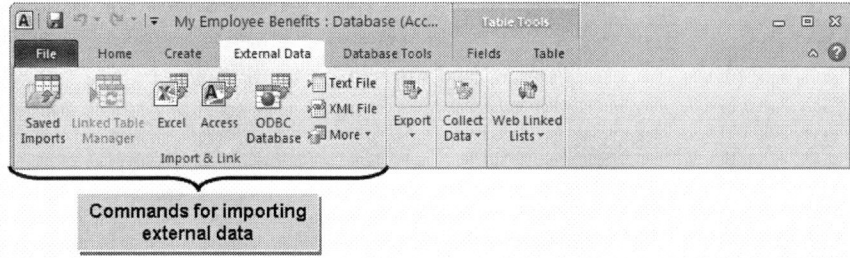

Figure 5-19: The options available in the Import & Link group for importing data into Access.

While importing data from sources such as an Excel worksheet, a text file, or an HTML page, you can specify various data storage options. Storage options include importing data into a new table, appending copies of records into a specified table, or linking to a data source by using a linked table. You can also save the import steps so that you do not need to run through them individually again in the future.

The Collect Data Group

The commands in the **Collect Data** group on the **External Data** tab allow you to collect and update external data via email by using Outlook 2010.

Options for Exporting Data

Access provides you with various options for exporting data from Access to different file formats such as Excel spreadsheets, text files, XML files, PDF or XPS files, Email, Access databases, Word, SharePoint lists, ODBC databases, HTML documents, or dBASE files. The commands in the **Export** group on the **External Data** tab allow you to export Access data with the help of user-friendly wizards. While exporting data to formats such as Excel or a text file, you can not only specify the file format but also retain most of the formatting and layout of different Access objects in the destination file. You can also save the export steps so that you do not need to run through them again in the future.

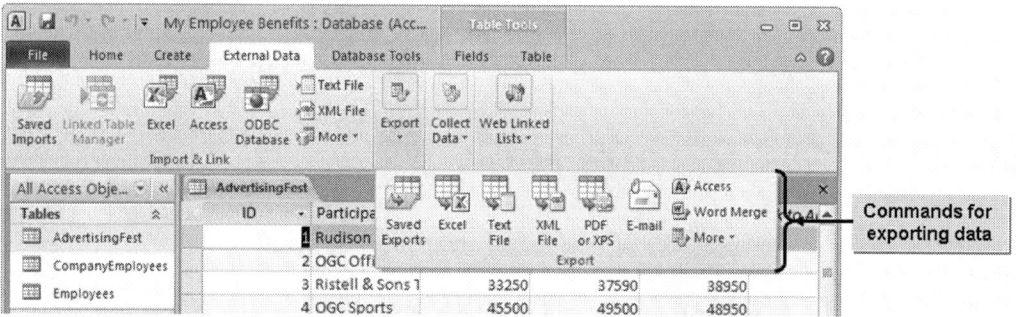

Figure 5-20: The options available in the Export group for exporting data.

SharePoint Lists

By using the commands in the **SharePoint Lists** group on the **External Data** tab, you can synchronize data between Access 2010 and a SharePoint server so that remote users can access various files and work in a collaborative environment.

How to Work with External Data

Procedure Reference: Specify the Source and Destination of Data to Import

To specify the source and destination of data to be imported:

1. Open the required database.
2. On the Ribbon, select the **External Data** tab.
3. In the **Import & Link** group, select the file format of the source file.
4. In the **Get External Data - [Source Data Type]** dialog box, in the **Specify the source of the data** section, click the **Browse** button and navigate to the desired location.
5. In the **File Open** dialog box, select the destination of the source file and click **Open**.

6. In the **Specify how and where you want to store the data in the current database** section, select an option.
   - Select the **Import the source data into a new table in the current database** option to create a table in the current database.
   - Select the **Append a copy of the records to the table** option, and from the drop-down list, select a table to add records to an existing table in the database.
   - Select the **Link to the data source by creating a linked table** option to create a table that retains its links to source data.
7. Click **OK**.

Procedure Reference: Import Data from an Excel Worksheet

To import data from an Excel worksheet:
1. Open the required database.
2. Specify the source and destination of the Excel data to be imported.
3. In the **Import Spreadsheet Wizard**, in the **Your spreadsheet file contains more than one worksheet or range. Which worksheet or range would you like** section, select the data to import.
   - Select the **Show Worksheets** option to import data into a worksheet.
   - Select the **Show Named Ranges** option to import named ranges into a worksheet.
4. In the list box, select the table to import and click **Next**.
5. If necessary, check **First Row Contains Column Headings** and click **Next**.
6. If necessary, select a field and click **Next**.
7. If necessary, specify field options.
   - In the **Field Name** text box, type the name of the field.
   - From the **Indexed** drop-down list, select the option to specify whether or not the field is to be indexed.
   - From the **Data Type** drop-down list, select a data type.
   - Check the **Do not import field (Skip)** check box to ignore the field when data is imported.
8. Click **Next**.
9. If necessary, specify the primary key.
   - Select the **Let Access add primary key** option to automatically add a primary key.
   - Select the **Choose my own primary key** option, and from the drop-down list, select an option to specify the desired field as the primary key.
   - Select the **No primary key** option if no primary key is required.
10. Click **Next**.
11. In the **Import To Table** text box, specify a different name for the table and click **Finish**.
12. If necessary, check the **Save Import Steps** check box to save the import steps.
    - In the **Save as** text box, specify the name of the import operation that is to be saved.
    - In the **Description** text box, describe the function of the import operation.
    - In the **Create an Outlook Task** section, check **Create Outlook Task** to create an Outlook task.
    - Click **Save Import**.

Procedure Reference: Export Data to a Text File

To export data to a text file:

1. Open a database.
2. Specify the database object from which you want to export data. You can export a table, form, query, or report.
3. On the Ribbon, select the **External Data** tab.
4. In the **Export** group, click **Text File** to export the file in the text file format.
5. In the **Export - Text File** dialog box, in the **Specify the destination file name and format** section, click **Browse** and navigate to the desired location.
6. Specify an export option.
    - Check **Export data with formatting and layout** to export data with the formatting and layout options intact.
    - Check **Open the destination file after the export operation is complete** to view the text file after the export.
    - Check **Export only the selected records** to export only the selected records.
7. Click **OK.**
8. In the **Encode** dialog box, select an encoding option and click **OK.**
9. If desired, save and close the text file.
10. If necessary, check **Save Export Steps** to quickly repeat the export process without using the wizard.
    - In the **Save as** text box, specify the name of the export operation that is to be saved.
    - If necessary, in the **Description** text box, describe the function of the export operation.
    - If necessary, in the **Create an Outlook Task** section, check **Create Outlook Task** to create an Outlook task to remind you when it is time to repeat the export operation again.
    - Click **Save Export.**

Procedure Reference: Export Selected Records

To export selected records:

1. Open a database.
2. Open a table and select the records to export.
3. On the Ribbon, select the **External Data** tab.
4. In the **Export** group, select the format in which the file will be exported.
5. In the **Export - [Destination Data]** dialog box, in the **Specify the destination file name and format** section, click **Browse** and navigate to the desired location.
6. In the **File Save** dialog box, click **Save.**
7. Specify an export option.
8. If necessary, close the Excel application.
9. If necessary, check **Save Export Steps** to quickly repeat the export process without using the wizard.

ACTIVITY 5-5
Working with External Data

Data Files:
Order Details.accdb, Computers.xlsx

Before You Begin:
From the C:\084574Data\Working with Databases Using Microsoft Office Access 2010 folder, open the *Order Details.accdb* database.

Scenario:
Your colleague has sent you an Excel workbook that contains details about the various orders placed by customers. You want to create a database by using this information. However, you do not want to type the data all over again. Also, because you are planning to go on vacation, your colleagues have volunteered to follow up on your contacts while you are away. You want to share your contact information database with them, but they do not have Access installed on their systems.

---

1. Specify the source of the Excel worksheet to be imported into Access 2010.

   a. On the Ribbon, select the **External Data** tab.

   b. In the **Import & Link** group, click **Excel**.

   c. In the **Get External Data - Excel Spreadsheet** dialog box, in the **Specify the source of the data** section, click **Browse**.

   d. Navigate to the C:\084574Data\Working with Databases Using Microsoft Office Access 2010 folder.

   e. In the **File Open** dialog box, select the **Computers.xlsx** file and click **Open**.

   f. Verify that the **Import the source data into a new table in the current database** option is selected and click **OK**.

---

2. Import data into the Access database.

   a. Verify that the **First Row Contains Column Headings** check box is checked and click **Next**.

   b. In the **Field Options** section, in the **Field Name** text box, verify that the **AssetTag** is displayed and also verify that its data type is **Text**.

   c. In the list box, click the **ManufacturerID** header, and in the **Field Options** section, from the **Data Type** drop-down list, select **Long Integer**.

   d. Click the headings for **DateReceived, PurchasePrice, Warranty,** and **EmployeeID** to review the data type that will be used for each heading and then click **Next**.

   e. Verify that the **Let Access add primary key** option is selected and click **Next**.

   f. In the **Import to Table** text box, verify that **tblComputers** is displayed and click **Finish**.

g. On the **Save Import Steps** page, read the message and click **Close.**

h. Double-click the **tblComputers** table to open it and view the records.

i. Close the tblComputers window.

3. Specify the destination of the Access file to be exported.

    a. Double-click the **Contacts:Table** table to open it.

    b. On the **External Data** tab and, in the **Export** group, click **Text File.**

    c. In the **Export - Text File** wizard, in the **Specify the destination file name and format** section, observe the destination file name and format.

4. Set the export options and export data into a text file.

    a. In the **Specify export options** section, check the **Export data with formatting and layout** check box.

    b. Check the **Open the destination file after the export operation is complete** check box and click **OK.**

    c. In the **Encode 'Contacts:Table' As** dialog box, verify that the **Windows (default)** option is selected as the encoding format to save the file and click **OK.**

    d. Observe that the text file opens up with the data that you exported from Access and close it.

    e. On the **Save Export Steps** page, read the message and click **Close.**

    f. Close the **Contacts:Table** window.

5. Save and close the database.

    a. Save the database as *My Order Details*

    b. Close the database.

TOPIC F
Design a Database for the Web

You created and designed tables, forms, and reports which were client-specific. To access a database on the web and enable other users to view the database, you need to design web-specific tables, forms, queries, and reports. In this topic, you will build a database for the web.

Businesses today are connected to a global network and sharing information with users across boundaries is vital to its smooth functioning. The smartest way to achieve this is to make information available in a real-time environment. Access 2010 provides you with new design tools that enable you to create a database that is easily accessible through a web browser. Understanding the design requirements for a web-specific database will ensure that you can create a database that holds up-to-date information anytime, anywhere.

Web Objects

Web objects refer to database objects such as tables, forms, queries, and reports in a web database. These objects that can only be created in Access 2010 are indicated by a small globe icon within the database icon. Web objects generally cannot reference client objects; however, they can reference other web objects. All the functional elements of a client object are not visible on the web objects. For example, tables in a web database do not support the Design view and can be displayed only in the Datasheet view.

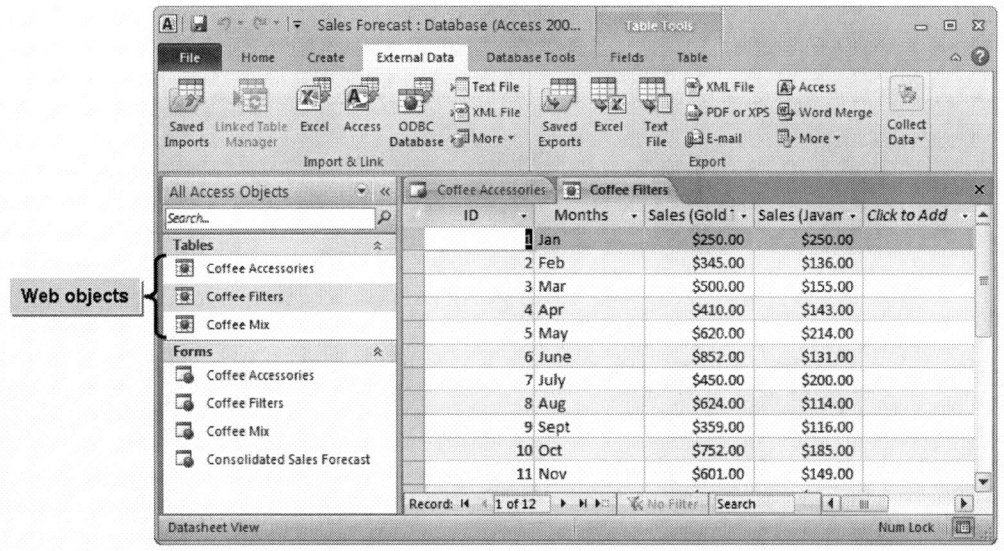

Figure 5-21: A table displayed in a web database.

The Web Compatibility Checker

The *Web Compatibility Checker* feature enables you to identify whether the web database objects that you create are supported on the web. Before publishing a database to the web, you must run the web compatibility checker to ensure that the contents in the database, such as text, images, or controls, are presented consistently. Once you run this feature, Access displays a table with the list of errors along with their descriptions and recommended resolutions.

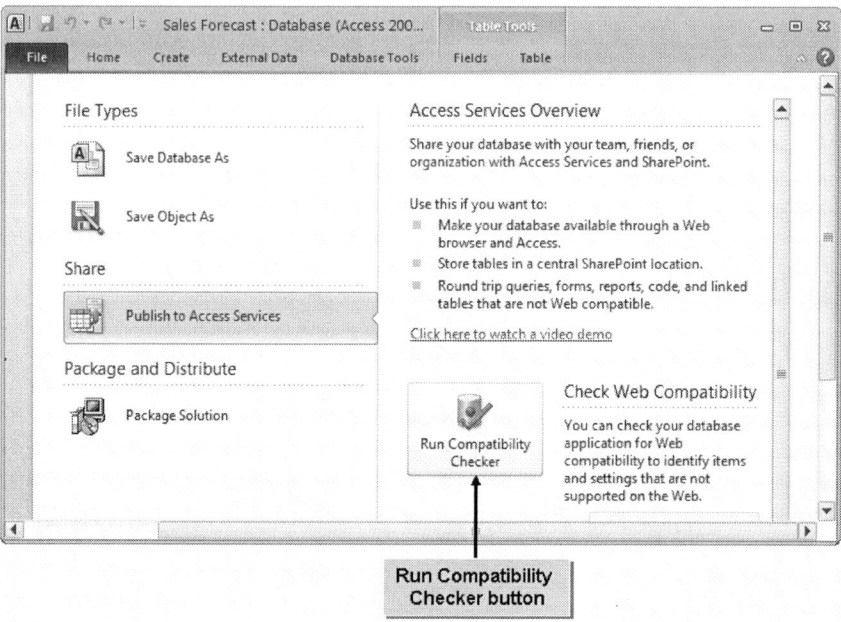

Figure 5-22: The Web Compatibility Checker button in the Backstage view that helps you identify web compatibility issues.

Navigation Forms

A *navigation form* is a layout that allows you to navigate within objects such as tables and forms within a web database. It provides you with easy navigation controls and subcontrols when working with Access on the web. There are six predefined navigation forms that are available by default in Access 2010. Once you add a navigation layout to the user interface, you can add controls and customize the layout according to your requirements. However, these controls can hold only Access forms and reports.

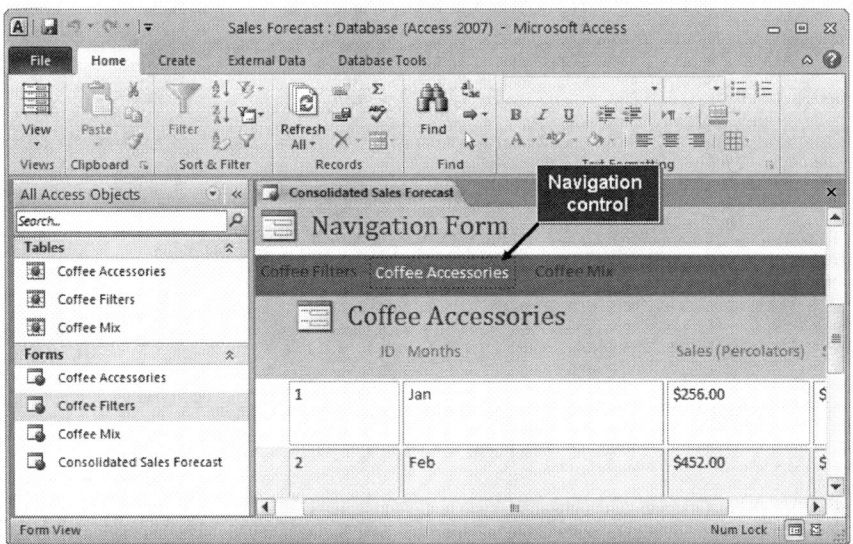

Figure 5-23: A navigation form displaying a control and a subcontrol.

Web Browser Control

Web Browser Control is a tool that allows you to view web content within the Access 2010 application. Clicking **Web Browser Control** displays the **Insert Hyperlink** dialog box, where you can enter the URL of the website that you want displayed in your database. This tool can be accessed only when you work on a web database form in the Form or Layout view.

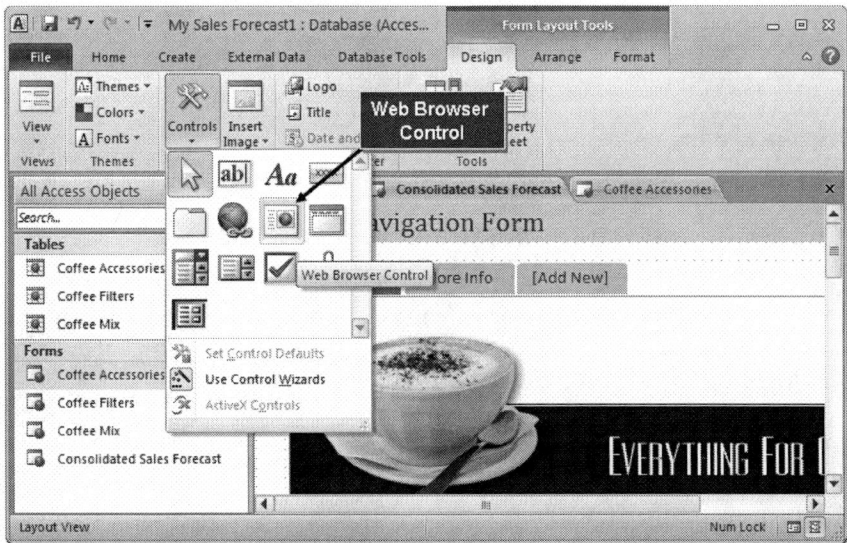

Figure 5-24: A website inserted into a form by using the Web Browser Control tool.

How to Design a Database for the Web

Procedure Reference: Create a Table in a Blank Web Database

To create a table in a blank web database:

1. In the Backstage view, in the **Available Templates** pane, click **Blank web database.**
2. In the **Blank web database** section, in the **File name** text box, type a file name.
3. If necessary, click the **Browse** button and navigate to the location where the database will be created.
4. In the **File New Database** dialog box, click **OK.**
5. In the **Blank web database** section, click **Create** to display a blank table.

Procedure Reference: Add Fields and Records to a Table in a Web Database

To add fields and records to a table in a web database:

1. Create a table in a web database and save it with the desired name.
2. Add fields to the table manually or by using the Data Type gallery.
3. Add a new record.
    a. In the table, specify the desired values in each row.
    b. On the **Home** tab, in the **Records** group, click **New** to create a new record.

Procedure Reference: Build a Form in a Web Database

To build a form in a web database:

1. Open a table in a web database, and on the Ribbon, select the **Create** tab.
2. In the **Forms** group, click a form type to generate a form.
3. Navigate to a record and update the desired fields, or insert a new record.
4. If necessary, on the **Design** contextual tab, in the **Controls** group, select a control tool and drag it to the form to add a control to the form.
5. If necessary, add a logo.
    a. On the **Design** contextual tab, in the **Header/Footer** group, click **Logo.**
    b. In the **Insert Picture** dialog box, select a graphic and click **OK.**
6. On the Quick Access toolbar, click the **Save** button.
7. In the **Save As** dialog box, in the **Form Name** text box, specify a name and click **OK.**

Procedure Reference: Add a Navigation Form to a Web Form

To add a navigation form to a web form:

1. If necessary, create a blank web form.
2. On the Ribbon, select the **Create** tab.
3. In the **Forms** group, from the **Navigation** drop-down list, select a navigation layout.
4. Drag a form or report from the Navigation Pane to the **Add New** navigation control.
5. If necessary, navigate by using the newly created tabbed views.

Procedure Reference: Add a Web Browser Control to a Web Form

To add a web browser control to a web form:

1. Open the form in which you want to add a web browser control.

2. If necessary, display the form in the Design or Layout view.
3. On the **Design** contextual tab, in the **Controls** group, click **Web Browser Control.**
4. In the form, click the field where you want the web page to be displayed. The **Insert Hyperlink** dialog box is displayed.
5. In the **Insert Hyperlink** dialog box, in the **Address** text box, type the address of the web page you want to display in your database and press **Enter.**
6. If necessary, resize the web page field by dragging the window to the desired length.

ACTIVITY 5-6
Building a Tabbed Navigation Form in a Web Database

Data Files:

Sales Forecast.accdb

Before You Begin:

From the C:\084574Data\Working with Databases Using Microsoft Office Access 2010 folder, open the Sales Forecast.accdb database.

Scenario:

You want to share the database of your department's sales forecast with the sales team in Asia. You also want to view information that is displayed on the company's website from the database and navigate through all the forms in your database.

1. Build forms by using table data.

    a. In the Navigation Pane, select the Coffee Mix table.

    b. On the Ribbon, select the **Create** tab.

    c. In the **Forms** group, click **Multiple Items**.

    d. Similarly, create forms by using the Coffee Filters and Coffee Accessories tables.

2. Save the forms.

    a. On the Quick Access toolbar, click **Save**.

    b. In the **Save As** dialog box, click **OK**.

    c. Close the form.

    d. Similarly, save and close the remaining forms.

3. Create a blank form and add a navigation form layout to it.

    a. Select the **Create** tab and, in the **Forms** group, click **Navigation**.

    b. In the **Navigation** gallery, select the **Horizontal Tabs, 2 Levels** form to create a blank form.

    c. Observe that the navigation controls are added to the blank form and close the **Field List** pane.

    d. In the Navigation Form tabbed window, in the first **Add New** button, click and type *Total Sales* and press **Enter.**

4. Add data to the navigation form.

    a. Below the Total Sales button, click the **Add New** navigation button.

b. In the Navigation Pane, click the **Coffee Filters** form and drag it to the **Add New** button below the Total Sales button.

c. Similarly, click the **Coffee Accessories** and **Coffee Mix** forms and drag them to the **Add New** button that is located in the Coffee Filters tabbed row.

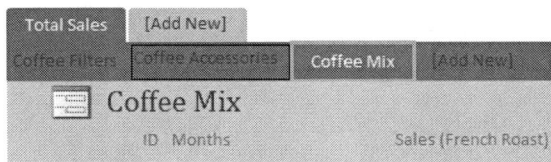

5. Add the **everythingforcoffee** web page to a form.

   a. In the **Add New** button that is to the right of the Total Sales button, click and type *More Info*

   b. On the **Design** contextual tab, in the **Controls** group, click **Web Browser Control.**

   c. In the Navigation Form tabbed window, click the **More Info** button to display the **Insert Hyperlink** dialog box.

   d. In the **Insert Hyperlink** dialog box, in the **Address** text box, type *www.everythingforcoffee.com* and press **Enter.**

   e. Close the everythingforcoffee pop-up window.

   f. Observe that the everythingforcoffee web page is displayed in the top half of the More Info tabbed window.

6. View the form in the tabbed window.

   a. Switch to the Form view.

   b. Close the everythingforcoffee pop-up window.

   c. Click the **Total Sales** button.

   d. Observe that the website **everythingforcoffee** is displayed at the top half of the tabbed window, while the Coffee Filters, Coffee Accessories, and Coffee Mix forms are displayed at the bottom of the tabbed window.

e. Navigate to the Coffee Accessories form by using the newly created tabbed view to view the respective sales forecast.

7. Save the form and close the database.

   a. On the Quick Access toolbar, click **Save.**

   b. In the **Save As** dialog box, in the **Form Name** text box, type ***Consolidated Sales Forecast*** and click **OK.**

   c. Close the Consolidated Sales Forecast form.

   d. Save the database as ***My Sales Forecast***

   e. Close the database and the Access 2010 application.

Lesson 5 Follow-up

In this lesson, you identified the new and enhanced features of Access 2010 from the earlier versions of Access. You used the new and enhanced features and tools to create and design databases, record and analyze information, and extract data for distribution in various formats. These skills not only enable a smooth transition from Access 2003 but also enable you to work effectively and efficiently with the Access 2010 application.

1. **What are the enhanced features that you may use while generating reports?**

2. **How do you think the ability of Access to import data from other formats will help you in your work?**

6 Managing Tasks with Microsoft Office Outlook 2010

Lesson Time: 1 hour(s), 30 minutes

Lesson Objectives:

In this lesson, you will manage tasks using the new features in Microsoft Office Outlook 2010.

You will:

- Manage mail messages.
- Locate information quickly.
- Share your Calendar information.
- Share information using an electronic business card.
- Add RSS feeds through Outlook 2010.

Introduction

You have represented information and statistical data in different formats. In an organization, apart from working on different data and reports, it is important to share data with others. In this lesson, you will work with Outlook 2010.

Communication with peers and clients is an integral part of working in any organization. You have probably managed your daily tasks using Outlook 2003, and are now migrating to Outlook 2010. The options in the 2010 interface are user friendly, making it much easier to manage, locate, and prioritize information.

TOPIC A
Manage Mail Messages

You have used some of the new components that are common to the Office 2010 environment, and you will now apply that knowledge to working with email messages in this new environment. In this topic, you will manage your mail messages using Outlook 2010.

Using Outlook, you can quickly and efficiently send information in a simple email message. There are times when you may also find it necessary to alter the content of a message. Perhaps, you may want to emphasize some text within the body of the message or correct a misspelled word. Outlook provides you with new tools to ensure that your messages are both accurate and easy to read.

Quick Steps

Quick steps are commands that facilitate the performing of common tasks that involve multiple actions in a single-click. Quick steps make repetitive tasks easier and faster to perform. They are displayed in the **Quick Steps** group on the **Home** tab of the Ribbon. There are various default quick steps available for common tasks performed in Outlook. You can also create custom quick steps by using the **Create New** command, which displays the **Edit Quick Step** dialog box. You can also edit, customize, or delete quick steps by using the **Manage Quick Steps** dialog box.

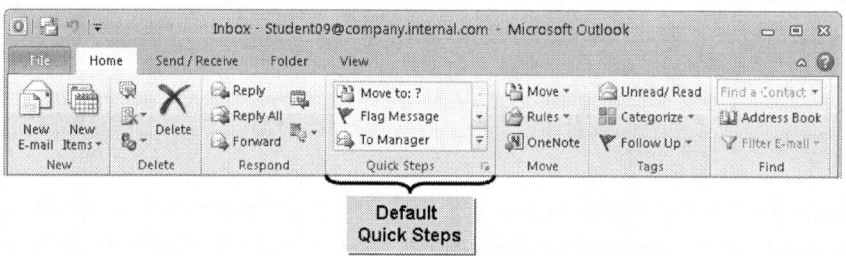

Figure 6-1: The Quick Steps displayed on the Home tab.

Default Quick Steps
Some of the default quick steps include:

- **Move To:** Marks an email message read and moves it to a specified folder.
- **Reply & Delete:** Allows you to reply to an email message and deletes the original message.
- **Done:** Marks an email message read and moves it to a specified folder.
- **Team E-mail:** Allows you to forward an email message to the members of your team, as specified in the Global Address List.
- **To Manager:** Allows you to forward an email message to your manager, as specified in the Global Address List.

The Manage Quick Steps Dialog Box
The **Manage Quick Steps** dialog box allows you to manage quick steps. You can also add shortcut keys and display tooltips for a quick step.

Component	Description
The **Quick step** drop-down menu	Displays all the quick steps such as **Move to, To Manager, Team E-mail, Done, Reply & Delete,** and **Create New.**
The **Description** section	Displays a description including the **Actions, Shortcut key,** and **Tooltip** for a selected quick step.
The up and down arrow buttons	Allows you to navigate between the quick steps, and reorder them in the **Quick step** list box.
The **New** drop-down list	Displays options to add a new quick step.
The **Edit** button	Allows you to edit a quick step.
The **Duplicate** button	Allows you to duplicate a quick step.
The **Delete** button	Allows you to delete a quick step.
The **Reset to Defaults** button	Allows you to reset quick steps to the default settings.

The Conversation View

In Outlook, email messages that share the same subject can be displayed together as a *conversation*. These message threads can be expanded or collapsed. The messages in a conversation are arranged with the newest message placed on top in the View pane. When there is a response to the email in a conversation thread, that particular conversation is also moved to the top. Conversations are displayed in the folders where you saved the messages and can be identified with an icon showing two envelopes. Conversations are useful when multiple ideas are exchanged in quick succession between a sender and a receiver.

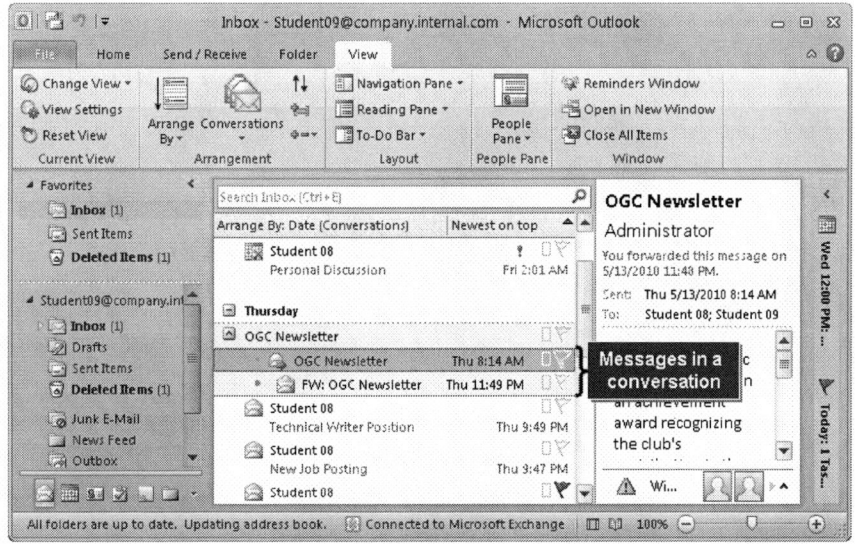

Figure 6-2: Messages listed under a conversation.

The Conversation view can be customized by using the **Conversations** option in the **Arrangement** group of the **View** tab. The following table describes the different options for customizing the Conversation view.

Option	Description
Show Messages from Other Folders	This is the default option, which allows you to display related messages from other folders such as Sent Items. It allows you to view the message without having to leave the Inbox.
Show Senders above the Subject	This option displays the name of the sender above the subject. It is useful for locating messages based on senders, rather than on the subject of the message.
Always Expand Conversations	This option allows you to view all the messages in a conversation. By default, only the latest messages in the conversation are displayed.
Use Classic Indented View	In this view, the replies and corresponding messages are indented and arranged in the Inbox.

The Clean Up Command

The **Clean Up** command, available in the **Delete** group of the **Home** tab allows you to move redundant messages. By default, messages that are cleaned up are sent to the **Deleted Items** folder. You can also move the cleaned-up messages into a folder of your choice. Cleaning up messages ensures that space is available in the Inbox for additional messages that are received. The options to clean up a specified set of messages and folders, and the location to which the cleaned-up items will be moved can be set in the **Outlook Options** dialog box.

 When you use the **Clean Up** command for the first time, the **Clean Up Conversation** message box is displayed.

The **Clean Up** command provides three options.

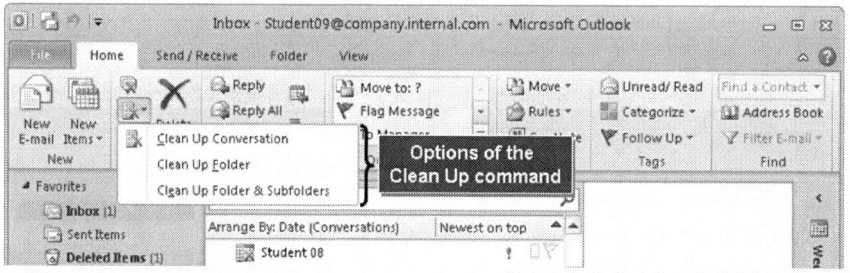

Figure 6-3: Clean Up command options.

Option	Description
Clean Up Conversation	Deletes redundant messages in a conversation.
Clean Up Folder	Moves all redundant messages from the current folder to the **Deleted Items** folder.
Clean Up Folders & Subfolders	Moves redundant messages from the current folder, as well as its subfolders, to the **Deleted Items** folder.

The Move Tool

The **Move** tool is present in the **Move** group of the **Home** tab and helps you organize conversations by moving them into specific folders. You can also choose the **Always Move Messages in This Conversation** option to move messages in a conversation to a specific folder in Outlook.

The Ignore Command

The **Ignore** command provides options to ignore messages in a conversation and move them to the Deleted Items folder. When you ignore a conversation thread, all the current and future messages relating to that conversation are also ignored. You can recover a conversation that has been ignored by selecting that conversation from the Deleted Items folder, and clicking the **Stop Ignoring** option of the **Ignore** command.

How to Manage Mail Messages

Procedure Reference: Format Text by Using the Mini Toolbar

To format text by using the Mini toolbar:

1. If necessary, create a new email message and enter text in the body of the message.
2. Select the text that needs to be formatted.
3. Apply the desired formatting changes from the displayed Mini toolbar.
   - From the **Font** drop-down list, select the desired font.
   - From the **Font Size** drop-down list, select the desired font size.
   - Click the **Grow Font** or **Shrink Font** button to increase or decrease font size.
   - Click the **Decrease Indent** or **Increase Indent** button to increase or decrease indent.
   - Click the **Bold, Italic,** or **Underline** button to bold face, italicize, or underline text.
   - Click the **Center** button to center the text.
   - Click the **Font Color** and **Text Highlight Color** options to change the color of the font or highlight.

Procedure Reference: Flag an Email Message for Follow-Up

To flag an email message for follow-up:

1. Display the **Follow Up** options.
   - In the Inbox, right-click the message that needs to be flagged and, from the displayed menu, choose **Follow Up.**
   - Select the message and, on the **Home** tab, in the **Tags** group, click **Follow Up.**
   - Or, open the message that needs to be flagged and, on the **Message** tab, in the **Tags** group, click **Follow Up.**
2. Select an option from the **Follow Up** options to add a flag.

 When a flagged message is due to be followed up on, the text in the message header will change from black to red.

3. If necessary, view the flagged message in the **For Follow Up** folder.
   a. On the **Folder** tab, in the **New** group, click **New Search Folder.**
   b. In the **New Search Folder** dialog box, in the **Select a Search Folder** list box, select **Mail flagged for follow up** and click **OK.**
   c. In the Navigation pane, click **Search Folders** to view the **For Follow Up** folder with the flagged messages.

Procedure Reference: Add a Reminder to an Email Message for Follow-Up

To add a reminder to an email message for follow-up:

1. Select the email message that needs to be flagged.
2. Display the **Custom** dialog box.
   - On the **Home** tab, in the **Tags** group, click **Follow Up** and, from the displayed menu, click **Add Reminder.**
   - Right-click the message and, from the displayed menu, choose **Follow Up→Custom.**

When the **Add Reminder** option is selected, the **Reminder** option is set by default. The **Reminder** option needs to be manually set only when the **Custom** option is selected.

3. In the **Custom** dialog box, set the required flagging options.
   - From the **Flag to** drop-down list, select the desired option.
   - Click the **Start date** drop-down arrow, and select a start date from the calendar.
   - Click the **Due date** drop-down arrow, and select an end date from the calendar.
   - If necessary, check the **Reminder** check box and, from the drop-down list, select the desired date, time, and sound alerts.
   - If necessary, click **Clear Flag** to clear the flag options that have been set in the **Custom** dialog box.
4. Click **OK** to close the **Custom** dialog box.
5. If necessary, in the Navigation Pane, click **Search Folders** to view the **For Follow Up** folder with the flagged messages.

Procedure Reference: Create a Quick Step

To create a quick step:

1. If necessary, switch to the Mail view.
2. In the Mail view, on the Ribbon, select the **Home** tab and, in the **Quick Steps** group, click **Create New.**
3. In the **Actions** section, select the actions for the quick step.
   - From the **Choose an Action** drop-down list, select an action.
   - Or, click **Add Action,** and from the **Choose an Action** drop-down list, select an action to add an additional action.
4. In the **Name** text box, enter a name for the new quick step.
5. If necessary, click the icon to the left of the **Name** text box and, in the **Choose an icon** dialog box, click an icon and click **OK** to change the icon for the new quick step.

ACTIVITY 6-1
Managing Mail Messages

Before You Begin:
Launch the Microsoft Outlook 2010 (Beta) application.

Scenario:
You have received an email message from a client with the product list of gourmet beans, and would like to follow up with the client about the products. You want to mark the email message and set a reminder, so that you can follow up with her about it. Because you will often want to flag email messages for following up on them later, you decide to create a quick step for the same. Moreover, you find that your mailbox is filled with messages you do not wish to keep. You decide to organize your mail by cleaning up your mail account.

1. Flag the **Product List** email message with a reminder.

    a. In the Inbox, select the **Product List** message and, on the **Home** tab, in the **Tags** group, from the **Follow Up** drop-down list, select **Add Reminder.**

    b. In the **Custom** dialog box, click the **Due date** drop-down arrow and, in the calendar that is displayed, select the next business day.

    c. In the **Reminder** section, from the **Time** drop-down list, select **10:00 AM.**

    d. Click **OK** to close the **Custom** dialog box.

2. Display the contents of the **For Follow Up** folder.

    a. On the Ribbon, select the **Folder** tab, and in the **New** group, click **New Search Folder.**

    b. In the **New Search Folder** dialog box, in the **Reading Mail** section, select the **Mail flagged for follow up** option and click **OK.**

    c. Observe that the **Product List** message is displayed in the **For Follow Up** folder and it is flagged with a red flag symbol to the right of the header.

    d. In the Navigation Pane, click **Inbox** to view the messages in the **Inbox.**

3. Create a quick step for flagging an email message.

    a. Select the **Home** tab and, in the **Quick Steps** group, click **Create New** to create a new quick step.

    b. In the **Edit Quick Step** dialog box, in the **Name** text box, type *Flag Message* and to the left of the text box, click the **Click here to change the icon for this quick step** button to change the icon for the quick step.

    c. In the **Choose an icon** dialog box, in the third row, click the third icon and then click **OK** to add it to the quick step.

d. In the **Edit Quick Step** dialog box, in the **Actions** section, from the **Choose an Action** drop-down list, from the **Categories, Tasks and Flags** section, select **Flag Message.**

e. From the **Choose flag** drop-down list, select **Next Week** to add an action to the quick step.

f. In the **Optional** section, in the **Tooltip text** text box, click and type *Flag an email message for follow-up next week.*

g. Click **Finish** to add the quick step.

h. Observe that the **Flag Message** quick step has been created, and is added to the **Quick Steps** group.

i. On the **Home** tab, in the **Quick Steps** group, click the **Manage Quick Steps** dialog box launcher and, in the **Manage Quick Steps** dialog box, below the **Quick step** section, click the down arrow button twice to move the new quick step to the third spot, and then click **OK.**

j. In the Inbox, select the **System Training** message, and from the **Quick Steps** group, in the displayed gallery, click **Flag Message** to add a flag.

4. Clean up a conversation.

    a. In your Inbox, select the **Lunch?** conversation that you want to delete.

    b. In the Inbox, in the **Home** tab, in the **Delete** group, click **Clean Up** and choose **Clean Up Conversation.**

    c. In the **Clean Up Conversation** message box, click **Clean Up** to clean up and move messages to the Deleted Items folder.

    d. Observe that the number of messages in the Inbox is reduced; and it contains only the latest messages in the conversation.

5. Change the settings for cleaning up conversations to prevent automatic deletion of unread messages during cleanup.

    a. Select the **File** tab and click **Options** to display the **Outlook Options** dialog box.

    b. In the **Outlook Options** dialog box, click **Mail,** and in the **Conversation Clean Up** section, check the **Don't move unread messages** check box and click **OK.**

6. Ignore future messages in the conversation.

    a. In the Inbox, select the **Lunch?** conversation, and in the **Home** tab, in the **Delete** group, click **Ignore** to ignore future messages in the conversation.

    b. In the **Ignore Conversation** message box, click **Ignore Conversation,** to ignore the conversation, and move them to the Deleted Items folder.

    c. Open the Sent Items folder, and open the **Lunch?** message.

    d. Click **Reply All,** and send the message to all the users in the conversation.

    e. Close the **Lunch?** message.

    f. Display your Inbox, and observe that you are no longer receiving messages from this conversation.

TOPIC B
Locate Information Quickly

You have managed some of your email messages. Now you are ready to search for messages that contain a specific piece of text or satisfy multiple criteria, and quickly view file attachments. In this topic, you will locate information efficiently.

Many people are hesitant to delete email, fearing they might need an email message again. This practice can result in having a folder with hundreds of messages, making it difficult to find an email message when needed. Outlook's Instant Search and attachment preview features make locating items that contain specific text, quick and easy.

The Instant Search Feature

Outlook's **Instant Search** feature allows you to quickly search for items by specifying certain search criteria. It enables you to search in different views using the Instant Search pane, and also specify different search options. It also allows you to modify different search criteria as needed. This feature works by indexing items, and then accessing the indexed items as needed. The Instant Search pane is available in different views such as **Mail, Calendar, Contacts, Tasks, Notes, Folder List,** and **Journal**.

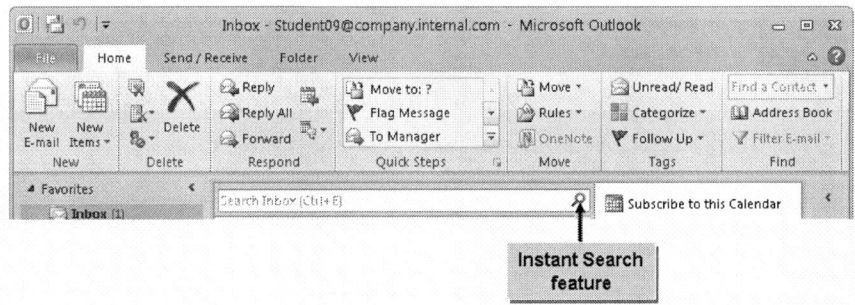

Figure 6-4: The Instant Search pane in the Mail view.

Searching for items in Outlook displays the **Search Tools** contextual tab that provides additional search options. You can change search options by clicking **Search Tools** in the **Options** group of the **Search Tools** contextual tab, and then choosing **Search Options.** This option displays the **Search** tab in the **Outlook Options** dialog box, where you can specify the options.

The Advanced Find Dialog Box

The **Advanced Find** dialog box is used to locate items by using specific criteria to narrow down the search. This is a contextual feature, with a default tab that is displayed based on the current view in Outlook.

The options in the **Advanced Find** dialog box are described in the following table.

Option	Allows You To
The **Look for** drop-down list	Select the types of Outlook items to search for, such as messages, tasks, notes, appointments, meetings, and contacts.

Option	Allows You To
The **Browse** button	Specify the folder in which the search needs to be performed.
The default tab	Enter the details of the selected item, depending upon the current view that is selected. The options displayed on this tab depend on the choice that is made in the **Look for** text box.
The **More Choices** tab	Categorize email messages, based on the read or unread status, attachments, the priority level, color categories, the flagged status, and size.
The **Advanced** tab	Define criteria based on different fields, conditions, or specific values.
The **Find Now** button	Look for a particular word or phrase that is specified in the **Search for the word(s)** text box.
The **New Search** button	Clear the current search and perform a new search.

How to Locate Information Quickly

Procedure Reference: Search for Items in Outlook

To search for items in Outlook:

1. Select the folders that are to be searched.
2. In the **Instant Search** text box, enter the search text. The items of the selected folder that contain the search text are displayed in the Instant Search Results pane, with the search text highlighted.
3. On the **Search Tools** contextual tab, in the **Scope** group, select the required option.
   - Click **All Mail Items** to search the mail items in all the folders.
   - Click **Current Folder** to search within the current folder.
   - Or, click **All Outlook Items** to search all the items.
4. On the **Search Tools** contextual tab, in the **Refine** group, select the required option.
   - Click **From** to search for messages from a particular sender.
   - Click **Subject** to search for messages with a particular subject.
   - Click **Has Attachments** to search for messages that contain attachments.
   - Click **Categorized** and, from the displayed menu, choose an option to search by category.
     - Choose **Any Category** to search for messages from any category.
     - Choose **No Categories** to search for messages that are not categorized.
   - Click **This Week** and, from the displayed menu, choose an option to search the message by date.
   - Click **Sent To** and, from the displayed menu, choose an option to search by sender.
     - Choose **Sent To: Me or CC: Me** to search for messages that were sent directly to you, or in which you were on the CC list.
     - Choose **Not Sent Directly to Me** to search for messages that were not sent directly to you.

- Choose **Sent to Another Recipient** to search for messages that were sent to another recipient.
- Click **Unread** to display the unread messages that match the search criteria.
- Click **Flagged** to display the flagged messages that match the search criteria.
- Click **Important** to display messages that have a specific priority level, and match the search criteria.
- Click **More** and, from the displayed menu, choose an option to display messages with the chosen field, and match the search criteria.

5. On the **Search Tools** contextual tab, in the **Options** group, select the required option.
   - Click **Recent Searches** and select a recent search to repeat the search.
   - Click **Search Tools** and choose an option to use advanced search tools.
     - Click **Indexing Status** to check the number of items remaining that need to be indexed.
     - Click **Locations to Search** and choose an email account.
     - Click **Advanced Find** to perform a search by using advanced search criteria.
     - Click **Search Options** to specify or modify the search options in the **Outlook Options** dialog box.
6. If necessary, in the **Close** group of the **Search Tools** contextual tab, click **Close Search** to close the current search.

Procedure Reference: Search for Items by Using Multiple Criteria

To search for items by using multiple criteria:
1. On the **Search Tools** contextual tab, in the **Options** group, click **Advanced Find.**
2. From the **Look for** drop-down list, select the item that you want to search for.
3. In the **Search for the word(s)** text box, type the search terms.
4. If necessary, click **Browse,** and in the **Select Folder(s)** dialog box, select the folder in which to search, and click **OK** to display the appropriate folder in the **In** text box.
5. In the **From** text box, specify a person's name whose email you need to search for.
6. Click **Find Now** to display the items that match the criteria in the **Advanced Find** dialog box.
7. If necessary, select the **More Choices** tab and choose the required options.
   - Click **Categories** and, from the **Color Categories** drop-down list, select a color category to filter the search results by.
   - Check the **Only items that are** check box to search for read or unread messages.
   - Check the **Only items with** check box to search for messages with attachments.
   - Check the **Whose importance is** check box to search for messages with a normal, low, or high priority.
   - Check the **Only items which** check box to search for messages that are flagged or completed.
   - From the **Size** drop-down list, select an option to specify the size of the message.

8. If necessary, select the **Advanced** tab and choose the required options.
    a. In the **Define more criteria** section, from the **Field** drop-down list, select a particular field and specify conditions and values.
    b. Click **Add to List** to add criteria to the **Find items that match this criteria** list box.
9. Click **Find Now** to search with the specified criteria.

ACTIVITY 6-2
Searching for an Email Message

Scenario:

You received an email message from your client with the product list for the gourmet beans that her company, Everything for Coffee, manufactures. As you have not yet responded to the message, you decide to search for the message so that you can follow up on it. You also want to specify advanced search options to customize the search.

1. Search for an email message with the subject "Product List."

    a. In the Inbox, above the View pane, in the **Search Inbox** text box, click the magnifying lens icon to display the **Search Tools** contextual tab.

    b. Observe that the **Search Tools** contextual tab is displayed on the Ribbon.

    c. In the **Search Tools** contextual tab, in the **Refine** group, click **Subject** and, in the **Search Inbox** text box, within parentheses, type *Product List*

    d. Observe that the **Product List** message you searched for is displayed in the search results.

2. Change the search preferences.

    a. In the **Search Tools** contextual tab, in the **Options** group, from the **Search Tools** drop-down list, select **Search Options** to display the **Outlook Options** dialog box with the **Search** tab as the active tab.

    b. In the **Outlook Options** dialog box, on the **Search** tab, in the **Results** section, in the **Include results only from** option, select the **All folders** option to include search results from all the folders.

    c. Uncheck the **Highlight search terms in the results** check box to remove highlighting search terms in the results.

    d. In the **Outlook Options** dialog box, click **OK** to apply the changed search preferences.

    e. In the Search contextual tab, click **Close Search** to close the search contextual tab.

TOPIC C
Share Calendar Information

You have worked with mail messages. You know how to view your own calendar. Now you are ready to share your calendar information with others. In this topic, you will assign permissions to have select email users view your calendar.

There may be situations where you want to share your calendar information with people who do not have Outlook. Also, you may want to share your calendar information with others. Outlook 2010 allows you to share your Calendar by using email, set permission levels for your delegates, and publish the calendar to Office Online.

The To-Do Bar

The *To-Do bar* is used to manage daily tasks and appointments. It displays the calendar, upcoming appointments, and a list of tasks to perform. The To-Do bar contains three parts: the Date Navigator that displays the current month, a list of appointments and meetings, and a list of tasks and to-do items. The To-Do bar can be customized to display only the required information.

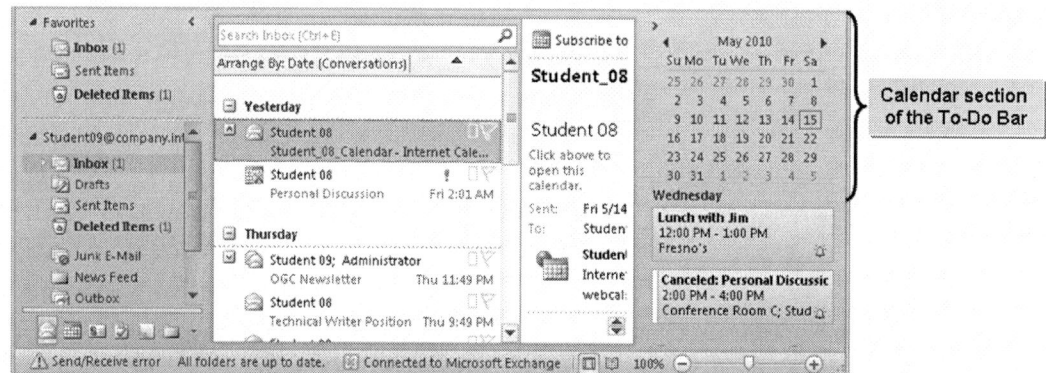

Figure 6-5: The To-Do bar displaying a calendar and a list of tasks and appointments.

Accessing the To-Do Bar

The To-Do bar can be accessed from the **To-Do Bar** command from the **Layout** group on the **View** tab. The To-Do bar can be minimized by clicking the **Minimize the To-Do Bar** button.

Schedule View

The *Schedule view* allows you to view multiple calendars to compare schedules. The calendars can be viewed in the horizontal layout. This view is useful when you select multiple calendars to check and schedule appointments or meetings. You can automatically view calenders either in the Vertical or Schedule layout depending on the number of calendars set using the **Calendar** tab of the **Outlook Options** dialog box. The option to display the calendar in the Schedule view is available in the **Arrange** group of the **Home** tab.

The Send A Calendar Via E-mail Dialog Box

The *Send a Calendar via E-mail* dialog box allows you to send calendars to other users through an email message. You can access the **Send a Calendar via E-mail** dialog box by clicking the **E-mail Calendar** option in the **Share** group of the **Home** tab in the Calendar view.

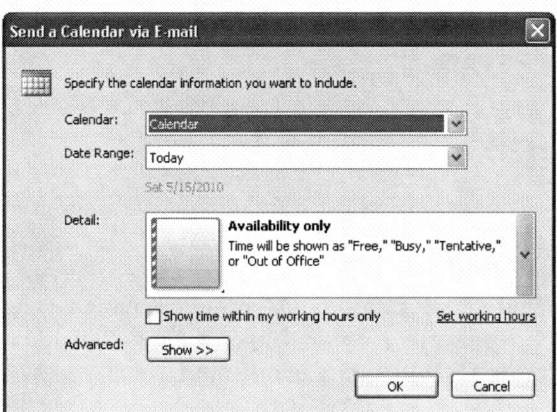

Figure 6-6: The options in the Send a Calendar via E-mail dialog box.

The **Send a Calendar via E-mail** dialog box options allow you to set the date range, working hours, time availability, and the free/busy information that can be sent to the email recipient.

Option	Enables You To
Calendar	Choose a calendar to send from a list of available calendars.
Date Range	Specify a date range you want to send from a list.
Detail	Set the details that can be sent with the calendar. The options are: • **Availability only:** Shows the availability status as free, busy, or out of the office. • **Limited details:** Limits details to availability and subjects of calendar items. • **Full details:** Shows the availability and full details of calendar items.
Show time within my working hours only	Specify your working hours, add holidays, propose new meeting times, and display options and time zones.
Advanced	Include items marked private, attach files, and set email layouts.

Calendar Overlays

Outlook provides you with the option of viewing multiple calendars at the same time. When you want to view multiple calendars, you can use the **Overlay** mode to stack calendars one on top of the other. You can access the **Overlay** option by right-clicking the calendar, and choosing **Overlay**. The **Overlay** mode can be used to stack default Outlook calendars, shared calendars from other people, Internet calendars, or Internet calendar subscriptions. This mode is useful for finding the free/busy information of other people and viewing any meeting requests they have accepted or saved.

Calendar Groups

A *calendar group* allows you to view multiple calendars of other users together to compare their schedules before you schedule a meeting. The **Calendar Groups** command can be accessed from the **Manage Calendars** group of the **Home** tab. You can either create a new calendar group using the **Create New Calendar Group** command or create a group of calendars that are being currently displayed using the **Save as New Calendar Group** command. Calendar groups are listed on the Navigation pane of the Calendar view.

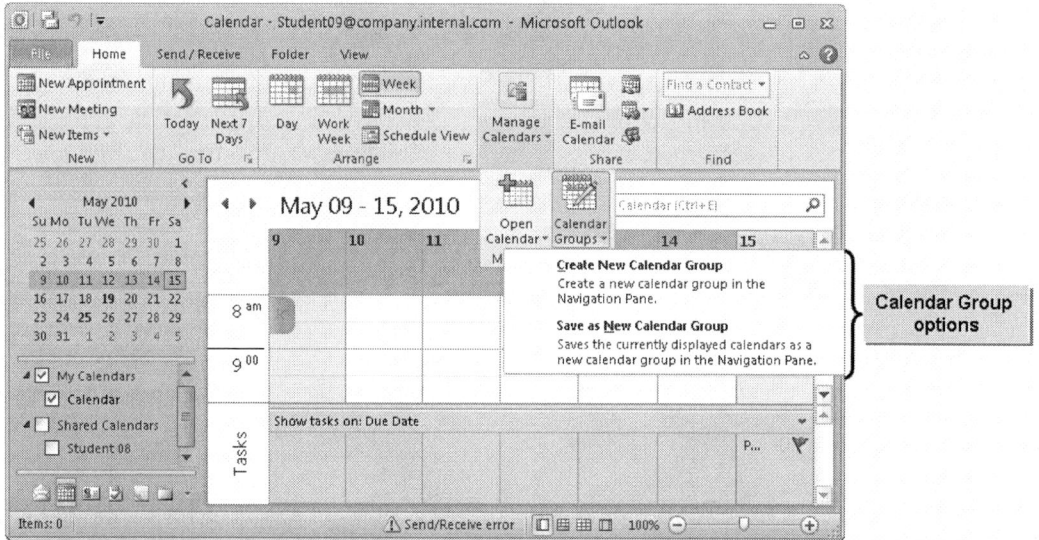

Figure 6-7: Options to create or save a new calendar group.

Delegate

A *delegate* is a person who is given permission to access another user's Outlook folders. You can add users and grant them permission to send and modify items using the **Delegate Access** option available in the **Account Setting** drop-down list. Once a user is added, you can set the required permission levels to the delegate using the **Delegate Permissions** dialog box. Permission levels include enabling delegates to author or review items in the various Outlook folders. You can also set permission to enable a delegate to view your personal items and to send a message to your delegate explaining the set permission levels. You can specify if any meeting requests or responses that are addressed to you must be delivered to your delegates.

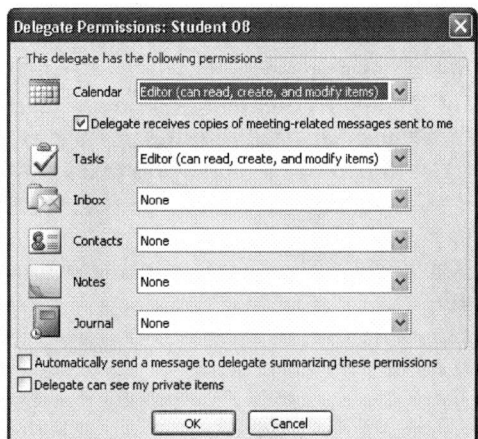

Figure 6-8: The Delegate Permissions dialog box used to set permissions to a delegate.

How to Share Calendar Information

Procedure Reference: Send Calendar Information via Email

To send calendar information in an email message:

1. If necessary, switch to the Calendar view.
2. On the **Home** tab, in the **Share** group, click **E-mail Calendar** to display the **Send a Calendar via E-mail** dialog box.
3. Specify the calendar information you want to include.

    a. In the **Send a Calendar via E-mail** dialog box, in the **Calendar** drop-down list, verify that **Calendar** is selected.

    b. From the **Date Range** drop-down list, select a desired date range to specify the calendar information for the selected date range: **Today, Tomorrow, Next 7 days, Next 30 days, Whole calendar,** or **Specify dates.**

    c. From the **Detail** drop-down list, select the desired option to specify the available details of calendar items: **Availability only, Limited details,** or **Full details.**

4. Click **OK** to close the **Send a Calendar via E-mail** dialog box, and to attach the calendar information in the message body.
5. Click **Send** to send the calendar information to the recipient.

Procedure Reference: Share Your Calendar

To share your calendar:

1. On the **Home** tab, in the **Share** group, click the **Share Calendar** button.
2. In the Sharing Invitation Message form, in the **To** text box, type the name of a contact with whom you want to share your calendar.
3. Send the message.
4. In the **Microsoft Outlook** dialog box that asks for confirmation, click **Yes** to share the calendar.

Internet Calendar Subscriptions

You can subscribe to and download a calendar from a calendar publishing service or a website and view it in Outlook. Using these calendars, you can exchange calendar information with other Outlook users regardless of the application that is used to create or view the information. All internet calendars use the "iCalendar" format with the .ics file extension. Once the calendar is downloaded and executed, it gets added to the Navigation pane in the Calendar view in the **Other Calendars** section and opens side-by-side along with the default Outlook calendar. The downloaded calendar checks for periodic updates made by the calendar publisher and automatically updates when an update is available. The websites that allow you to download calendars begin with the protocol **webcal://**.

Procedure Reference: View a Shared Calendar

To view a shared Calendar:

1. Open the desired Sharing Invitation Message form.
2. In the Sharing Invitation Message form, on the **Share** tab, in the **Open** group, click **Open this Calendar** to view your default calendar and your partner's calendar side-by-side.

Procedure Reference: View Calendars in Overlay Mode

To view calendars in Overlay mode:

1. In the Navigation pane, in the **All Calendar Items** section, right-click the other user's name and choose **Overlay** to view the calendar in Overlay mode.
2. If necessary, right-click the other user's name and choose **Overlay** again to switch back to the default calendar view.

Procedure Reference: Delegating Access to Your Folders

To delegate access to your folders:

1. On the **File** tab, choose **Info.**
2. In the Backstage view, in the **Account Information** section, from the **Account Settings** drop-down list, select **Delegate Access.**
3. In the **Delegates** dialog box, click **Add.**
4. In the **Add Users** dialog box, select the person you want as a delegate, and click **OK.**
5. In the **Delegate Permissions** dialog box, from the **Calendar** drop-down list, select an option to set the permission levels for your **Calendar** folder.
    - Select **Editor (can read, create, and modify items)** to allow the delegate to read, create, and modify items on your calendar. It is the default option.
    - Select **Author (can read and create items)** to allow the delegate to read and create items on your calendar.
    - Select **Reviewer (can read items)** to allow the delegate to only review items on your calendar.
    - Select **None** to deny the delegate to access your calendar folder.
6. Similarly, select an option each from the **Tasks, Inbox, Contacts, Notes,** and **Journal** drop-down lists and click **OK.**

7. In the **Delegates** dialog box, set options to decide on the delivery of responses for meeting requests you have organized.
   - Select the **My delegates only, but send a copy of meeting requests and responses to me (recommended)** option to send responses to delegates and a copy to the organizer.
   - Select the **My delegates only** option to send the response only to the delegate.
   - Select the **My delegates and me** option to send the response both to the delegates and the organizer.
8. Click **OK** to close the dialog box.

Procedure Reference: Publish Calendar Information to Office Online

To publish calendar information to Office Online:

1. If necessary, connect to the Exchange server.
2. Display the calendar you want to publish.
3. In the Navigation pane, in the **Calendar** section, right-click **Calendar** and choose **Share→Publish to Office.com.**
4. In the **Office.com Registration** wizard, click **Sign in.**
5. In the **Microsoft Outlook Calendar Sharing Service** page, in the **E-mail address** text box, type your Windows Live Mail ID.
6. In the **Password** text box, type your password.
7. Click **Sign in** to sign in to the Office Online service.
8. On the **Sign In Complete** page, click **Finish.**
9. In the **Publish Calendar to Office.com** dialog box, in the **Permissions** section, select an option.
   - Select **Only invited users can view this calendar** to allow only invited users to view your calendar.
   - Select **Anyone can subscribe to this calendar** to allow all users to view the calendar.
10. Click **OK** to publish the calendar.
11. Specify whether to send the sharing invitation to other users.
    - In the **Send a Sharing Invitation** dialog box, click **Yes** to send the invitation.
    - In the **Send a Sharing Invitation** dialog box, click **No** to prevent the invitation from being sent.
12. In the Internet Calendar - Share Message form, in the **To** text box, type the user name to whom you want to send the invitation.
13. Send the invitation.

ACTIVITY 6-3
Sending Calendar Information in an Email Message

Before You Begin:
Display the calendar with the current date selected.

Scenario:
A colleague has asked you to send him your calendar information for the next 30 days. He says he wants to view the details of your schedule. You decide to send him your schedule details in an email message. The Director of your company has requested that you share your calendar, so that she can view the calendar details easily to plan some important meetings. You also want to specify how you want your calendar items to be viewed when you share your calendar.

1. Specify the calendar information you want to include.

    a. In the Calendar view, on the **Home** tab, in the **Share** group, click **E-mail Calendar**.

    b. In the **Send a Calendar via E-mail** dialog box, in the **Calendar** drop-down list, verify that **Calendar** is selected.

    c. From the **Date Range** drop-down list, select **Next 30 days** to specify how long calendar information is to be sent.

    d. From the **Detail** drop-down list, select **Full details** to specify that all the details of calendar items be sent, and click **OK**.

    e. In the Message form, scroll down to view the details attached to the message body.

2. Send the calendar information.

    a. In the **To** text box, type your partner's name.

    b. In the Message form, click **Send** to send the calendar information.

3. Send an invitation to share your calendar.

    a. On the **Home** tab, in the **Share** group, click **Share Calendar**.

    b. In the Sharing Invitation Message form, in the **To** text box, type your partner's name and click **Send**.

    c. In the **Microsoft Outlook** message box, click **Yes** to share the Calendar.

4. View the shared calendar in Overlay mode.

    a. Display the Inbox.

    b. Open the Sharing Invitation Message form.

    c. In the Sharing Invitation Message form, in the **Open** group, click **Open this Calendar**.

d. If necessary, maximize the Outlook window.

e. Observe that the Calendar view displays your partner's calendar and your calendar side-by-side.

f. In the Navigation pane, in the **Calendar** section, right-click your partner's calendar and, from the displayed menu, choose **Overlay.**

g. Observe that the calendars are displayed in Overlay mode.

h. In the **Calendar** section, right-click your partner's calendar, and from the displayed menu, choose **Overlay** again to remove the calendars from overlay mode.

: Transition from Office 2003 (First Look)

ACTIVITY 6-4
Delegating Access to Your Calendar Folder

Before You Begin:
1. Make sure that your Calendar is shared with the user to whom you are delegating access to your Calendar.
2. Schedule a meeting on the upcoming Wednesday from 2.00 to 4.00 PM with your partner with the subject "Personal Discussion" and set the location as Conference Room A.

Scenario:
You are unable to come in to office for about two months due to health reasons, and your Director is planning to take over your work responsibilities during the period of absence. He will need to know your plans and schedule for these two months, so you need to give him access-only permission to your calendar. Also, you had already scheduled a meeting with a member of your team for a personal discussion. As you want to handle this meeting yourself, you need to cancel the meeting with a message stating the reason.

1. Delegate the Calendar folder access to your partner.
    a. Select the **File** tab.
    b. In the **Account Information** section, from the **Account Settings** drop-down list, select **Delegate Access**.
    c. In the **Delegates** dialog box, click **Add**.
    d. In the **Add Users** dialog box, select your partner's name, click **Add** and then click **OK**.
    e. In the **Delegate Permissions: [User name]** dialog box, in the **Calendar** drop-down list, verify that the **Editor (can read, create, and modify items)** option is selected.
    f. From the **Tasks** drop-down list, select **None** to deny access to your **Tasks** folder and click **OK**.
    g. In the **Delegates** dialog box, verify that the **My delegates only, but send a copy of meeting requests and responses to me (recommended)** option is selected and click **OK**.
    h. Select the **File** tab again to close it.

2. Cancel the meeting organized by your partner.
    a. In the Calendar view, in the **Shared Calendars** section, check the check box against your partner's name to display your partner's calendar along with your calendar in overlay mode.
    b. In the Date Navigator, select the upcoming Wednesday.
    c. In your calendar, scroll down, and double-click the **Personal Discussion** meeting request.
    d. In the Meeting form, in the **Actions** group, click **Cancel Meeting**.

e. In the message body, click and type *Due to illness, I need to cancel this meeting.* and click **Send Cancellation.**

f. Observe that the meeting request is removed from the Calendar.

ACTIVITY 6-5
Publishing the Calendar to Microsoft Office Online

Before You Begin:
Switch to the Calendar view, and display just your calendar.

Scenario:
You are the captain of the soccer team at your company. You regularly update your calendar information with the practice schedule and game dates. Since you may need to update your calendar after office hours, you decide to publish your calendar to Office Online, and invite all your teammates to view the calendar. This allows your team as well as others attending the game to view the updated game times from Office Online.

1. Register with Office Online to publish the Calendar.

   a. On the **Home** tab, in the **Share** group, from the **Publish Online** drop-down list, select **Publish to Office.com**.

   b. In the **Office.com Registration** wizard, in the **Microsoft Outlook Calendar Sharing Service** page, click **Sign in**.

   c. In the **Microsoft Office Online Registration** page, in the **E-mail address** text box, type your Windows Live Mail ID.

   d. In the **Password** text box, type the password, and click **Sign in** to sign in to the Office Online service.

   e. On the **Sign In Complete** page, click **Finish**.

   f. In the **Publish Calendar to Office.com** dialog box, in the **Permissions** section, select the **Anyone can subscribe to this calendar** option and click **OK**.

   g. In the **Send a Sharing Invitation** message box, click **Yes**.

   h. In the Message form, in the **To** text box, type the desired user name and click **Send** to send the share invitation to the user.

2. View the calendar published to Office Online.

   a. Display your Inbox, and open the calendar message from your partner.

   b. In the **[User name]_Calendar - Internet Calendar - Share** message, in the **Share** tab, in the **Open** group, click **Subscribe to this Calendar**.

   c. In the **Microsoft Outlook** message box, click **Yes** to add this calendar to Outlook, and subscribe to updates.

   d. On the Navigation pane, observe that the other user's Internet calendar is displayed in the Shared Calenders section.

   e. Close the Internet Calendar Message form.

TOPIC D
Share Information by Using an Electronic Business Card

You are familiar with creating contacts. Outlook provides you with the option of sending contact information to another recipient through email. In this topic, you will share information using an electronic business card.

There may be times when someone will ask you to send them information on one of your contacts. Instead of writing down all the details in an email, you can attach the contact's information in an email and send it. It is also better if the recipient can view the contact information in a format similar to the paper-based business card format. Outlook makes the task easier by allowing recipients to save the contact as a contact record.

Contact Cards

The **Find a Contact** text box, in the **Find** group on the **Home** tab, allows you to find contacts from your address book. You can find contacts from within the Mail view itself. The search result then displays not only the contact window for the searched for contact but also different ways of communicating with the contact.

Electronic Business Cards

An *Electronic Business Card (EBC)* is the electronic version of a business card that displays contact details. It is automatically created when you create a contact entry. Contact details displayed can include the name of the contact, employer, designation, phone numbers, and email address. Other contact information specified in the contact entry can also be displayed on an electronic business card. An EBC can also include an image of the contact. The background and layout of an EBC can be modified to suit individual preferences. You can insert an EBC of a contact in an email message, or even include an EBC in your email signature.

Figure 6-9: Display of an electronic business card on a contact form.

The Edit Business Card Dialog Box

The **Edit Business Card** dialog box enables you to format the appearance of a business card and the contact information in it. The following table describes the sections of the **Edit Business Card** dialog box.

Section	Description
Fields	Lists fields that have been added as contact information in the business card. New fields can be added to the business card and existing fields edited or deleted.
Card Design	Used to modify the design of the card. An image can be added by clicking **Change,** and then choosing an image in the **Add Card Picture** dialog box. The card can then be customized by changing the layout, alignment, background color, and area of the image.
Edit	Displays text in the format appropriate for the field selected in the **Fields** section. The text and labels for the field can then be customized by choosing an option from the different formatting options provided in the **Edit** section for the text.
Preview	Shows a preview of the business card. Any changes made to the business card are reflected here.

The People Pane

The People pane displays the details, related files, appointments, notes, and also any updates from social media about a contact. It provides a single point of access for all items in Outlook associated with a contact. You can add accounts from social networking sites and receive updates from those accounts on the People pane. The **People Pane** option on the **View** tab of the Ribbon enables you to add such accounts. The People pane is also present on the Message, Contact, and Meeting forms. On the Meeting form, the People pane displays all the attendees for a meeting. Clicking an individual attendee displays information about that particular contact. You can also choose to minimize or disable the People pane.

How to Share Information by Using an Electronic Business Card

Procedure Reference: Edit a Business Card

To edit a business card:

1. In the Contacts view, open a contact.
2. Display the **Edit Business Card** dialog box.
   - In the Contact form, on the **Contact** tab, in the **Options** group, click **Business Card.**
   - In the Contact form, double-click the business card.
   - Or, in the Contact form, right-click the business card and choose **Edit Business Card.**
3. In the **Edit Business Card** dialog box, in the **Fields** list box, select the desired field.
4. If necessary, below the **Fields** list box, click **Add,** and from the displayed menu, choose a category, and from the submenu, choose the field that you want to add to the list box.
5. In the **Edit** section, in the text box, type the information for the corresponding field that has been added.
6. If necessary, from the **Label** drop-down list, select an option to specify the location of the label.
   - Select **Left** to display the label on the left side of the business card.
   - Select **Right** to display the label on the right side of the business card.
7. If necessary, in the **Label** text box, type a name for the label.
8. If necessary, remove a field from the business card.
   a. In the **Fields** list box, select the field that needs to be removed.
   b. Click **Remove** to remove the selected field.
9. Click **OK** to save the business card and close the **Edit Business Card** dialog box.

Procedure Reference: Format the Appearance of a Business Card

To format the appearance of a business card:

1. In the Contacts view, open a contact.
2. On the **Contact** tab, in the **Options** group, click **Business Card.**
3. In the **Edit Business Card** dialog box, in the **Card Design** section, specify settings to format the business card.
   - From the **Layout** drop-down list, select an option to specify the location of the image.
     - Select **Image Left** to place the image at the left of the business card.
     - Select **Image Right** to place the image to the right of the business card.
     - Select **Image Top** to place the image at the top of the business card.
     - Select **Image Bottom** to place the image at the bottom of the business card.
     - Select **Text Only** to display only text on the business card.
     - Select **Background Image** to display the image as the background image.
   - Set a background color for the business card.
     a. Click the **Background Color** button.
     b. In the **Color** dialog box, from the displayed palette, select a color.

c. If necessary, define a color.

   A. Click **Define Custom Colors** to display the rainbow color palette.

   B. Select a color, and click **Add to Custom Colors** to add the selected color to the **Custom Colors** section.

d. Click **OK.**

- Insert an image for the business card.

   a. From the **Image** drop-down list, select **Change.**

   b. In the **Add Card Picture** dialog box, select an image.

   c. Click **OK** to insert the selected image in the business card.

- In the **Image Area** spin box, click the up or down arrow to set the size of the image.
- From the **Image Align** drop-down list, select an option to align the image in the business card.

4. In the **Edit Business Card** dialog box, in the **Fields** list box, select a field so that the corresponding text for the field is displayed in the **Edit** text box.

5. In the **Edit Business Card** dialog box, in the **Edit** section, format the text displayed in the **Edit** text box.

   - Click the **Increase Font Size** button to increase the font size of the selected field.
   - Click the **Decrease Font Size** button to decrease the font size of the selected field.
   - Click the **Bold** button to apply bold formatting to text.
   - Click the **Italic** button to italicize text.
   - Click the **Underline** button to underline text.
   - Click an alignment option button to set text alignment.
   - Click the **Font Color** button, and in the **Color** dialog box, select a color and click **OK.**
   - From the **Label** drop-down list, select an option.
   - Click the **Label Color** button and select the color that you want to apply to the label.

6. In the **Edit Business Card** dialog box, click **OK** to apply formatting to the business card.

7. Save and close the contact.

Procedure Reference: Create a Personal Signature

To create a personal signature:

1. Select the **File** tab and choose **Options.**

2. In the **Outlook Options** dialog box, select the **Mail** category and, in the **Compose Messages** section, click **Signatures** to display the **Signatures and Stationery** dialog box.

3. In the **Signatures and Stationery** dialog box, on the **E-mail Signature** tab, below the **Select signature to edit** list box, click **New** to display the **New Signature** dialog box.

4. In the **New Signature** dialog box, in the **Type a name for this signature** text box, type a name and click **OK** to create a new signature.

5. In the **Edit signature** section in the text area, type the text for the signature.

6. If necessary, change the font, font size, and font color of the signature text.
    a. In the **Edit signature** section in the text area, select the signature text that you entered.
    b. From the **Font** drop-down list, select a font.
    c. From the **Font Size** drop-down list, select a font size.
    d. From the **Font Color** drop-down list, select a font color.
7. If necessary, include a business card in the signature.
    a. In the **Edit signature** section, in the text box, click where you want the card to be displayed.
    b. Click **Business Card.**
    c. In the **Insert Business Card** dialog box, in the **Filed As** list box, select a contact and click **OK.**
8. If necessary, include a picture in the signature.
    a. In the **Edit signature** section, in the text box, click where you want the picture to be displayed.
    b. Click the **Picture** button.
    c. In the **Insert Picture** dialog box, select an image and click **Insert.**
9. If necessary, include a hyperlink in the signature.
    a. In the **Edit signature** section, in the text box, click where you want the link displayed.
    b. Click the **Insert Hyperlink** button.
    c. In the **Insert Hyperlink** dialog box, select the hyperlink, or type an address, and click **OK.**
10. In the **Signatures and Stationery** dialog box, in the **Choose default signature** section, from the **New messages** drop-down list, select **(none)** to prevent the signature from being automatically inserted in all the messages.

 By default, **(none)** is displayed in the **New messages** drop-down list. You need to explicitly select the option again to prevent the insertion of the signature in all of the messages.

11. If necessary, from the **Replies/forwards** drop-down list, select a signature to include in the messages that you forward or reply to, or select **(none)** to prevent a signature from being automatically inserted in the messages.
12. Click **OK** to apply the changes and close the **Signatures and Stationery** dialog box.
13. Click **OK** to close the **Outlook Options** dialog box.

Procedure Reference: Send a Business Card in an Email Message

To send a business card in an email message:
1. Open a new Message form.
2. Enter the required information in the **To, Cc,** and **Subject** fields.
3. Click the body of the message, select the **Insert** tab, and in the **Include** group, click **Business Card.** From the displayed list, select a business card to insert it in the message.

ACTIVITY 6-6
Editing a Business Card

Data Files:

Card_Image.jpg

Scenario:

You have a new Instant Messaging address and want to update your business card. You also want to add your home phone number to the business card. Finally, you want to add an image to, and format and design the business card, to improve its appearance.

1. Add an IM address and a home phone number to the business card.

   a. Switch to the Contacts view, and double-click the **Angela Barry** contact.

   b. In the **Internet** section, in the **IM address** text box, click and type *angela@example.com* and press **Enter**.

   c. Observe that the IM address has been added to the business card.

   d. In the **Phone numbers** section, in the **Home** text box, click and type *585–555–5555*

   e. On the **Contact** tab, in the **Options** group, click **Business Card.**

   f. If necessary, in the **Location Information** dialog box, in the **What area code (or city code) are you in now?** text box, click and type *06430* and click **OK.**

   g. If necessary, in the **Phone and Modem Options** dialog box, click **OK.**

   h. In the **Edit Business Card** dialog box, in the **Fields** list box, click the **Home Phone** field.

   i. In the **Label** drop-down list, verify that **Right** is selected and, in the text box to its right, the text "Home" is displayed. This label text will be displayed to the right of the telephone number in the business card.

   j. In the **Edit** section, in the **Label** text box, double-click and type *IM* to add the label text to the right of the IM address in the business card.

2. Add the Angela.jpg image and change the background color of the business card.

   a. In the **Card Design** section, next to the **Image** text box, click **Change.**

   b. In the **Add Card Picture** dialog box, navigate to the C:\084574Data\Working with Microsoft Office Outlook 2010 folder.

   c. Select **Angela.jpg** and click **OK.**

   d. In the **Card Design** section, from the **Image Align** drop-down list, select **Fit to Edge.**

   e. Observe that the image has been inserted and is displayed on the left edge of the business card.

   f. In the **Card Design** section, click the **Background Color** button.

g. In the **Color** dialog box, in the **Basic Colors** section, select the color in the last row, sixth column and click **OK** to apply the color.

3. Format the name and label text.

   a. In the **Fields** list box, select **Full Name,** and in the **Edit** section, click the **Italic** button to italicize the name.

   b. Click the **Font Color** button, and in the **Color** dialog box, in the **Basic Colors** section, select the color in the third row, fifth column and click **OK.**

   c. In the **Edit Business Card** dialog box, click **OK** to apply the formatting.

   d. Save and close the contact.

ACTIVITY 6-7
Including a Business Card in a Personal Signature

Before You Begin:
Display the Inbox.

Scenario:
Being the director of the marketing department of a company, you need to share your contact information with clients. Therefore, you want to include your business card in your signature so that the business card is automatically included in all of the messages being sent from your Inbox.

1. Create a new signature.

    a. Select the **File** tab and choose **Options** to display the **Outlook Options** dialog box.

    b. In the **Outlook Options** dialog box, select the **Mail** tab and, in the **Compose messages** section, click **Signatures.**

    c. In the **Signatures and Stationery** dialog box, on the **E-mail Signature** tab, below the **Select signature to edit** list box, click **New.**

    d. In the **New Signature** dialog box, in the **Type a name for this signature** text box, type *Angela* and click **OK** to create the new signature.

    e. In the **Edit signature** text area, click and type *Regards,* and press **Enter.**

    f. Type *Angela* and press **Enter.**

2. Insert the Angela Barry business card in the signature.

    a. In the **Edit signature** toolbar, click **Business Card.**

    b. In the **Insert Business Card** dialog box, in the **Filed As** list, select **Barry, Angela** and click **OK.**

    c. In the **Edit signature** section, verify that the business card of Angela Barry is inserted below the signature text.

3. Set the option to automatically insert the signature in all email messages.

    a. In the **Choose default signature** section, from the **New messages** drop-down list, select **Angela** to automatically insert the signature in all the email messages.

    b. From the **Replies/forwards** drop-down list, select **Angela** to automatically insert the signature in all the messages that are replied to or forwarded, and then click **OK.**

    c. In the **Signatures and Stationery** dialog box, click **OK.**

    d. In the **Outlook Options** dialog box, click **OK.**

4. Verify that the business card is used with the signature.

a. Switch to the Mail view.

b. Open a new email message.

c. Observe that the new message form is opened with the signature and business card of Angela Barry automatically inserted in the message body.

d. Close the email message.

TOPIC E
Add RSS Feeds Through Outlook 2010

You worked with SharePoint content from the Outlook environment. Now, you want to collect information from various websites and receive updates in your Outlook Inbox. In this topic, you will add RSS feeds through Outlook 2010.

When you are designing a project, you may have to collect and browse through information from various websites. Rather than browsing separately through each website, you can collect the information through Outlook. This helps you receive information, without revealing your email address to any of the site owners.

Really Simple Syndication Feeds

Really Simple Syndication (RSS) is a method for distributing information in a standardized XML format. This XML format allows you to publish information just once so that the information can then be viewed by subscribers by using various client software programs such as Outlook. These programs are known as RSS aggregators or RSS readers, and the delivery method for RSS content is known as an *RSS feed*.

Outlook includes the functionality of an RSS aggregator. You can get RSS feeds that you have subscribed to from the RSS Feeds folder in the Navigation pane. When the sites publish content, they update the RSS feed, and users who have subscribed to the feed will get a list of the newly published content. You can use RSS feeds to keep up with websites, news sites, or blogs that you frequently read.

How to Add RSS Feeds Through Outlook 2010

Procedure Reference: Add an RSS Feed Through Outlook 2010

To add an RSS feed through Outlook 2010:

1. Select the **File** tab and choose **Info.**
2. In the **Info** section, click **Account Settings** and, from the displayed menu, choose **Account Settings.**
3. In the **Account Settings** dialog box, select the **RSS Feeds** tab.
4. On the **RSS Feeds** tab, click **New.**
5. In the **New RSS Feed** dialog box, in the text box, type the RSS feed link and click **Add** to display the **RSS Feed Options** dialog box.
6. In the **RSS Feed Options** dialog box, specify settings for the RSS feed.
    - In the **General** section, in the **Feed Name** text box, type the desired name.
    - If necessary, in the **Delivery Location** section, click **Change Folder** and, in the **New RSS Feed Delivery Location** dialog box, choose a location for the RSS Feeds folder or create a new RSS Feeds folder, and click **OK**.
    - In the **Downloads** section, check the **Automatically download enclosures for this RSS feed** check box to download all the articles attached to the feed.
    - Check the **Download the full article as an .html attachment** check box to download the article attached to the feed as an HTML file.
    - If necessary, in the **Update Limit** section, check the **Use the publisher update recommendation** check box for updating the feed every one hour.

7. Click **OK** to add the feed.
8. In the **Account Settings** dialog box, click **Close.**
9. If necessary, in the Navigation pane, in the **Mail Folders** section, expand the RSS Feeds folder and select the particular feed folder to view feeds.

Procedure Reference: Share an RSS Feed with Other Users

To share an RSS feed with other users:

1. In the Navigation pane, in the **Mail Folders** section, expand the RSS Feeds folder.
2. Select the desired feed folder and open the feed article that you want to share.
3. On the **RSS Article** tab of the **RSS Article** form, in the **Respond** group, click **Share This Feed.**
4. In the **RSS Feed - Share** form, in the **To** text box, type the name of the user with whom you want to share the feed.
5. If necessary, in the message body, enter message text.
6. Click **Send** to share the RSS feed.

Procedure Reference: Add an RSS Feed Received from Other Users

To add an RSS feed received from other users:

1. Display the Inbox.
2. In the Inbox, open the message with an article attached as an RSS feed.
3. On the **RSS Article** tab of the **RSS Article** form, in the **Open** group, click **Add This Feed.** The **Microsoft Outlook** dialog box is displayed prompting you to confirm whether the RSS feed can be added to Outlook.
4. If necessary, click **Advanced,** and in the **RSS Feed Options** dialog box, configure options for the RSS feed.
5. Click **Yes** to add the RSS feed to Outlook.

ACTIVITY 6-8
Adding an RSS Feed Through Outlook 2010

Scenario:
You know that Outlook 2010 allows receiving RSS feeds from within the application. As you would like to subscribe to some feeds, you decide to add the feeds to Outlook.

1. Add an RSS feed to your account.

   a. Select the **File** tab, and verify that **Info** is selected.

   b. In the **Info** section, click **Account Settings,** and from the drop-down list, select **Account Settings,** and in the **Account Settings** dialog box, select the **RSS Feeds** tab.

   c. On the **RSS Feeds** tab, click **New.**

   d. In the **New RSS Feed** dialog box, in the text box, type **http://office.microsoft.com/download/afile.aspx?assetid=HX102367541033**

   e. Click **Add** and, in the **RSS Feed Options** dialog box, in the **General** section, in the **Feed Name** text box, type *Microsoft Office*

   f. Click **OK** to add the feed and close the **RSS Feed Options** dialog box.

   g. In the **Account Settings** dialog box, click **Close.**

2. View the RSS feeds.

   a. In the Navigation pane, in the **Mail Folders** section, expand the **RSS Feeds** folder.

   b. Select the Microsoft Office folder to view the displayed items.

   c. Close the application.

Lesson 6 Follow-up

In this lesson, you managed various tasks using the new features of Outlook. Knowledge of the new features and their functionality will give you the confidence to use these features when you are working with the latest version of Outlook.

1. What Outlook tools do you expect to use most often to manage your email messages?

2. Which feature for scheduling meetings in Outlook do you think will help you the most in scheduling meetings?

7 Sharing Microsoft Office 2010 Files

Lesson Time: 30 minutes

Lesson Objectives:

In this lesson, you will share files in Microsoft Office 2010.

You will:

- Protect files.
- Share files using Office Web Apps.

Introduction

You familiarized yourself with the various new features of Office 2010 applications. File protection and sharing are features that are common to all Office applications. In this lesson, you will protect and share Office files, thereby finalizing them.

Irrespective of what software you use to create a file, you still need to protect the file against unauthorized access and modification. Office 2010 is packaged with enhanced protection and sharing options that enable users to authenticate and share content in a secure manner.

TOPIC A
Protect Files

You worked on different kinds of files using various applications of Office 2010. Protecting files enables you to ensure their safety and integrity. In this topic, you will protect files.

When data is easily accessible to multiple users, it runs the risk of getting tampered with. Some amount of data loss might also occur if it does not reach the right hands. Protecting files gives you the flexibility to share them knowing that the data is secure.

The Document Inspector

The *Document Inspector* feature removes personal information, comments, hidden text, and tracked changes from a file. Files usually contain hidden details such as the author and company name, the comments placed, presentation notes, and other document properties, all of which you may not want to share with other users. The Document Inspector feature is used to prevent other users from viewing or retrieving such hidden information.

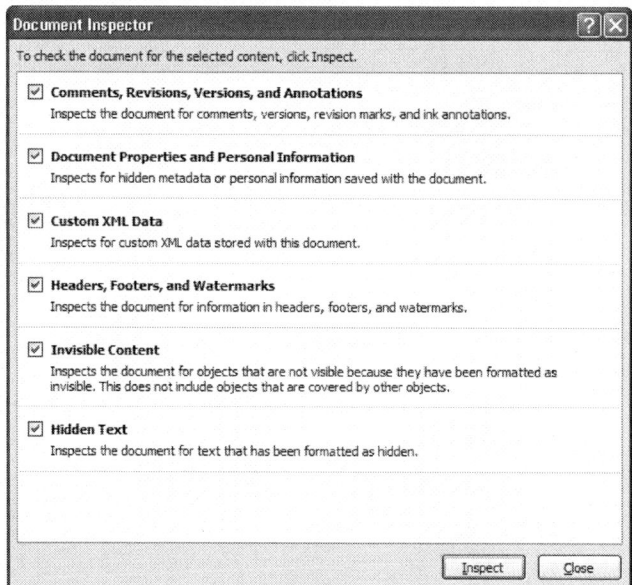

Figure 7-1: The Document Inspector dialog box.

Types of Hidden Data

Microsoft Office 2010 files can contain the following types of hidden data and personal information.

Information Type	Function of the Document Inspector
Comments and Annotations	Scans and removes comments and annotations.

Information Type	Function of the Document Inspector
Document Properties and Personal Information	Scans and removes file properties such as the author name, the subject and title of a file, statistical information such as the number of slides and hidden slides, and other details such as the person who last saved the file. In addition, it can also find information such as the creation date and the location of the file.
Custom XML Data	Removes custom XML data that is not visible in a file. This XML data defines the structure and visual appearance of any data in the file.
Invisible On-Slide Content in Micosoft Office PowerPoint.	Scans and removes the objects in the presentation that have been formatted and made invisible.
Off-Slide Content in Microsoft Office PowerPoint.	Allows you to check the presentation and remove objects that are outside the slide area. These objects are not visible because of their placement. Objects may include text boxes, clip art images, graphics, and tables. However, objects to which animation effects have been added are not checked.
Presentation Notes in Microsoft Office PowerPoint.	Allows you to check and remove any text that is present in the Notes section and that you may not want to share, especially if it was specifically added for the use of the presenter while delivering the presentation.

The Mark As Final Option

The *Mark as Final* feature enables you to save a file as the final version and make it read-only. Marking a file final ensures that the file cannot be tampered with when it is shared.

Information Rights Management (IRM)

Information Rights Management (IRM) is a feature that helps prevent sensitive information from being forwarded, copied, printed, or otherwise manipulated by unauthorized recipients. You can restrict permission for a file using this feature and restrictions are carried through along with the presentation or document as part of the file.

Digital Signatures

A *digital signature* is designed to ensure the authenticity of a digital document and verify the identity of the person who signed the document. It validates the authenticity, integrity, and origin of the document. In Word, Excel, and PowerPoint 2010, a digital signature can be added by going to the Office Backstage View and the digital signature will not be visible in the content of the file.

A *digital ID* is commonly known as a digital certificate. To apply a digital signature to a document in a file, you need a valid digital certificate or ID because it enables the recipient to authenticate the document.

When you try to apply a digital signature to a Office application document without a digital ID, the **Get a Digital ID** dialog box provides you with options to either purchase a digital ID from a Microsoft partner or create your own digital ID.

After you create a digital ID, the Office application will always use the same digital ID. You do not have to create a new digital ID each time you need to add a digital signature to a document.

How to Protect Files

Procedure Reference: Inspect a Presentation

To inspect a presentation:

1. Ensure that the presentation that needs to be marked final has been saved.
2. Select the **File** tab and choose **Info.**
3. In the Information pane, from the **Check for Issues** drop-down list, select **Inspect Document.**
4. In the **Document Inspector** dialog box, check or uncheck the desired options that need to be inspected and click **Inspect.**
5. In the **Review the inspection results** section, click **Remove All** to remove information such as comments and annotations, document properties and personal information, metadata information, invisible on-slide and off-slide content, and presentation notes.
6. If necessary, click **Reinspect** and repeat steps 4 through 6 to reinspect the presentation.
7. Click **Close.**

Procedure Reference: Mark a Presentation Final

To mark a presentation final:

1. Select the **File** tab and choose **Info.**
2. In the Information pane, from the **Protect Presentation** drop-down list, select **Mark as Final.**
3. In the **Microsoft PowerPoint** message box, click **OK** to mark the presentation final, and then save the file.

ACTIVITY 7-1
Restricting Document Access

Data Files:

OGC Informations.pptx

Before You Begin:

1. Launch the PowerPoint application.
2. Navigate to the C:\084574Data\Sharing Microsoft Office 2010 Files folder and open the OGC Information.pptx file.

Scenario:

Your manager has given some feedback on the document that you are working on. Now, you want the other functional managers to give their feedback too, but you do not want them to view your manager's comments. Therefore, before sending the document to the other managers, you decide to remove all the comments and personal information from it.

---

1. Inspect the presentation.

    a. Select the **File** tab and, in the Information pane, from the **Check for Issues** drop-down list, select **Inspect Document**.

    b. In the **Document Inspector** dialog box, uncheck the **Custom XML Data** check box to avoid checking the XML data.

    c. Check the **Off-Slide Content** check box to inspect the objects that are outside the slide area.

    d. Click **Inspect** to inspect the presentation.

e. Observe that the slide contains comments, annotations, document properties, personal information, and presentation notes.

2. View the inspection results.

   a. In the **Document Properties and Personal Information** section, click **Remove All**.

   b. In the **Presentation Notes** section, click **Remove All**.

   c. In the **Comments and Annotations** section, click **Remove All**.

   d. Click **Reinspect,** and then click **Inspect** to confirm the changes.

   e. In the **Document Inspector** dialog box, observe that there is no hidden data or personal information that needs to be removed and click **Close**.

3. Mark the presentation final.

   a. On the **File** tab, from the **Protect Presentation** drop-down list, select **Mark as Final**.

   b. In the **Microsoft PowerPoint** warning message box, click **OK** to mark the presentation final and save it.

   c. In the **Microsoft PowerPoint** message box, click **OK** to confirm that this version of the presentation is the final one.

4. Save and close the presentation.

   a. On the **File** tab, click **Save As**.

   b. Save the file as *My OGC Information*

   c. On the status bar, observe that an icon is displayed, indicating that the presentation has been marked final, and in the slide, in the Message bar, observe the message indicating that the file cannot be edited because it is marked final.

   d. Close the presentation.

TOPIC B
Share Files Using Office Web Apps

You saved documents in different formats. To access documents from a web browser, you need to save them to the web. In this topic, you will save documents to the web.

Sharing your documents with other users using the desktop application is not always possible. Saving your files to the web not only ensures that anyone can access them, but also you will be able to work with the files in real time.

The Save to SkyDrive Feature

Microsoft Office 2010 allows you to save Office files to the web through a Windows Live ID. You can then sign in to SkyDrive by inputting your Windows Live credentials to access the file from any other computer and from any location. Using this feature, you can also view, edit, or download files.

Windows Live SkyDrive

Windows Live SkyDrive is an online repository that lets you save files and share them with other users. To access a SkyDrive account, you need to have a Windows Live ID.

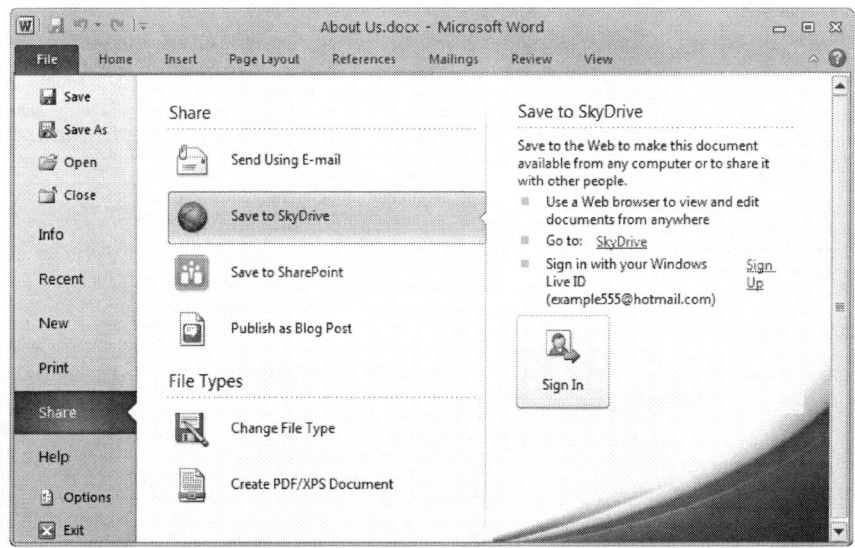

Figure 7-2: The Save to SkyDrive option used to save files to the Web.

Office Mobile 2010

Office Mobile 2010 is a feature that allows you to work on your Office file using an enhanced mobile version of Word, Excel, and PowerPoint. With Office Mobile 2010, you can easily open, view, edit, and copy and paste information in your file. You can email your Office documents from your mobile device or post them to your SharePoint workspace. Office Mobile 2010 is not part of Office 2010, but the application will be available at the release of Office 2010 for phones using Windows Mobile 6.5 or later.

How to Share Files by Using Office Web Apps

Procedure Reference: Save a Presentation in PowerPoint on the Web by Using the Save to SkyDrive Option

To save a presentation on the web by using the **Save to SkyDrive** option:

1. Select the **File** tab and choose **Share.**
2. Select the **Save to SkyDrive** option.
3. Click **Sign In** and enter your Windows Live credentials.
4. In the **My Folders** section, select the folder you want to save the presentation in, and click **Save As.**
5. In the **Save As** dialog box, enter the name of the presentation, and click **Save.**

Procedure Reference: Broadcast a PowerPoint Presentation as a Slide Show

To broadcast a slide show:

1. Open the PowerPoint presentation that you wish to broadcast.
2. Select the **File** tab to display the Backstage view.
3. Click **Share** and, in the **Share** pane, select the **Broadcast Slide Show** option.
4. In the **Broadcast Slide Show** pane, click **Broadcast Slide Show.**
5. In the **Broadcast Slide Show** dialog box, click **Start Broadcast.**
6. On the **.NET Passport** wizard, click **Next.**
7. On the **Do you have an e-mail address** page, click **Next.**
8. On the **Have you already signed up** page, select the **No, sign up now** option and click **Next.**
9. On the **Sign up with Windows Live ID** page, click **Next.**
10. On the **Sign in with my Windows Live ID** page, enter the email address and password and click **Next.**
11. On the **You're done** page, click **Finish.**
12. In the **Broadcast Slide Show** dialog box, click **Copy Link** to copy the link or click **Send in Email** to transmit it as an email message.
13. Click the **Start Slide Show** button to view the slide show.
14. If necessary, press **Esc** to end the slide show.
15. On the presentation slide, below the Ribbon, in the **Broadcast View** message bar, click **End Broadcast** to end the broadcast.
16. In the **Microsoft PowerPoint** warning message box, click **End Broadcast** to end the broadcast and disconnect all the remote viewers.

Procedure Reference: Access and Work with Excel Workbooks on the Web

To access and work with Excel workbooks on the web:

1. Open a web browser of your choice.
2. In the address bar, type *http://skydrive.live.com*
3. Enter your Windows Live login credentials.
4. Work with the workbook.
    a. Browse to the workbook you want to view and click **View.**
    b. Click the **Open in browser** button to make changes to the workbook.

5. Click the sign out link to log out of SkyDrive.

Procedure Reference: Work with Presentations on the Web

To work with presentations on the web:
1. Open a web browser of your choice.
2. In the address bar, type *http://skydrive.live.com*
3. Enter your Windows Live login credentials.
4. Browse to the presentation that you want to view and click **View.**
5. Work with the presentation.
   a. Browse to the presentation that you want to view and click **View.**
   b. Click the **Open in browser** button to make changes to the presentation.
6. Click sign out to log out of SkyDrive.

ACTIVITY 7-2
Saving Presentations to the Web

Data Files:

OGC Properties Overview.pptx

Before You Begin:

Navigate to the C:\084574Data\Sharing Microsoft Office 2010 folder and open the OGC Properties Overview.pptx file.

Scenario:

You have completed work on a presentation. You plan to send the presentation in an email message to a reviewer in a different location. However, you are aware that the reviewer does not have the Office 2010 suite installed. You decide to share the presentation on the web so that he can access it without having to install the Office 2010 suite.

1. Enable sharing options.

    a. Select the **File** tab and choose **Share**.

    b. In the **Share** pane, select the **Save to SkyDrive** option.

    c. In the **Save to SkyDrive** pane, click **Sign In**.

    d. In the **.NET Passport Wizard**, click **Next**.

    e. If necessary, in the **Security Alert** message box, click **Yes**.

    f. On the **Do you have an e-mail address** page, verify that the **Yes, use my existing e-mail address** option is selected and click **Next**.

    g. On the **Have you already signed up** page, click **Next**.

    h. On the **Sign in with your Windows Live ID** page, in the **E-mail address** text box, type your Windows Live email address.

    i. In the **Password** text box, type the password and click **OK**.

2. Save the file to SkyDrive.

    a. In the **Save to SkyDrive** pane, in the **My Folders** section, verify that the **Public** folder is selected and click **Save As**.

    b. In the **Save As** dialog box, in the **Save in** text box, observe that the SkyDrive location where the file will be stored is displayed.

    c. Save the file as *File for Review* and close it.

    d. Close the PowerPoint application.

ACTIVITY 7-3
Working with Shared Presentations on the Web

Scenario:
You have saved a presentation on the web. Before you send information about the presentation and its location details to the reviewer, you want to preview the presentation on the web to ensure that all the necessary details have been entered. Therefore, you decide to access the presentation from the Internet.

1. Display the OGC for Review.pptx presentation from a web browser.

    a. Choose **Start→Internet**.

    b. In the Internet Explorer window, on the address bar, click and type *http://skydrive.live.com* and press **Enter**.

    c. On the **Windows Live** page, in the top-right corner, click **Sign in**.

    d. On the **Windows Live** page, in the **Sign in** section, in the **Windows Live ID** text box, type your user name.

    e. In the **Password** text box, type your password and click **Sign in**.

    f. In the **Recent folders** section, select the **Public** folder to display the presentation.

2. View and edit the presentation.

    a. Select the **File for Review** file to view it.

    b. On the toolbar above the presentation file, click the **View** link, close the message bar that is displayed below the **File** tab, and at the bottom of the Internet Explorer window, click the **Next Slide** button to navigate to the next slide.

    c. Click **Edit in Browser** to edit the presentation in the Internet Explorer window.

    d. On the displayed slide, select the bulleted list.

    e. On the **Home** tab, in the **Font** group, click the **Italic** button to italicize the selected text.

    f. In the **Font** group, from the **Font** color drop-down list, in the **Theme Colors** section, in the fifth row, sixth column, select the **e5cb92** color, and click away from the bulleted list to view the change.

    g. Select the **File** tab and choose **Close** to close the presentation.

    h. In the top-right corner of the Internet Explorer window, click **sign out** and close the Internet Explorer window.

Lesson 7 Follow-up

In this lesson, you saved a document to the web and viewed it by using Office Web Apps. This provides you with the flexibility to access and modify your Office files on the fly.

1. **What are the features you find beneficial by using the Save to SkyDrive feature while sharing presentations?**

2. **What are the advantages of sharing an Office document over the web ?**

Follow-up

In this course, you customized the redesigned user interface and modified documents using the Microsoft Word application. You also added visual elements to the slides in a PowerPoint presentation. Additionally, you saved Office application files to the web, so that they can be accessed by users who do not have Microsoft Office installed on their workstations. These skills will enable you to use various user friendly features available in Microsoft Office 2010 and will help work with various Office applications.

1. **How do the new features of Office 2010 help reduce the time taken to carry out various functions?**

2. **Where might you become more efficient while working in a document by using the new features in PowerPoint 2010?**

3. **How will you use the new features in Access 2010 for developing databases in your organization?**

What's Next?

This course does not form part of any specific series.

Lesson Labs

Lesson labs are provided as an additional learning resource for this course. The labs may or may not be performed as part of the classroom activities. Your instructor will consider setup issues, classroom timing issues, and instructional needs to determine which labs are appropriate for you to perform, and at what point during the class. If you do not perform the labs in class, your instructor can tell you if you can perform them independently as self-study, and if there are any special setup requirements.

Lesson 1 Lab 1
Getting Started with Microsoft Office 2010 Application Interface

Activity Time: 15 minutes

Data Files:

OGC Properties.docx

Before You Begin:

Open C:\084574Data\Getting Started with Microsoft Office 2010 folder and open the OGC Properties.docx file.

Scenario:

You are working on the file OGC Properties.docx in a Word application, and to simplify the functionality you want to add certain commands in the Quick Access tool bar. You decide to format the appearance of the title previewing the various available options in the gallery. After printing a copy of the document you want to save a new copy of the document in earlier Word format just to make sure you can work with the document in other workstations which do not have the Word 2010 installed.

1. In the Quick Access toolbar, add the **New** button.

2. Bold format the title "OGC PROPERTIES, INC." using the Mini Toolbar.

3. Apply the QuickStyle **Heading 1** to the title text "OGC PROPERTIES, INC."

4. Preview the document in **Portrait Orientation** and print it.

5. Save the document as My OGC Properties.doc in the Word 97–2003 (*.doc) format.

Lesson 2 Lab 1
Working with Documents Using Microsoft Office Word 2010

Activity Time: 10 minutes

Data Files:

OGC Annual Report.docx

Before You Begin:

Open the C:\084574Data\Working with Documents Using Microsoft Office Word 2010, and open the Annual Report.docx file.

Scenario:

You are working on the document Annual Report.docx. You want to add style enhancements to the text for better visual appeal. Also you want to add a SmartArt graphic for better illustration and make changes to the structure of the document using the Navigation Pane.

1. Use the Navigation pane to **Promote** the title "Market Forecast".

2. Insert a SmartArt **Linear Venn** under the heading "Strategy" above the caption "Figure A" and in the shapes click and type *Residential, Rental, Corporate* and *Relocation*

3. Create a QuickStyle named "ogc_prop" and apply it to the title "OGC Properties, Inc." and add it to the Styles gallery..

4. Save the file as My OGC Annual Report.docx.

Lesson 3 Lab 1

Presenting Data in a Spreadsheet

Activity Time: 10 minutes

Data Files:

Revenue Summary.xlsx

Before You Begin:

From the C:\084574Data\Working with Spreadsheets folder, open the Revenue Summary.xlsx workbook.

Scenario:

You need to analyze and prepare a report on the previous year's revenue summary of your company. Before making decisions based on figures, you decide to highlight and segregate the low, medium, and high revenue figures and also filter the highest revenue figures from the data. Also, you need to calculate the average high revenue figure for the first quarter.

1. Convert the range of data to a table.

2. Apply appropriate icon sets to conditionally format the sales figures.

3. Sort data by the color of the icon to analyze data.

4. Filter the revenue values for January and February.

5. In the C:\084574Data\Working with Spreadsheets folder, save the Excel workbook as *My Revenue Summary.xlsx* and close it.

6. In the Revenue.xlsx workbook, in the European Sales worksheet, create a column chart for the data.

7. In the Revenue.xlsx workbook, in the European Sales worksheet, insert a Line Sparkline to display the sales trend for each region.

8. Add a high point for the Sparkline and format the Sparkline.

9. Based on the Revenue worksheet, create a PivotChart and PivotTable to analyze sales data by month and sales.

10. In the C:\084574Data\Working with Spreadsheets, save the Excel workbook as *My Revenue.xlsx* and close it.

Lesson 4 Lab 1
Creating Dynamic Presentations

Activity Time: 10 minutes

Data Files:

Enhance Presentation.pptx

Before You Begin:

From the C:\084574Data\Creating Dynamic Presentations folder, open the Enhance Presentation.pptx file.

Scenario:

While reviewing a presentation, you find that the presentation is not in the correct format and is not visually appealing. You want to change the layout to suit the overall theme of the presentation. You also want to apply some graphical effects to enhance the visual appearance of the presentation.

1. Create a custom theme color with the following specifications and save it as *Company Theme Color.*
   - Text/Background - Dark 2: Olive Green, Accent 3
   - Accent 1: Tan, Text 2, Darker 50%
   - Accent 2: Dark Blue, Background 2, Lighter 60%

2. In slide 8, apply the **Inside Diagonal Bottom Right** shadow effect.

3. In slide 8, apply the **Offset Center** shadow effect to the picture.

4. Save the file as *My Enhanced Presentation* in the PPTX format in the C:\084574Data\ Creating Dynamic Presentations to a Presentation folder.

5. Save the presentation as My Enhance Presentation.ppsx and close it.

Lesson 5 Lab 1
Working with Databases

Activity Time: 10 minutes

Data Files:

Inventory.accdb

Before You Begin:

From the C:\084574Data\Working with Databases Using Microsoft Office Access 2010 folder, from the Inventory.accdb database, display the Computers table.

Scenario:

You want to examine the procurement price for the inventory in your organization. You want to generate a report which can be used as a quick reference when needed. You also want to export the data to a text file so that you can share the inventory data with others.

1. Create a report with the fields for the manufacturer ID, the manufacturer name, and the current and previous years' purchase price.

2. Group the data by manufacturer.

3. Format the gridlines by applying a solid border with a black color from the Standard Colors section.

4. Apply conditional formatting using data bars for the purchase prices for the current and previous years.

5. Export the data into a text file and save the file as Inventory Data.

6. Save and close the database.

Lesson 6 Lab 1
Managing Your Calendar in Outlook

Activity Time: 10 minutes

Scenario:

Being the HR manager, you want to attend a meeting scheduled in your head office regarding HR policies. Since you will be out of office for a week, you are delegating the Reviewer access to your personal assistant in order for her to manage and maintain your schedule. Also, you are to interview a candidate for the Multimedia Developer position. You decide to schedule a meeting for the same, and as there are other managers who also will be on the interviewing panel for the candidate, you decide to share your calendar with them, so that they can view your schedule in case there are any changes to be made to the schedule.

1. Schedule a meeting with required and optional attendees with a subject of "Interview for the Multimedia Developer position." for an hour in a conference room.

2. Share your calendar with two other users.

3. Add a delegate.

4. Set the Reviewer permission to the delegate for accessing your Calendar.

Lesson 7 Lab 1

Sharing Presentations Through the Web

Activity Time: 10 minutes

Data Files:

OGC Overview.pptx

Before You Begin:

To perform this activity, you must have a registered Windows Live ID account and Internet connection.

Scenario:

Now that the presentation is complete, you need to send it out for review. You need feedback for this presentation by next week and your reviewer is out of the office. You decide to save the presentation on the web for your reviewer to access and preview the presentation on the web easily.

1. Navigate to the C:\Sharing Microsoft Office 2010 Files folder and open the OGC Overview.pptx file.

2. Mark the presentation final.

3. Save the file to the **Public** folder in your SkyDrive account.

4. Open your browser and access the SkyDrive account using **http://skydrive.live.com**

5. Navigate to the file available in the Public folder.

6. View the file from skydrive.

Solutions

Glossary

alternate background color feature
A feature using which you can set a specific color for every other row in a table.

anchoring
A feature that enables you to tie a control or a section of a control to another control so that you can move and resize them simultaneously.

Animation Painter command
A command that allows you to replicate the animation of the existing objects on a slide and apply it to other objects.

Application Parts gallery
A gallery that lists database objects such as tables, queries, reports, and forms as templates.

Attachment data type
A new data type that enables you to store external documents and binary files in a record, and attach multiple files to a single record.

Auto Calendar
An icon that pops up at the right side of the Date/Time data type cell when you select the cell.

backstage view
An interface that contains a series of tabs that group similar commands, and display the compatibility, permissions, and version information of a file. Additionally, it contains options to save, share, print, and publish files.

calendar group
An option in the Calendar view that allows you to view multiple calendars of other users together so as to compare their schedules before you schedule a meeting.

calendar overlays
An option of viewing multiple calendars at the same time.

Compare feature
A feature that is used to combine or compare different versions of a document and to check for information that might have been deleted, modified, moved, or replaced in the original document.

Compatibility Checker
A feature that enables you to identify the compatibility of objects used in your Office 2010 document when it is saved in an earlier version.

conditional formatting
The application of formatting to values based on conditions they fulfill.

contextual tabs
Tabs with specialized commands that are displayed when the object they operate on is selected.

conversation
A view that enables you to view groups of messages that share the same subject.

data bar
A new conditional formatting technique that is used to depict data as a shaded bar.

data macro
A feature that allows you to attach macros to table data.

Data Type gallery
A gallery that displays common field types such as attachment and currency, and used for inserting a new field into a table.

data type
A categorization of data associated with a particular field based on certain predefined characteristics.

Dialog Box Launchers
The miniature buttons that accompany button groups on command tabs, and display an associated dialog box with additional commands and tools, when clicked.

digital ID
A digital certificate required to apply a digital signature to a document.

digital signature
Ensures the authenticity of a digital document, such as a presentation or email.

Document Inspector
A feature that enables you to scan and remove personal information, comments, hidden data, and tracked changes within a file.

EBC
(Electronic Business Card) The electronic version of the business card that displays contact details.

Edit Business Card dialog box
A dialog box that enables you to format the appearance of a business card and the contact information in it.

embedded macros
The macros that are part of the property attached to an event.

Expression Builder dialog box
A dialog box that allows you to select database objects and build formulas and calculations that are used with queries and reports.

field insertion feature
A feature with which you can easily insert a new field by typing the field name in the first row of a new column in the Datasheet view.

filter
A feature that enables you to filter data based on the data type in a column.

Formula AutoComplete feature
A dynamic feature that allows you to conveniently choose and enter formulas and functions.

Formula Bar
An interface component of Excel 2010 that contains the Name Box and the Insert Function button, and is used for specifying formulas.

galleries
Libraries that list the varying outcomes of using certain commands found within the Ribbon.

Grouping feature
A feature that enables you to have a clear view of data groupings when you preview the changes as you are applying them in a report.

Insert Function button
A button in the Function Library group that displays the Insert Function dialog box, which holds numerous functions in several categories.

Instant Search
Allows you to quickly search for items in Outlook by specifying certain search criteria.

IntelliSense feature
A feature in Access 2010 that allows you to build expressions by automatically displaying the expression that you might use in a given context when you type.

layouts
The groups of controls that enable you to make design changes to an interface element.

ligatures
Are two-letter characters that are formed into one by joining the letters.

Live Preview
A feature that enables you to view the results of editing and formatting changes made to an Office application, without actually applying them.

Macro Designer
A macro builder that enables you to create macros.

Mark as Final
A feature that enables you to save a file as the final and latest version and also convert the file to read-only mode.

Microsoft Office Status Bar
A frame that displays a number of options relating to document functionality in a well-organized manner.

Mini toolbar
A floating toolbar that is displayed beside selected text, and consists of commonly used font and paragraph tools.

multivalued field
A field that is used for storing multiple values.

navigation form
A layout that allows you to navigate within objects in the application.

options for importing data
The options located in the Import & Link group on the External Data tab that enable you to import data from various data sources into Access.

People pane
A pane that displays the contact details, related files, appointments, notes, and updates from social media about a contact.

Picture Tools Format contextual tab
A tool with commands to modify and enhance a picture graphic.

PivotChart option
An option in the PivotTable drop-down list that allows you to insert a PivotChart and PivotTable.

PivotChart
A chart whose data can be reoriented, analyzed, and dynamically represented.

PivotTable button
A button used to display the Create PivotTable dialog box for creating a new PivotTable.

PivotTable
A table whose fields can be reoriented for performing selective analysis.

PowerPivot
A tool that enables you to model and analyze data on worksheets.

Property Sheet
A collection of tools that enable you to set properties for the controls in a form such as a text box, image, label, or combo box.

Protected view
A view that opens a file in the read-only mode and is a safe mode that allows the user to check whether the file is from a trusted source or not.

Quick Access toolbar
A toolbar that provides easy access to core commands such as save, undo, and repeat.

quick step
A command that facilitates performing common tasks that involve multiple actions as a single-click option.

Ribbon
A panel on the top portion of a Office document that contains a selection of easy-to-browse commands, which you may need to work on a document.

rich text memo field
A field that enables better formatting of data in tables, forms, or reports.

rich text support feature
A feature that provides enhanced formatting capabilities such as bold, underline, text alignment, font colors, and indentation.

RSS feed
A delivery method for RSS content.

RSS
A method for distributing information in a standardized XML format.

Schedule view
A calendar view that allows you to view multiple calendars to compare schedules.

ScreenTip
A description of the task performed by the tool when the mouse pointer is placed over the tool.

Send a Calendar via E-mail dialog box
A dialog box that allows you to send calendars to other users in an email message.

Slicers
A feature that enables you to slice data and include only the elements you want in PivotTables and PivotCharts.

SmartArt graphics
The layouts that are used to show a time line or developmental progression, or the sequential steps in a process or workflow.

Sparklines
Miniature charts that appear within the worksheet, depicting the numbers in a worksheet table.

Stacked layouts
The form layouts that display controls vertically.

Styles command
A command that contains sets of styles packaged together to apply a set of design and formatting changes to a document.

stylistic sets
Styles which can be applied to a font to give it a slightly different look in a document.

tab groups
A logical group of commands on a tab that contain features designed to perform specific tasks.

Tabular layouts
The form layouts that display controls in a horizontal table format with one row per record.

themes
Design templates that provide a consistent visual look and feel for a presentation.

To-Do bar
A bar that displays the calendar, upcoming appointments, and a list of tasks.

Totals feature
A feature that enables you to add a totals row to a report.

Tri-Pane Review panel
A panel that is used to view and compare two different versions of a document along with the view that combines the changes from each of the two compared documents.

Web Browser Control
A control tool that allows you to view web content within the Access 2010 application.

Web Compatibility Checker feature
A feature that enables you to identify whether the web database objects that you created are supported on the web.

web objects
The database objects such as a form, table, query, or report in a web database.

WYSIWYG interface
(What You See Is What You Get) A feature that enables you to modify the layouts in a form when you are working on it.

Index

A
Access databases
 interconverting to different formats, 22
Advanced Find dialog box, 179
Auto Calendar, 122

B
Background Removal tab, 49
backstage view, 4
 Excel templates in, 62
 printing slides in, 27
buttons
 Conditional Formatting, 65
 Insert Function, 70
 PivotTable, 89
 Reset Button, 44

C
calendar groups, 186
calendar overlays, 186
chart templates, 79
charts in Excel, 77
 creating, 79
commands
 Animation Painter, 107
 Clean Up, 174
 for video tools, 110
 Ignore, 175
 Report, 145
 Styles, 36
 Totals, 147
 Trigger, 107
Compatibility Checker, 22
conditional formatting, 65
 applying, 65
 clearing, 66
 printing reports using, 147
contacts, 195
contextual tab groups, 13
contextual tabs, 11
 formatting objects using, 17
 objects that display, 11
 Picture Tools Format, 103
 types of, 12
controls
 anchoring, 131
conversation view, 173

D
data bars, 148
data types, 120
delegates, 186
digital IDs, 211
digital signatures, 211
 Also See: IRM
Document Inspector, 210

E
EBCs, 195
Edit Business Card dialog box
 sections in, 196
enhanced animation effects, 107
enhanced chart tools, 78
Excel tables
 building from existing data sources, 61
 enhancements to, 60
 filtering data in, 62
Excel templates
 enhancements to, 61
Expression Builder dialog box, 148

F

features
  alternate background color, 123
  Compare, 53
  field insertion, 120
  Formula AutoComplete, 69
  Grouping, 146
  Instant Search, 179
  Office Mobile 2010, 215
  rich text support, 147
  SkyDrive, 215
  Slicers, 90
  Web Compatibility Checker, 162
fields
  multivalued, 123
  rich text memo, 121
files
  opening, 7
  reviewing & comparing, 54
  saving in an earlier version, 23
Formula Bar in Excel, 69

G

galleries, 15
  Add Animations, 107
  Application Parts, 132
  Data Type, 122
groups
  SharePoint Lists, 156

H

hidden data
  types of, 210

I

IntelliSense, 139
Internet calendars, 188
IRM, 211

L

layouts, 131
ligatures, 37
Live Preview, 15

M

Macro Designer, 138
macros
  creating & running, 140

  data, 139
  embedded, 139
Manage Quick Steps dialog box, 172
Microsoft Office 2010 User Interface
  customizing, 7
Mini toolbar, 14
  formatting text using, 17

N

navigation forms, 162
Navigation pane, 32
  displaying, 33

O

options
  Compare, 53
  for advanced querying, 145
  for enhanced conditional formatting, 147
  for enhanced filtering/sorting, 146
  for exporting data, 156
  for importing data, 155
  for pasting, 16
  for printing, 26
  for slide sections, 114
  Mark as Final, 211
  Paste Preview, 16
  PivotChart, 90
Options dialog box
  tabs in, 5

P

panels
  Tri-Pane Review, 53
panes
  People, 196
  PivotTable Field List, 91
PDF formats, 22
PivotTables
  creating, 91
PowerPivot, 90
presentations
  broadcasting a slide show, 216
  inspecting, 212
  previewing, 27
Print tab, 5
Property Sheets, 131
protected view, 5

Q

Quick Access toolbar
  adding a group to, 8
  customizing, 7
quick steps, 172

R

reports
  grouping data in, 149
Ribbon
  and screen size, 3
  benefits of, 3
  tabs in, 3
Ribbon tabs
  that are customizable, 3
RSS feeds, 204
  adding through Outlook, 204

S

schedule view, 184
screenshots
  capturing, 50
ScreenTips, 6
SmartArt graphics, 43
  applying graphic/3D effects to, 44
  categories of, 43
  inserting, 44
Sparklines, 85
  creating, 86
status bar
  customizing, 8
  differences in display across Office applications, 3

Styles command, 36
  creating a style, 37
  modifying an existing style, 37
stylistic sets, 37

T

table tools in Excel, 14
themes, 98
  formatting, 100
  types of, 98
To-Do bar, 184
  accessing, 184
tools
  Background Removal, 49
  for form creation, 130
  Move, 175
  Screenshot, 49

V

video styles, 111
videos
  manipulating, 111

W

Web Browser Control, 163
web objects, 161
Windows Live SkyDrive, 215
WYSIWYG interface, 131

X

XML formats, 20
  advantages of, 21
  upgrading a file to, 23